Praise for *The Revenge*

"How did the 'end of history' turn into th
Moisés Naím brings his incisive analysis and global perspective to
the most disturbing question of the twenty-first century, showing
how populism, polarization, and 'post-truth' politics have powered
the rise of leaders from Berlusconi to Bolsonaro, Orbán to Erdoğan,
Duterte to Donald Trump. Anyone who cares about the future of
truth and democracy should read this book."
— Alan Murray, CEO of FORTUNE

"*The Revenge of Power* is wide-ranging in scope, providing insights
into our current crisis without trying to ferret out a single cause of
democratic decline. . . . Filled with illustrative histories of various
autocrats and the ways they honed their craft in their rise to power."
— *The Washington Post*

"A foreign-policy maven's account of how recent demagogues have
come to power and used the tools of our time—social media, television, the society of spectacle—to promote one-man rule and the
suppression of dissent." — Adam Gopnik, *The New Yorker*

"Naím delivers a cogent and accessible overview of the new authoritarianism. Readers will agree that the matter is of urgent concern."
— *Publishers Weekly*

"An authoritative and intelligent portrait of the global spread of authoritarianism and its dangers." — *Kirkus Reviews*

"Another original book by an original thinker, offering a unique global
perspective on populism and power."
— Anne Applebaum, Pulitzer Prize–winning
historian and staff writer, *The Atlantic*

"An unusually smart, insightful, and elegantly written book about
why authoritarians and autocrats have risen to power around the
globe—and how we can defend democracy in our own backyards."
— Adam Grant, #1 *New York Times* bestselling author of
Think Again and host of the TED podcast *WorkLife*

Published in the United States by St. Martin's Griffin, an imprint of
St. Martin's Publishing Group

THE REVENGE OF POWER. Copyright © 2022 by Moisés Naím. All rights
reserved. Printed in the United States of America. For information, address
St. Martin's Publishing Group, 120 Broadway, New York, NY 10271.

www.stmartins.com

Designed by Meryl Sussman Levavi

The Library of Congress has cataloged the hardcover edition as follows:

Names: Naím, Moisés, author.
Title: The revenge of power: how autocrats are reinventing politics
    for the 21st century / Moisés Naím.
Description: First edition. I New York: St. Martin's Press, 2022. I
    Includes bibliographical references and index.
Identifiers: LCCN 2021042262 I ISBN 9781250279200 (hardcover) I
    ISBN 9781250279217 (ebook)
Subjects: LCSH: Power (Social sciences)—Political aspects. I Polarization
    (Social sciences)—Political aspects. I Truthfulness and falsehood—Political
    aspects. I Populism. I Democracy.
Classification: LCC JC330 .N335 2022 I DDC 320.01/1—dc23
LC record available at https://lccn.loc.gov/2021042262

ISBN 978-1-250-87582-2 (trade paperback)

Our books may be purchased in bulk for promotional, educational,
or business use. Please contact your local bookseller or the Macmillan
Corporate and Premium Sales Department at 1-800-221-7945, extension
5442, or by email at MacmillanSpecialMarkets@macmillan.com.

First St. Martin's Griffin Edition: 2023

D 10 9 8 7 6 5 4 3 2

THE REVENGE OF POWER

How Autocrats
Are Reinventing Politics
for the 21st Century

MOISÉS NAÍM

ST. MARTIN'S GRIFFIN
NEW YORK

To Nusia Feldman

CONTENTS

We know that no one ever seizes power with the intention of relinquishing it.

—George Orwell, *Nineteen Eighty-Four*

We do not know what is happening to us, and that is precisely the thing that is happening to us.

—José Ortega y Gasset, *Man and Crisis*

INTRODUCTION: THE PERIL

Free societies all around the world face an implacable new enemy. This foe has no army, no navy; it comes from no country we can point to on a map. It is everywhere and nowhere, because it is not *out there* but *in here*. Rather than threatening societies with destruction from without, like the Nazis and the Soviets once did, this foe threatens them from within.

A peril that is everywhere and nowhere is elusive, hard to discern, to pin down. We all sense it, but we struggle to name it. Torrents of ink are spilled describing its components and features, but *it* remains elusive.

Our first task, then, is to name it. Only then can we grasp it, fight it, and defeat it.

What is this new foe that threatens our freedom, our prosperity, even our survival as democratic societies?

The answer is *power, in a malignant new form.*

Every era has seen one or more forms of political malignancy. What we're seeing today is a revanchist variant that mimics democracy while undermining it, scorning all limits. It is as if political power had taken stock of every method free societies have devised over the centuries to domesticate it and plotted to strike back.

That is why I think of it as the *revenge* of power.

In this book, I look at the rise of this malignant new form of political power, noting the way it has developed around the world. I document how it stealthily eats away at the fundamentals of a free society. I show how it has arisen from the ashes of an older form of power, devastated by the forces that spelled its end. And I argue that wherever it develops, whether in Bolivia or North Carolina, in Britain or the Philippines, it relies on a compact core of strategies to weaken the foundations of democracy and cement its malignant dominance. I also sketch out ways of fighting back to protect democracy and, in many cases, to salvage it.

The clash between those with power and those without it is, of course, a permanent fixture of the human experience. For the vast bulk of human history, those with power hoarded it for their own benefit, passing it on to their children to found dynasties of blood and privilege, with little regard for those without. The tools of power—violence, money, technology, ideology, moral suasion, spying, and propaganda, to name just a few—were the domain of hereditary castes, far outside the reach of most people. Yet beginning with the American and French revolutions of the late eighteenth century, a seismic transformation took hold of power relations, making power contestable and placing new constraints on those who wielded it. That form of power—limited in scope, accountable to the people, and based on a spirit of lawful competition—was at the center of the great expansion in prosperity and security the world saw after the end of World War II.

But at the turn of the twenty-first century, unsettling transformations began to shake that postwar settlement. In a previous book, *The End of Power*, I examined the way power was decaying across a whole range of human institutions. Technology, demography, urbanization, information, economic and political change, globalization, and changed mindsets conspired to fragment and dilute power, making it easier to gain but harder to use and easier to lose.

A backlash was inevitable. Those determined to gain and wield unlimited power deploy old and new tactics to protect their power from the forces that weaken and constrain it. Those new behaviors are designed to stem the decay of power, to allow power to be reconstituted, concentrated, and wielded without limits once more—but with twenty-first-century technologies, tactics, organizations, and mindsets.

Put another way, the centrifugal forces that weaken power called forth a new set of centripetal forces that tend to concentrate it. The clash between these two sets of forces is one of the defining characteristics of our time. And the outcome of that clash is far from predetermined.

The stakes couldn't be higher, and nothing is guaranteed. What's at stake is not just whether democracy will thrive in the twenty-first century but whether it will even survive as the dominant system of government, the default setting in the global village. Freedom's survival is not guaranteed.

Can democracies survive the attacks of aspiring autocrats bent on wrecking the checks and balances that limit their power? How? Why is power concentrating in some places while in others it is fragmenting and degrading? And the big question: What is the future of freedom?

Power is seldom ceded voluntarily. Those who have it naturally try to contain and counter the attempts of their rivals to weaken or replace them. The newcomers who attack the incumbents are often innovators who not only use new tools but also follow a very different playbook. Their political innovations have deeply altered the way power is conquered and retained in the twenty-first century.

This book identifies and scrutinizes these innovations, showing their possibilities, inner logic, and contradictions—and then identifies the key battles democrats will need to win to prevent them from destroying freedom in our time.

A limited, contingent form of power will not be enough to satisfy aspiring autocrats who have learned how to leverage trends like migration, the economic insecurity of the middle class, identity politics, the fears globalization gives rise to, the power of social media, and the advent of artificial intelligence. In all sorts of geographies and under all sorts of circumstances, they've shown they want power with no strings attached, and they want it for keeps.

These aspiring autocrats face a new set of options, and they have new sets of tools they can use to lay claim to unlimited power. Many of these tools did not exist just a few years ago. Others are as old as time but combine in new ways with emerging technologies and new social trends to become far more powerful than they have ever been before.

That's why, in recent years, we have seen the success of a new breed of power-seekers: unconventional leaders who witnessed the decay of traditional power and realized that a radically new approach could open hitherto untapped opportunities. They have arisen all over the world, from the richest countries to the poorest, from the most institutionally sophisticated to the most backward. We have in mind here Donald Trump, of course, but also Venezuela's Hugo Chávez, Hungary's Viktor Orbán, the Philippines' Rodrigo Duterte, India's Narendra Modi, Brazil's Jair Bolsonaro, Turkey's Recep Tayyip Erdoğan, El Salvador's Nayib Bukele, and many others. This book dissects their approach because one cannot defeat what one cannot understand.

These new autocrats have pioneered new techniques for gaining unlimited power and then keeping it for as long as they can. The ultimate goal—not always attainable but always fought hard for—is power for life. Any trends that weaken their power are seen as vital threats, things to be contained. Their success is emboldening others to try to emulate them all around the world. They've enjoyed many successes along with some notable failures. And more turn up seemingly every other week. These leaders—and this *style* of leadership—are at the forefront of *The Revenge of Power*.

These leaders are adapting to the new landscape, improvising new tactics and reengineering old ones to boost their ability to impose their will on others. Despite the enormous national, cultural, institutional, and ideological differences between the countries where they arise, their playbooks look uncannily similar. Jair Bolsonaro, Brazil's president, and Mexico's Andrés Manuel López Obrador, for example, couldn't be more ideologically different, nor more similar in their style of leadership. The tiny, impoverished Central American backwater of El Salvador and the massive, sophisticated superpower that is the United States could not be more different as countries, yet Nayib Bukele and Donald Trump governed from an eerily similar playbook.

What is this formula? What are its components? And how does it operate in the real world? These are the questions at the heart of this book. To my mind, the formula can be summed up in three words: populism, polarization, and post-truth.

We call them the 3Ps. And those who deploy them are the 3P autocrats.

What Is a 3P Autocrat?

3P autocrats are political leaders who reach power through a reasonably democratic election and then set out to dismantle the checks on executive power through populism, polarization, and post-truth. As they consolidate their power, they cloak their autocratic plans behind walls of secrecy, bureaucratic obfuscation, pseudolegal subterfuge, manipulation of public opinion, and the repression of critics and adversaries. Once the mask comes off, it's too late.

Authoritarianism is a continuum. One extreme is in totalitarian regimes like North Korea's, where power is fully concentrated in the hands of a dynastic dictator who wields it openly and brutally. On the other end lie democratically elected leaders with authoritarian proclivities. Twenty-first-century autocrats begin on this milder end and work to maintain democratic appearances while furtively undermining democracy.

How do they do it? Through populism, polarization, and post-truth.

Much has been written about each of these three Ps. Here we will integrate them, bringing them into a framework that's at the center of how twenty-first-century autocrats gain, wield, and keep power.

The specifics vary from place to place and leader to leader—power is always contextual—but the basics of this approach are recognizable wherever it is deployed. It spans geographies and circumstances as it destabilizes old institutions and opens opportunities for newcomers. In isolation, none of the three Ps is enough to explain the mutations of power in our time. But deployed in tandem, they can counteract the forces that tend to fragment and dilute power.

Populism may be the most persistently discussed of the three Ps and the most often misunderstood. Because it ends with "-ism," it is often mistaken for an ideology, a counterpart to socialism and liberalism in the competition for a coherent governing philosophy. It is no such thing. Instead, populism is best understood as a *strategy for gaining and wielding power*. Its draw is versatility: populism as a strategy can work in a very wide variety of contexts and be made compatible with virtually any governing ideology or with no ideology at all.

As Cas Mudde and Cristóbal Rovira Kaltwasser have shown, populists portray a political realm neatly cleft into two: the corrupt, greedy elite versus the noble and pure—but betrayed and aggrieved—*Volk*, the people. All the people's problems stem from the decisions—often conspiratorial, always corrupt—of a venal elite. Populist leaders portray themselves as embodying the will of the people and championing their cause against the corrupt elite. The effectiveness of this frame is tried and true and adaptable nearly without limit, since ultimately *any* position can be described as championing the pure people, and *any* contrary voice can be dismissed as furthering the ends of a corrupt elite.[1]

Recent years have seen an explosion of scholarship on democratic backsliding. Scholars like Tim Snyder,[2] Yascha Mounk,[3] Daron Acemoglu,[4] Anne Appelbaum,[5] Enrique Krauze,[6] and Larry Diamond[7] have all noted that similar patterns emerge when we study the way populists organize their bids for power.

Among them are:

- **Catastrophism.** Populists are marked pessimists about the current situation in which they find themselves. The world around them is corrupt, dysfunctional, and failing. The Augean stables must be cleared to enable a new start. There is nothing redeeming in a past dominated by the anti-people elite.
- **The criminalization of political rivals.** Political opponents are

not compatriots with different opinions but lawbreakers who belong in prison. Populists are prone to move the confrontation with their political rivals from the electoral arena to the courts, where they are likely to have friendly judges ready to jail pesky (or too popular) members of the opposition. "Lock them up" is their chant. Corruption, sedition, treason, terrorism, sexual abuse, or conspiracies to overthrow the government are commonly used excuses to jail opponents.

- **Using external threats.** In addition to the internal threat, there is the external threat. It's an age-old practice: The populist leader claims that the nation is threatened by a foreign enemy. This national emergency calls for unity and requires nothing short of the people's unconditional support for the government. Under these circumstances, opposing the government is akin to treason. The foreign enemies can be nations, immigrants who steal jobs, or abusive foreign companies that exploit the homeland.

- **Militarization and paramilitarization.** Populists have a long history of glorifying military imagery and of turning to military and paramilitary groups to intimidate their own dissidents.

- **Crumbling national borders.** National borders are portrayed as "too open," "porous," and therefore in urgent need of strengthening in order to stop the invasion of "job-stealing immigrants."

- **Denigrating experts.** Experts and scientists are, by definition, part of the intellectual elite and therefore are complicit in the mistreatment of the noble people that the populist leader represents. Experts also obtain data and evidence that reveal realities that are inconvenient for the populist in power. Populism inhabits a world of belief and gut feeling rather than facts and science.

- **Attacking media.** The (unfriendly) media are as much foes as the experts. They, too, have data and often unveil governmental corruption and incompetence. They are also prone to expose actions that the government would rather keep secret.

- **Undermining checks and balances.** Any institutions that act as barriers or checks to the unfettered will of the populist are held in distrust and are sometimes openly attacked and undermined.

- **Messianic delivery.** The answer to all these common woes lies within the strong individual who leads the populist cause. The embodiment of populism is frequently the charismatic individual leading the fight against the elites who oppress the people.

Once a populist frame is established, the stage is set for the second strategy used to gain and retain power: polarization. Relentlessly demonizing opponents and portraying both long-simmering and newly introduced wedge issues that divide the nation are the divisive strategies that, sadly, often yield great results. It's an approach that Marxists used to call "sharpening the contradictions"—and its effectiveness is beyond doubt.

The differences pit not just political opponents against each other but even family members, friends, colleagues, and neighbors. Such divisions can have many sources: ideology, race, religion, regional rivalries, historic grievances, economic inequality, social injustice, language, and many more.

Polarization eliminates the possibility of a middle ground, pushing every single person and organization to take sides. In our age, it operates through the dynamics of *fandom*: a pattern of identification with roots in the celebrity culture of the music industry and sports, where followers come to identify intensely with their favorite stars and feel visceral animosity toward rival stars.

Another important source of polarization is identity. As Francis Fukuyama aptly characterized it, "[Identity] focuses people's natural demand for recognition of their dignity and provides language for expressing the resentments that arise when such recognition is not forthcoming."[8] Again, politicians have always used identity as a wedge to energize and mobilize people and recruit followers. In recent years, this recruiting has been facilitated and amplified by an explosion in political polarization.

In a polarized political environment, fandom and identity leave no room for hedged support, cross-party bridge building, or temporary truces between the sides. As polarization advances, political rivals come to be treated as enemies. Contending sides no longer seek to accommodate each other in a quest for minimum viable governing arrangements. Instead, they deny the basic legitimacy of the other side's right even to contend for power, dispensing with the typical democratic norm that sees alternation in office as a normal, natural, and healthy pillar of democratic coexistence.

Populism and polarization are old instincts in the political realm: examples could be cited dating back to antiquity. The most peculiarly contemporary aspect of the revenge of power is its final ingredient: post-truth. Here, we run into a largely new phenomenon—not because politicians never used to lie, which they certainly did, but because the concept of post-truth goes much deeper than simply lying. In their current approach to post-truth, leaders go far beyond fibbing and deny the existence of a verifiable independent reality. Post-truth is not chiefly about getting lies accepted as truths but about muddying the waters to the point where it is difficult to discern the difference between truth and falsehood in the first place.

The term "post-truth" was first used in a 1992 article by Steve Tesich, a screenwriter and novelist.[9] In 2016, Oxford Dictionaries named it "the word of the year," explaining that it detected a spike in the frequency of its use "in the context of the EU referendum in the United Kingdom and the presidential election in the United States. It has become associated with a particular noun, in the phrase *post-truth politics*."[10] This concept tries to capture what according to Sean Illing is "the disappearance of shared objective standards for truth"[11] and what Barbara A. Biesecker describes as the "circuitous slippage between facts or alt-facts, knowledge, opinion, belief, and truth."[12]

Populism, polarization, and post-truth are high-level mechanisms, abstractions that need to be brought down from their Olympian heights to become usable power-seeking and power-retaining practices. Skillfully deployed by a power-hungry practitioner, they can scramble the defenses societies have developed to protect democracy from the encroachment of unaccountable power.

Together, they have the capacity to stop power's tendency to decay, but at a terrible price. Because the 3Ps sketch out a recipe for pursuing and maintaining power that is fundamentally undemocratic, uncontained by constitutional principles or institutional restraint.

Autocracy Remade

How did it come to this? To grasp the roots of this moment, we need to look back on the one just before. The end of the Cold War saw the hardening of a new consensus about the nature of political legitimacy. According to the new view, the power of a ruler is legitimate if that person checks the boxes of democratic government. That means, first and foremost, being chosen in a free and fair election but also respecting the rule of law and the rights of minorities, facing proper institutional checks and balances from courts and parliaments that are not unduly beholden to the executive, tolerating a free and independent media, and respecting voters' right to change the government through periodic elections. Where formal term limits exist, it means respecting them, and where they don't, it means resisting the temptation to try to stay in power for life. It is this high-level statement of principles that's usually referred to as "the liberal consensus," using the word "liberal" not in the contemporary American sense of center-left but in the historical sense of "centered on liberty."

It's important to grasp that there's nothing natural about this consensus. In fact, as a source of governing legitimacy, the liberal consensus is a relative newcomer. For the bulk of the ten thousand years since the first permanent government developed in ancient Mesopotamia, the ruler's right to rule stemmed from his connection with some deity. Around a thousand years ago, as David Stasavage has shown, some kings in Europe began to accept some checks on their power and to rule in cooperation with councils or assemblies of the highest-ranking nobles in their domains.[13] More recently, the revolutionary aspirations of the working class, the hereditary prerogatives of monarchs, and the ancestral connections of native peoples to their land have been put forward as alternative bases for a ruler's legitimacy.

No longer. Since the collapse of the Soviet Union, democratic legitimacy has been the only game in town. This was the seminal shift that Francis Fukuyama memorably dubbed the "end of history"[14]— not, of course, because history had literally ended, but because the competition over different systems for establishing that a government was legitimate had ended. After the Cold War, people would surely still try to set themselves up in power based on religion, heredity, class, or ethnicity—but such attempts would no longer be recognized as fully legitimate and acceptable by the most important actors in the international community.

But if liberal democracies, with all their vexing limits on executive power, can't be openly challenged from the outside, how are aspiring autocrats to establish rule? Their solution: by undermining democracies furtively, from the inside.

The 3P framework is a system for taking, wielding, and maintaining unlimited power in a world that doesn't recognize that kind of power as legitimate. It solves that problem by faking fealty to the liberal consensus, all the while eating away at it from the inside.

This new technology for aspiring autocrats developed in the twenty-first century because the need for it arose only recently. In the twentieth century, dictators did not need to hide their dominance over the political sphere: if they could amass power, they could wield it quite openly, through force of arms or by offering fealty to one of the dominant superpowers, which would in turn protect their ally from external enemies. Propaganda was often heavily deployed to cement a dictator's power, but its object was seldom obscuring the dictator's authority. Just the opposite—there was generally little need to dress up as a democratic nation or as a liberal leader. Back then, autocrats had options beyond the consent of the governed when it came to establishing the legitimacy of their rule. Those on the right wing could appeal to "order and progress," and those on the left could carry the mantle of the dictatorship of the proletariat. Whichever justification they chose, they had little incentive to pass it off as liberal democracy—though some, like East Germany and North Korea, sought to co-opt the word "democracy" and put it to Marxist ends.

Some legacy old-school dictatorships that reached power before the "end of history" are still around—more than a few, in fact. They've kept their grip on countries like China, Syria, Belarus, and Cuba, examples that confirm that such regimes remain viable all around the world. But for aspiring autocrats who came onto the world stage after the end of the Cold War, the old way wasn't a viable path. They needed a new solution

In a world where people, goods, and ideas are constantly on the move, and the old instinct to defer to higher-ups or to tradition is on the wane, any attempt to claim absolute authority is swimming against the historical tide. In the twenty-first century, marked by an explosion in personal freedom, mobility, and access to information, blunt appeals to force are less tolerated than in the past. This is why today's 3P autocrats, as they begin to establish their power, try to pass themselves off as something they're not: democracies in the Western mold.

That is the circle that only populism, polarization, and post-truth can square. The 3P framework allows new autocrats to portray themselves as embodying the people's true will, which is denied by the corrupt elites that lord power over them, and hidden from view by a corrupt media. It allows them to claim the mantle of the true voice of the people even as they dismantle the institutions that allow the people's true voices to be heard.

That is how 3P autocrats establish their legitimacy in an environment where unassailable power remains taboo. The 3P framework allows these new players to hypocritically mimic the forms of the liberal consensus, appearing to shore up its legitimacy while stealthily undermining the old order. Throughout this book, we will examine the mechanisms that allow this to happen. For now, perhaps the simplest way to cut through the haze is to grasp that, in their quest for absolute power, today's aspiring autocrats are duplicitous in ways their twentieth-century predecessors seldom needed to be.

Indeed, deception is at the center of the 3P path to power. And if hypocrisy is, as the French memoirist La Rochefoucauld once said, the tribute that vice pays to virtue, 3P power is a happy tributary to the democracies it corrodes.[15]

In the twenty-first century, new autocratic regimes typically emerge not by toppling democracies via force but by passing themselves off as democracies. As Erica Frantz of Michigan State University puts it in her 2018 book, *Authoritarianism: What Everyone Needs to Know*, today's autocracies often arise by eating democracy from within, in the same way the larvae of some wasps will eat their host spiders from the inside.[16]

The trend runs across continents, from countries as poor as Bolivia to those as rich as the United States. Even a threadbare facsimile of democracy can be crucial to sustaining the viability of power maintained by 3P strategies. As Stanford University's Larry Diamond put it, "There is still enough resonance today of the democracy principle so that leaders like [Egyptian dictator Abdel Fattah] el-Sisi and [Russia's Vladimir] Putin feel the need to show that they have won in a superficially competitive election, that they are the people's choice."[17] They're stuck with the phraseology of the liberal consensus—and so they turn to stealth, sneakily undermining the systems they rode to power.

For two decades, 3P practitioners have been pioneering this new take on authoritarianism. Their approach is aware of its own indefensibility. Lacking an alternative explanation that they can use to bolster their legitimacy, they go to considerable trouble to dissemble, trying to pass themselves off as exemplars of a system they're determined to dismantle.

Stealth, then, is one of the central tactics used by autocrats to concentrate power in an environment where its natural tendency is to disperse. Stealth becomes the necessary adjunct to the 3P framework, a tactical imperative needed to deliver on aims too shocking to be acknowledged. So much so that, in many cases, concealing the real operations of power becomes a central strategy for amassing and retaining it. It is useful to think of these cases as *stealthocracies*.

Of course, not all politicians who used the 3P strategies to gain and retain power were stealthocrats maneuvering in the dark. Some, like Rodrigo Duterte in the Philippines and Hungary's Viktor Orbán, were transparently explicit about their penchant for autocratic power. But most of those seeking to supplant established democracies with authoritarian regimes find, in the 3Ps, a cunning solution to the problem of introducing autocracy to a population accustomed to democracy and to an international community that demands it. Indeed, even the most shamelessly dictatorial leaders find themselves compelled to put up at least a thin façade of democratic legitimacy now and then—witness the "elections" that Putin feels bound to simulate every few years to sustain his rule.

The "how" of the 3P power—how it arises, how it operates, how it corrupts both formal institutions and informal norms, and how it devolves into anti-politics in some cases and into mafia states in others—makes up the bulk of this book.

There's little point, however, in diving deep into the how without a strong grasp of the *why*. 3P power is a reaction to the fragmentation and degradation of traditional forms of power. It's a way that those determined to wield power without limits adapt to a world where the power of incumbents is under constant challenge and in which prolonged tenures are rare.

This adaptation isn't some technical matter, nor is it a morally neutral evolutionary change. 3P power is a malign form of power, incompatible with the democratic values at the center of any free society. It hides, until it no longer needs to hide. Then it strikes. And by the time this type of power sets aside the cloak of stealth, it's often too late.

In the pages ahead, we'll look at each of these tactics in detail, and get under their surface to decode how they operate and how they can be challenged. The challenge 3P autocracy poses to free and democratic societies is existential. There is simply no room for complacency here.

PART I

THE ERA OF POPULISM, POLARIZATION, AND POST-TRUTH

1

THE GLOBAL WAR ON CHECKS AND BALANCES

Warsaw, Poland, December 2019: After a string of embarrassing defeats for the government in the lower courts, a new law empowers the country's supreme court, dominated by ruling party appointees, to unseat lower court judges found to have "engaged in political activities." Such activities include questioning the political independence of the body that would administer the penalties.[1]

New Delhi, India, June 2017: Charging fraud, India's Criminal Bureau of Investigations raids the home of the founder of news channel NDTV, known for its sharply critical coverage of the government, even as the station denounces "concerted harassment of NDTV and its promoters" intended to silence it.[2]

La Paz, Bolivia, November 2017: The country's highest court rules that the right to stand for election is a universal human right, applicable to all citizens. The right is so universal that it applies even to the sitting president, who is nearing the end of his two-term limit—and who appointed the members of that tribunal.[3]

Washington, DC, April 2019: The White House announces it will fight all congressional subpoenas, and President Trump instructs all executive branch officials to refuse to cooperate with congressional demands for information or testimony.[4]

On its own, each example seems relatively small. Come across them in a newspaper headline and you might be tempted to skip the article. None on its own seems like a cause for alarm. Nor, at first, is it entirely obvious what they all have in common. Nothing seems to unite the America First conservatives in Washington with the Hindu chauvinists in New Delhi, the paleo-nationalists in Warsaw with the indigenist socialists in La Paz.

Yet a silent thread runs through them. Each shows a leader picking away, furtively, at strategic safeguards that protect democracy, limit leaders' options, and guarantee fair competition for power. This is the revenge of power at work.

Poland, India, Bolivia, the United States—countries big and small, rich and poor, East and West. It's difficult to imagine more different locations or leaders. And yet all these leaders alighted on a similar set of strategies to strengthen their grip on power without calling too much attention to themselves. The moves are couched in legalese, but each carries a political intent that is plain for anyone to see. Sometimes they attack the oversight powers of the legislative branch, other times the watchdog role of the press, the independence of the courts, or key checks on limitless executive power.

They don't always succeed: America's aspiring autocrat was thrown out of office, as was Bolivia's. But Bolivia's socialists found a way back to power, and America's leading populist-nationalist is plotting his own comeback. What unites them all is that they grasp that to consolidate power, they need to dismantle existing checks and balances, whether those be term limits, prosecutorial independence, a free and adversarial press, or the independence of the courts. Their aim? To undo any mechanism that stands in the way of their ability to rule without limits.

People in rich, developed democracies were long used to a comfortable, somewhat smug feeling that what happens politically in the poorest countries has nothing to do with them. But after Trump and Brexit, that confidence lies in tatters. Turns out that the tactics that worked there *can* work here, too.

This chapter shows how 3P practitioners worldwide have settled on a common set of approaches and strategies, building up shared knowledge on how to reconstitute absolute power in a moment that's hostile to it. Although often practiced by self-styled anti-globalists, the revenge of power is itself a thoroughly globalized affair.

In this chapter, we'll trace some of the common features 3P autocrats employ across vastly different landscapes. We'll see how the same kinds of strategies arise again and again in places and cultures as disparate as Italy and Bolivia, India and Hungary, the Great Smoky Mountains of North Carolina and the sweltering jungles of Mindanao, the Philippines. Scratch the surface and you see common themes and threads in the politics of such disparate places, always used to the same end: to coax a world hostile to absolute power into making room for autocracy.

The first order of business for leaders aspiring to wield unchecked political power is to bend the institutions of the state to their will. This is no easy feat: in today's democracies, such institutions are designed so that they will not readily bend to a single person's will. Overcoming this resistance without appealing to old-style power grabs with tanks on the streets takes a certain amount of dexterity as well as mastery of a common set of 3P techniques. This chapter examines those techniques and traces their worldwide spread.

Who Will Guard the Guardians?

The most basic problem in designing a government that truly answers to the people it governs is so old it's best known in its Latin form: *Quis custodiet ipsos custodes?* Who will guard the guardians?

A government needs power to operate, but that power needs to be limited somehow lest it run amok and dominate all of society. Somebody needs to guard the guardians, to keep a watchful eye on those trusted with authority to ensure they do not, and indeed cannot, abuse it.

The way modern societies do that is through a clever institutional design built into the liberal consensus: an interlocking system of government bodies, each guarding the others, each ensuring no single one of them can run off with power and use it for private rather than public ends.

In the American tradition, such a system is commonly referred to as "checks and balances." It's an old idea but a good one. In fact, it must rank as one of America's most successful global exports.

Having suffered under the uncheckable growth of the British monarch's power, America's founders were famously consumed with the problem of ensuring the same tendency wouldn't grip their own executive branch. The system of checks and balances they embedded into the U.S. Constitution, drafted over four months in 1787, became the blueprint for constitution-makers across the globe. Today, the influence of America's founders resonates far beyond the United States. All over the world, safeguards such as term limits, congressional oversight, judicial review, press freedom, apolitical law enforcement, judicial and parliamentary independence, frequent elections, and a military that is subservient to the civilian government are written into law.

Today, budding autocrats hoping for absolute power need, more than anything else, a reliable system for sidestepping these checks on their power. The worldwide spread of checks and balances means that the push to render them meaningless is now a worldwide phenomenon, too. Wherever limits on executive authority have gone, stealthy methods for nullifying them have followed.

Core checks and balances are enforced through the rule of law. So to exercise autocratic control free from those constraints, the first order of business is to find a reliable way to subvert the rule of law. This cannot be done out in the open. The first rule of 3P is: always maintain the outward trappings of legality and constitutional order. The unabashed despot in an epauletted uniform shutting down courts and barking orders at subordinates is a relic of the twentieth century, fading in the rearview mirror of history. What twentieth-century autocrats did by force, their twenty-first-century counterparts do by stealth. While their twentieth-century predecessors set out to destroy the rule of law with brute force, twenty-first-century autocrats undermine it through the corrosive power of insincere mimicry.

Sustaining the appearance of legality, however threadbare, is not some superficial aspect of this endeavor. It's often its crux. Appearances must be kept up if the system of checks and balances at the heart of the liberal democratic consensus is to be taken apart. But how?

Pseudolaw: Corroding the Rule of Law from the Inside

One key strategy to this end is pseudolaw: a corrupt facsimile of the rule of law that is, in fact, its mortal enemy.

Pseudolaw is to real law what pseudoscience is to real science. Just like pseudoscience appropriates the outward forms of science to pervert it, pseudolaw borrows the look and feel of the rule of law to render law meaningless.

Think of the oil industry's efforts to subvert climate science. For decades, giant oil companies spent freely to commission academic "studies" that invariably found the threat from carbon pollution overblown. The papers these researchers produced looked and felt just like real scientific papers—they were conscious mimics of science. But as writers such as Steve Coll[5] and David Michaels[6] have amply documented, these papers weren't science; they were pseudoscience, designed to cast doubt on the real thing. Similar dynamics have played out in support of tobacco and sugary drinks and in favor of the mass prescription of opioids: junk science, dressed up to look like the real thing, is used again and again to justify the unjustifiable.

It's easy to see why powerful interests reliably pursue this path. It would be futile to attack science as such because science is universally accepted as the way we arrive at legitimate knowledge about the natural world. That's why special interests seeking to sow doubt about mainstream science typically choose to mimic it rather than deny it. The final goal, of course, is to avoid, delay, or water down any government regulations that could impair profits.

Instead of attacking science head-on, lobbyists invest decades and huge amounts of resources to subvert it, financing experts to produce reports that have the look and feel of science but are no such thing, with the aim of creating the appearance of controversy where none really exists. The basic move is always the same: appropriating the outward trappings of science to obscure real scientists' findings.

Pseudolaw follows the same pattern. It embraces the formalities of the law in a bid to undermine its essence.

What does pseudolaw look like in practice? Pseudolaw looks like Donald Trump in 2017 unveiling a hastily assembled executive order banning travel from several Muslim-majority countries and claiming it as a national security measure. Pseudolaw looks like Argentine president Cristina Fernández de Kirchner in 2009 slapping an export ban on Argentine beef on "food security" grounds, which everyone could see was the barest of fig leaves to hide an attempt to punish her critics in the beef industry. It looks like the Polish constitutional court's disciplinary chamber sanctioning judges who ruled against the government's interests after cursory hearings before politically docile magistrates who kept to the usual protocols of court proceedings.

This is similar to what Javier Corrales of Amherst College calls "autocratic legalism." Corrales notes this practice has taken surprisingly similar form in countries as different as the United States and Venezuela: "Presidents across the world use diverse tactics to achieve unlimited government, but a common approach is to erode the impartiality of the law. The goal is always to use and abuse the law to protect yourself and your allies. This is autocratic legalism."[7]

The insidious part is that once 3P autocrats begin to use pseudolaw to entrench themselves in power, their opponents often find it hard to resist the urge to use pseudolegal measures of their own to suppress them when and if they come to power. Pseudolaw is also the Thai constitutional court in May 2013 ordering the popular but autocratic prime minister and her entire cabinet to resign and yield power to a military junta. Pseudolaw is Brazil's congress, in which three out of four deputies were under investigation for corruption in 2016 but still was able to impeach President Dilma Rousseff. Pseudolaw was Donald Trump in 2018 ordering the postmaster general of the United States to raise the cost of shipping a parcel, a move that would undermine the profitability of Amazon, a company whose owner, Jeff Bezos (who also owned the *Washington Post*), was perceived by Trump as a political adversary.

Pseudolegality has been a boon to would-be autocrats all over the world. The Hindu nationalist Bharatiya Janata Party (BJP) government of Indian prime minister Narendra Modi cemented its 3P credentials with an incendiary new "citizenship law" that excluded millions of Muslims who had immigrated from neighboring countries decades earlier (the hated "them" in the BJP's sectarian "us vs. them" narrative) from keeping Indian citizenship. The move was classic pseudolaw—using a legal instrument specifically for the purpose of dividing the nation in a way that the autocrat seeks. At around the same time, Israel's Benjamin Netanyahu was himself cementing his 3P bona fides with a remarkably similar manufactured controversy: a new "nation-state law" that refused to commit Israel either to legal equality between its citizens or even to democracy, refounding the state in ways that exclude full participation by its Arab minority. Law, once more, is made an appendage of a 3P strategy: a political wedge in the form of a statute.

At times, the extent of pseudolegal contortion can seem almost comical. In 2017, Hungary approved a new law affecting branch campuses of foreign universities that was written in such a way that it could apply only to Central European University (CEU), which is technically a U.S.-registered university whose main campus operated in Hungary. The reason? Hungarian American financier and philanthropist George Soros had donated the money to establish the university, which had long provided a secure livelihood to independent academics, many not aligned with Viktor Orbán's budding 3P regime. Remarkably, the law was so narrowly written that beyond applying only to CEU, it was also impossible for CEU to comply with it. After a protracted fight, the university campus was forced to decamp two hundred miles west to Vienna. To outsiders, the 3P autocrats' obsessive commitment to pseudolaw can be hard to figure out. It might seem much simpler for Orbán to simply send some cops to shut CEU down without this complicated rigamarole involving passage of absurd absurd new pseudolaws. As is so often the case, the legal patina intended to obscure the move was ridiculously thin.

This is often the MO for 3P autocrats. A pretense of legality is typically built on the sort of obvious nonsense no sensible person could take seriously. In some cases, these power-concentrating tricks take place deep inside the governmental bureaucracy and are so arcane that, in practice, they are invisible to the public.

Why bother? Why go to all the trouble? Who, exactly, is being fooled?

These are the wrong questions. The commitment to pseudolaw is not really meant to fool anyone, at least not in the sense of getting them to accept a falsehood as truth. Instead, pseudolaw should be seen as an instrument of post-truth. Its goal is to muddy the waters, to create just enough murkiness around the legitimacy of a course of action to allow it to go forward, to draw opponents into intractable legal debates accessible only to the elite, to create enough room for doubt for imposition to go forward, and to defang the legal system itself, corrupting it and rendering it meaningless as a check on executive power.

To truly understand the 3P power, you must learn to spot pseudolaw and grasp the nihilism at its core for what it is. This can be tricky. Just as pseudoscientific arguments are often obvious shams to trained scientists but superficially convincing to laypeople, pseudolaw exploits the public's thin understanding of constitutional principles. The exasperated rebuttals it elicits from elites are a feature, not a bug. By riling the "corrupt elite," pseudolaw helps align post-truth with populism and polarization.

Pseudoscientific arguments are designed not so much to win the argument as to force an intellectual stalemate: to create a controversy that regular people feel incompetent to adjudicate. For years, the tobacco industry deployed pseudoscience to cast doubt on the link between smoking and lung disease. The goal was not so much to convince anyone that smoking was safe as to generate enough doubt and confusion about the question to muddle and slow down efforts to regulate smoking. "Teach the controversy" was, after all, the real policy goal of pseudoscientific hucksters hoping to bring creationism into U.S. classrooms. The strategy of the religious advocates of "intelligent design" was to simply argue that they had a different theory than mainstream scientists, and that it was only fair that both points of view be given equal billing in the science curriculum.[8]

The new breed of aspiring autocrats often put pseudolaw in the service of post-truth. The purpose of absurd rulings and wildly dis-ingenuous interpretations of the law is to create confusion and cast doubt about what is and isn't legal, a debate that helps them move forward with their plans.

The collateral damages of such projects are considerable. In his last op-ed before passing away, Paul Volcker, the respected former chairman of the U.S. Federal Reserve, described the new autocrats' approach as a "nihilistic force" that "seeks to discredit the pillars of our democracy: voting rights and fair elections, the rule of law, the free press, the separation of powers, the belief in science, and the concept of truth itself."[9]

The Limits of Term Limits

As 2008 approached, Vladimir Putin knew he had a problem. He was already well on his way to consolidating authoritarian control over the Russian state. But his second term as president was nearly finished and, under Russia's 1993 constitution, he was not allowed to run for a third. What to do?

These kinds of term-limit conundrums are a recurring problem for today's autocrats, both established and new. At least 134 coun-tries have some sort of formal term limit or bar on consecutive terms for the executive branch, so aspiring autocrats will more likely than not eventually have to deal with this problem. Keeping control of the executive branch is, in all cases, priority number one. But the means of doing so vary depending on each country's political and institu-tional circumstances.

Russia's constitutional design offered Putin one intriguing possi-bility. In the Kremlin's organizational chart, just beneath the vastly powerful presidency, was the post of prime minister—on paper a clearly inferior office, closer to the role of a White House chief of staff in the U.S. system. Still, this gave Putin an opening: with a sufficiently pliant figure in the presidency, the prime minister's office would be a fine place to lie low for a while. At any rate, the constitution only limited how many consecutive terms one could serve: there was noth-ing to bar Putin's return to the top job again four years later, in 2012.

And this is exactly what he did. At a grand ceremony of the ruling party, United Russia, Putin announced he would be swapping jobs with his long-serving prime minister, Dmitry Medvedev, for the 2008–12 term. Immediately after that, Putin and Medvedev would swap again . . . but not before approving a constitutional reform to extend the president's term from four years to six.

The Putin-Medvedev arrangement was classic pseudolaw: blatantly designed to defeat a constitutional check on the accumulation of power without exactly violating it. Term limits are designed to prevent a ruler from accumulating excessive power by making it impossible to stay in power too long. This Putin-Medvedev arrangement made a mockery of the term limit's intent. But in fine pseudolegal fashion, it shredded the spirit of the rule without quite technically breaking it. Through the years, Putin would continue to push back his term limit as needed. In March 2020, he had the Duma, his rubber-stamp parliament, pass a law allowing him to run for a further two terms, through 2036—thirty-seven years after he first came to power. The vote tally for this change on the floor of the Duma was 383 in favor, 0 against. The proposal then went to the voters: with a 65 percent turnout, 78 percent of Russia's voters agreed to the proposal.[10]

The institutional contortions that the autocrats in power perform in order not to lose have become common. A study published in 2020 in the *Columbia Law Review* by Mila Versteeg, Tim Horley, and Anne Meng et al found that since the year 2000, presidential term-limit evasion has become "exceedingly common." "About one-third of all presidents who reached the end of their term made a serious attempt to overstay," the study finds. "Two-thirds of those who tried succeeded." As Versteeg and her coauthors show, amending the constitution is the most common path, accounting for two-thirds of attempted overstays. But constitutions have also been rewritten entirely to extend term limits—a strategy they found in 8 percent of attempted overstays. Challenging the legality of term limits before the courts accounts for 15 percent of cases, with Bolivia the stand-out case. And appointing a Medvedev-style stand-in/stooge rounds out the remainder of cases.[11]

The amendment strategy is especially popular in Africa. Just since 2015, leaders in Burundi, Benin, the Democratic Republic of Congo, and Rwanda expressed plans to scrap or extend their countries' term limits. Egypt's president, Abdel Fattah el-Sisi, a former general, had notional term limits removed in early 2019. When the Ugandan constitution's age limit of seventy-five years for the presidency threatened the reelection prospects of the seventy-three-year-old incumbent, Yoweri Museveni, he had the Ugandan parliament, full of his supporters, amend it.

In Latin America, Bolivia's president Evo Morales broke records for shamelessness in trying to circumvent term limits. First he held a constitutional referendum in 2016 to ask the voters to abolish term limits. When 51.3 percent of Bolivians rejected Morales's proposal at the ballot box, he turned to the courts, getting his hand-picked constitutional tribunal to rule, in November 2017, that the constitution itself was unconstitutional because its term limits violated the president's innate human right to stand for election. By 2019, it looked as though Morales had pushed his luck too far: his reelection in a process riddled with irregularities provoked a military coup, and Morales had to flee the country. A year later, the candidate he supported won the presidential election, and Morales triumphantly returned to Bolivia.

Evo Morales's gambit was an especially glaring example but not at all isolated. In Venezuela, Hugo Chávez opted instead to keep asking this referendum question as many times as it took for voters to give the right answer. After having proposed a broad constitutional reform lifting term limits that was defeated by the voters in 2007, he refused to take no for an answer, asking the question again in a 2009 vote (when the voters finally gave him the answer he'd wanted). There was no specific legal impediment to just proposing the same referendum question again and again until voters gave in—the tactic didn't so much break the law as render it meaningless.

Perhaps one of the clearest cases of a democratically elected leader who sets out to terminate term limits right after winning an election is that of Sri Lanka's president Gotabaya Rajapaksa. In mid-2020, his party, the People's Front, won a majority in parliament, which meant that the president's brother, Mahinda, could continue as prime minister. The two brothers used their parliamentary supermajority to pass the Twentieth Amendment to Sri Lanka's constitution. This gave them the power to revoke a two-term limit on the presidency, grant the president blanket immunity from persecution while in office, and annul the provision that made presidential appointments subject to parliamentary oversight.

The Reversal: When Politicians Pick their Voters

When we read about such behaviors in impoverished, faraway countries, we risk feeling a certain sense of immunity, a self-satisfied feeling that such a thing could never happen in consolidated democracies. But the Trump era has, if nothing else, had the salutary effect of puncturing Americans' dangerous complacency about the perilous spread of populism.

The sense of panic about the damage Donald Trump and his enablers inflicted on the American republic captures the problem only partially. Some of the most dangerous trends toward pseudolaw in the United States long precede him.

Certainly, America's most distinguished contribution to the canon of pseudolaw is gerrymandering—the art of drawing election district lines to maximize one party's representation over another. This practice is anything but new: after all, it's named after Elbridge Gerry, one of the signers of the Declaration of Independence. As governor of Massachusetts between 1810 and 1812, Gerry put together a district map for the state senate that gave a huge electoral advantage to his own party's candidates.[12] Gerrymandering has survived until today and consists of manipulating the borders of a territorial unit in a way that ensures that one's party has an advantage.

This bizarre practice allows representatives to pick their voters rather than the other way around. It is undemocratic, primitive, and untouchable until now. The practice, with a sordid history that dates back to the founding of the republic, has been completely transformed and deeply radicalized in the twenty-first century by the development of sophisticated mapping software. Historical gerrymanders were artisanal affairs crudely cooked up in smoke-filled rooms by political bosses and operatives using paper and pen. Now big data and mapping applications allow leaders granular control over the demographic profile of the districts they wish to serve. Gerrymandering as a concept may not be new, but computer-assisted gerrymandering is so much more powerful than the heritage variety that it has become one of the most powerful tools in the 3P arsenal.

In a gerrymandered election map, the party that has the power to define the boundaries of an electoral district will win many districts by relatively comfortable margins and lose a small number of districts by huge margins. This is achieved by "packing and cracking" the opposing party's supporters. First, the party that controls the redistricting planning will "pack" as many of the opposing party's supporters (often minority voters) into a small handful of districts, where they will have huge permanent supermajorities. This ensures that the opposing party "wastes" many votes in a small number of districts that are specifically designed never to be competitive.

Then the gerrymanderer "cracks" the remainder of the opposition's voters by spreading them thinly among a bigger number of remaining districts, where they don't have a realistic chance of victory. Cracking thus creates many districts where one party wins consistently by comfortable but not overwhelming margins. Skillfully applied, the "packing and cracking" approach can turn a minority of voters into a comfortable majority of elected seats.

This is a key part of the reason the United States has districts that are two-thirds black, like Mississippi's Second Congressional District, or 80 percent Latino, like Texas's Fifteenth District. When Democratic-voting minorities are packed at such densities, the rest of the state is left with many more reliably Republican districts. The outcome is pseudolaw painted in bright hues of red, white, and blue.

Through the aggressive application of new mapping technology, for instance, North Carolina's partisan gerrymander turned the Republicans' 53 percent share of the popular vote in the 2016 House of Representatives into 77 percent of the state's seats in the U.S. House of Representatives, with the GOP winning ten of those thirteen seats. A state that is 22 percent black ended up with a congressional delegation that was less than 8 percent black. Worse, not even one of North Carolina's thirteen congressional districts was decided by less than

12 percentage points. When gerrymandering is this aggressive, a state often heads into election day with perfectly predictable outcomes of its congressional races.

And North Carolina is far from unique in its willingness to countenance an extreme partisan gerrymander. In 2016, Pennsylvania, a "purple" state closely divided between Republicans and Democrats, ended up with a congressional delegation that was 72 percent Republican. In Wisconsin in 2018, a state where voters gave 53 percent of their support to Democratic candidates for the state assembly, who nonetheless ended up with Democrats holding only 36 percent of that assembly's seats.[13]

These departures should make clear that democracy is safe nowhere, not even in the nation that pioneered it in the modern world. When issues of real power come to the fore, politicians' rhetorical commitment to democracy turns out to be paper-thin.

"When highly committed parties strongly believe in things that they cannot achieve democratically," argues David Frum, "they don't give up on their beliefs—they give up on democracy."[14] Frum makes this argument in *Trumpocracy*, his 2018 broadside against the corrupting effect of the Trump administration.[15] But even before Donald Trump was elected, American democracy had displayed worrying signs of serious backsliding. Such backsliding deepened enormously during Trump's time in power, to the point that a violent insurrection broke into the actual halls of Congress on January 6, 2021, under the president's influence.

Gerrymandering is by no means the only kind of 3P shenanigan that flourishes in the richest countries as well as in the poorest. An even more consequential one involves stacking the judiciary with reliable political appointees.

Working the Ref: When the Powerful Pick Their Own Judges

Among the most startling cases of 3P autocracy are those in central and eastern Europe, where a new breed of right-wing populists has applied the 3P framework with rapid success. Hungary, Poland, the Czech Republic, and Bulgaria have each seen the rise of governments that clash strongly with European standards, creating repeated clashes between national governments and the Brussels-based EU institutions. Hungary and Poland, in particular, show the operations of 3P autocracy with special clarity under leaders who have moved decisively to consolidate their power and shield it from any form of challenge. And to do that, it becomes crucial to control the judges.

In Poland, to take one example, the hard-right Law and Justice Party (PiS) took power in 2015 and moved quickly to make sure meddlesome judges could not short-circuit its governing program. Pseudolaw demands that such a power grab be justified as a defense of democracy, and PiS hewed closely to the script.

Throughout the 2010s, PiS leaders argued that after the fall of the Berlin Wall a generation earlier, Poland had undertaken an "incomplete transition to democracy," with secret supporters of the old communist regime packed into powerful posts within the judiciary disguised as liberals. The style of reasoning behind this justification should already be sounding alarm bells to those with a feel for the 3P framework—a sweeping, unproven allegation is put at the center of a program of political reform that, by "coincidence," can only be addressed by placing substantial new powers in the hands of the executive. This was very much PiS's program for Poland's courts: an aggressive push to dislodge existing judges and replace them with loyal PiS cronies was presented as a move to bolster the rule of law.

Poland's European neighbors were having none of it, and soon the European Commission found itself in a long, testy battle with Warsaw over its commitment to the rule of law. But criticism of Europe was baked into the PiS plan from the beginning: posturing as the defenders of Polish sovereignty facing down meddling from leftist intellectuals in the rest of Europe had always been a key part of PiS's populism and polarization strategy. The howls of outrage from Brussels, Paris, and Berlin were a feature of their plan, not a bug.

Membership in the European Union has hardly been an effective obstacle to the spread of these techniques. In 2017, the PiS-controlled Polish supreme court created a disciplinary chamber, which quickly set about harassing and threatening judges for a variety of perceived misdeeds. Since 2016, at least sixty judges have faced proceedings before the chamber, with some threatened with sentences of up to three years in jail for handing down rulings the government disapproved of. In some cases, judges were punished merely for seeking opinions from the European Court of Justice—now an "offense" that can result in up to 40 percent of a judge's salary being docked.

This sort of grab for the judiciary is another recurring theme in any bid to entrench a new stealthocracy. Courts can hinder any other part of the authoritarian program: making sure they are on the autocrat's side is very commonly the next priority, second only to controlling the nation's executive office. Which is why aggressive moves to tilt the courts in one's political direction are among the most powerful signs that stealthocracy is on the prowl.

In the United States, the GOP-controlled Senate's decision to hold a Supreme Court seat open throughout 2016, the entire final year of the Obama administration, is justly famous as a canary in the coal mine of judicial independence—an early sign that the basic liberal democratic order would soon come under unprecedented pressure. The justifications given about "giving the voters a chance to decide who would appoint the new justice" were vintage pseudolaw—blatantly prejudicial to the rule of law as a whole without necessarily ever breaking any specific law.

The eventual appointment in 2017 of a conservative stalwart, Neil Gorsuch, was worrying, but arguably not the most worrying aspect of the new Trump administration's approach to justice. Supreme Court appointments are high-visibility affairs that attract intense public scrutiny, but less visible appointments lower down the judicial totem pole often do as much to shape the legal landscape.

Here, things were worse. Soon after taking office in 2017, President Trump moved quickly to appoint and get Congress to confirm an unprecedented twelve appellate court judges. In the lower courts, too, Trump moved decisively, appointing an unprecedented number of judges who were plainly not qualified for their posts. Several amounted to little more than GOP political operatives in robes. One, Matthew Petersen, made headlines when a video surfaced of him during a hearing in which he could not answer the kinds of basic questions about legal procedures that any first-year law school student would be expected to master. He had been nominated to the U.S. District Court for the District of Columbia.

The blithe dismissal of long-established norms of behavior in office played its role in Trump's approach to the courts as well. For decades, federal judgeships were appointed following a set process that saw "home-state senators"—senators elected in the state where the judge would serve—play the leading role. The tradition varied from state to state, but in many cases, home-state senators were expected to defer to the state bar or other local institutions, allowing them a formal role in the decision-making process. The Trump administration discarded these norms and traditions, which together had created obstacles to the arbitrary appointment of political cronies, without a second thought.

Take this approach to its furthest logical extreme and you find yourself in Turkey, under the helm of another of the world's most ruthless and effective 3P leaders: Recep Tayyip Erdoğan. When he took office as prime minister, in 2003, he faced an unusual predicament: while he campaigned on a promise to radically progress the Turkish state away from its secular tradition and toward a more Islamic-infused style of nationalism and conservatism, he faced an entrenched military and legal establishment put in place in the 1920s by Kemal Ataturk, the founder of modern Turkey, precisely to prevent any move away from secularism. Those institutions had given rise to a doggedly secularist ruling establishment popularly known as Kemalism. Obsessed with enforcing a strict separation between mosque and state, Kemalism went to lengths that would be controversial in the West, such as barring women from wearing Islamic headscarves in state-funded universities. It would take unusually determined action to bring down this decades-long status quo, but Erdoğan achieved it through a sustained, patient war of attrition followed by a shockingly aggressive final push.

In 2010, Erdoğan's AKP party put a referendum to Turkey's voters that, among other things, drastically strengthened his control over the judiciary. The proposal deprived sitting senior judges of their long-standing role in vetting the appointments of junior judges, giving the AKP's majority in parliament final say over the board that makes judicial appointments. That board was also—wait for it—packed, with new seats created specifically to be filled by AKP loyalists. These reforms promised to gradually loosen the Kemalist hold over the judiciary. But events would soon end Erdoğan's patience for gradualism.

In July 2016, military commanders alarmed by the Islamist and authoritarian angle Erdoğan seemed to be pursuing attempted to overthrow his government by force. The coup failed and, in its wake, Erdoğan seized his chance: a broad-based purge of both the military and the judiciary followed. By the end of 2016, the American Bar Association warned that more than four thousand Turkish judges, prosecutors, and other high-ranking legal professionals had been not just fired but jailed. They were held in squalid, overcrowded facilities amid a broad purge of the state that, at its height, saw nearly two hundred thousand suspects detained. Turkey simply didn't have anywhere near enough prison cells to put away all the people Erdoğan felt threatened by, and the state of emergency made possible by the coup enabled him to move against them all at once, with no possibility of judicial review. After all, the judges who normally would be doing the reviewing were, by and large, themselves in jail.

Where 3P autocrats try to consolidate power, a sprawling, shadowy conspiracy theory supported by little evidence is never far behind. After his success in subduing Kemalism, Erdoğan pivoted to an enemy with roots in his own Islamist camp. Here, the pivotal figure was Fethullah Gülen, an exiled cleric living in the United States, who, Erdoğan said, led a vast, secret network of conspirators against him.[16] As usual, the absence of actual evidence of a conspiracy perversely reinforced Erdoğan's belief in the theory; that they could not be located only confirmed the skill of the conspirators.

Erdoğan's push against the Gülenists alleged to be hiding in every nook and cranny of the Turkish state stuck to the letter of Turkey's secular constitution, all the while emptying it of practical meaning. With emergency powers used to justify the arbitrary arrest of hundreds of thousands of people given no hope of being brought before a judge, Erdoğan abolished habeas corpus in practice, though never in theory. Pseudolaw has seldom been pursued at a greater cost to human rights than in Turkey's anti-Gülenist purges. One upshot was a court system utterly purged of judges independent enough to act as a real check on Erdoğan's power. Moves to control the courts need not be as over the top as Turkey's. One venerable old mechanism is court-packing: simply expanding the number of seats on a court to create a majority of cronies. Famously attempted—unsuccessfully—by Franklin D. Roosevelt in 1937, court-packing is an idea that would be picked up in later decades by others with far less credible democratic credentials.

In 2004, Hugo Chávez created an additional twelve seats on the Venezuelan supreme court in addition to the twenty already in place. The move was not specifically prohibited by the Venezuelan constitution, and yet the practical effect was what you would expect: what had been a closely divided court came to have a permanent pro-government majority. The practice effectively ended the judiciary as a check on government power. In 2014, a team of Venezuelan legal scholars reviewed some 45,474 decisions handed down by the supreme tribunal between 2004 and 2013 and failed to find even a single ruling against the government.

The debasement of the Venezuelan supreme tribunal continued for years thereafter. In 2017, a jurist by the name of Maikel Moreno was appointed chief justice, despite a criminal rap sheet rumored to contain a murder charge. A Reuters investigation of the allegation found all records of the case had conveniently disappeared.[17] Moreno was indicted by the U.S. Department of Justice in early 2020 on a slew of corruption charges stemming from bribes he had taken from defendants before the court. According to the indictment, in the past few years Moreno had spent as much as a million dollars on private charter flights, and many times that on luxury real estate in south Florida.

But in some situations, court unpacking can have the same effect. In 2016 in North Carolina, when the Republican-led legislature realized a number of GOP-appointed appeals court judges would reach retirement age in the coming years and their replacements would be appointed by the new Democratic governor, they passed a law to reduce the number of judges on the state appeals court from fifteen to twelve—a decision that would safeguard the Republican majority just as effectively. Again, nothing in North Carolina's constitution specifically prohibited the move—but its political effects were never exactly in doubt. Tortured pseudolegal interpretations were put in the service of raw power, all the while retaining a patina of legality too thin to be credible but thick enough to shroud the controversy in a fog of partisanship. In this case, pseudolaw, stealth, and post-truth all operated in tandem a few hours' drive from the capital of the world's oldest democracy.

The move to unpack North Carolina's appeals court came only after the GOP-controlled legislature saw the governor replaced with an incoming Democrat. As such, it represents a particular kind of shenanigan that illustrates the perils of the lame-duck session.

The Logic of Preemption and the Perils of the Lame-Duck Session

By and large, autocrats would prefer to do away with elections—and do so as soon as it's politically feasible. Electorates being fickle, it isn't always possible to prevent an election loss. But in most places, power isn't handed over immediately after an election—only weeks or months later. Legislators still get to legislate, and executives still get to execute in this so-called lame-duck session, even if they've been voted out.

Electoral defeats of incumbents who happen to be aspiring autocrats often spark bold attacks against precedent and democratic norms. The case of Donald Trump's bold attempt to overturn his election loss at the end of 2020 and the beginning of 2021 is the most notable recent case. But it's far from the only one. Take Venezuela. As we have seen, Hugo Chávez had already moved to pack his supreme court once, back in 2005. A decade later, the Venezuelan regime decided to do it again.

In a 2015 election for parliament, Nicolás Maduro's political party was stunned to lose two-thirds of the seats in the unicameral National Assembly. The outgoing pro-Maduro National Assembly moved swiftly to repack Venezuela's supreme tribunal. Whereas the judges appointed in 2004 had been, for the most part, plausible-seeming legal scholars who were ideologically sympathetic to the government, the 2015 appointees were hardly lawyers. Instead, they were a who's who of Maduro's most extreme supporters, including a member of parliament for the ruling party who had lost his bid for reelection in 2015 and during the lame-duck session voted for himself to sit on the court. Within two years, this crew had elected as its chief justice the First Lady's schoolmate.

Maduro seemed to calculate that this far more tightly controlled supreme court would be willing to go places the previous supreme court would not have countenanced. Control of the court allowed the government to completely neuter the new opposition-dominated National Assembly. At one point, in 2017, citing alleged irregularities in the elections for the legislature, the new court ruled that it would transfer to itself all the powers the constitution assigned to the National Assembly. In short, the supreme court that Maduro had swiftly packed declared itself Venezuela's parliament. It turns out that if you have enough control over a sufficiently brazen court, winning elections becomes entirely optional.

Once such tricks become established in a country's political culture, it turns out to be enormously difficult to root them out. Perversely, opponents of the new powers sometimes find themselves tempted to adopt stealthocratic behaviors themselves as a last-ditch effort to slow the advance of a looming autocracy. Faced with losing power, the logic of preemption takes place—and those threatened by the rise of a 3P autocracy sometimes end up adopting the 3P autocrats' own techniques.

What makes pseudolaw so dangerous is that it's a contagious disease. Think once more of Poland. When the Law and Justice Party won the 2015 parliamentary election, the outgoing liberals panicked. Justifiably concerned by the prospect of looming PiS judicial appointments, they decided to use the lame-duck session, the period between the election and the swearing-in of the new administration, to preempt them. To prevent PiS from stacking the constitutional court with its supporters, the outgoing liberal government rushed to place as many new liberal justices on the bench as possible. The move was done in accordance with the law—but it was also, quite plainly, calculated to box in the new PiS government and prevent it from carrying out the reforms it had promised to undertake if elected.

Of course, this preemptive move only deepened the incoming PiS majority's sense that it had been wronged. And it had been: PiS came into power with a legitimate grievance over the makeup of the Polish constitutional court and with a powerful case that its opponents were the ones undermining democratic norms.

When a major, difficult-to-reverse policy decision is made during a lame-duck session by a government that's just been voted out of power, it's a fair bet that democratic norms are under serious strain. In Poland, these decisions were legal and made just before power came to a 3P autocrat.

But lame-duck-session abuses don't need to be this extreme to establish a disturbing pattern of authoritarian drift. In some cases, politicians reveal the full extent of their authoritarianism only after being voted out.

As we've already seen, North Carolina's 2016 lame-duck session set the high-water mark for stealthocracy in America. Republican governor Pat McCrory was, by all accounts, stunned by a narrow loss to his Democratic challenger, Roy Cooper. After initially refusing to concede the election, McCrory eventually realized that he would have no choice but to accept his loss. He then set out to work with the Republican majority in the state legislature to push a series of laws during the lame-duck session that would strip key powers from the incoming governor.

The new laws forced Cooper to submit his cabinet choices to approval by the Republican-led legislature. The legislature also removed the incoming governor's power to name new members to the board of trustees of the University of North Carolina, stripped his power to oversee elections, and cut the number of appointments he could make to state government jobs by two-thirds. A long court battle ensued, which Cooper, the incoming governor, ultimately lost in 2018 at the hands of the Republican state supreme court majority.[18]

Cooper did indeed become governor, but the office he was handed had a fraction of the powers it had had under his predecessor. It's not quite Venezuelan-level encroachment, but the instinct to subvert democracy by hamstringing elected leaders before they can take office is entirely similar.

McCrory defended his moves as an attempt to safeguard North Carolina's elections and to improve the quality of education in the state. The justification was classic pseudolaw: it observed the outward appearance of legality, but that legality was of the paper-thin kind, barely able to conceal its authoritarian intent.

The Hollowness of Illiberal Democracy

Sometimes 3P autocracy spreads by imitation. Poland's Law and Justice Party did not arrive at its political and economic reform program by chance. Jarosław Kaczyński, its charismatic leader, never hid his admiration for Viktor Orbán, the hard-core nativist prime minister elected next door in Hungary and, arguably, the most successful of the 3P autocrats in Europe.

"Viktor Orbán has demonstrated that in Europe things are possible," Jarosław Kaczyński said in 2016. "You have given an example, and we are learning from your example."[19]

Since coming to power in 2010, Orbán's Fidesz party has pursued one of the most comprehensive programs of 3P autocracy in recent memory. In fact, Fidesz began its bid with a comprehensive approach to stealthocracy: packing the courts, furtively purging the bureaucracy, and ending the independence of the state broadcaster. Crucially, it manipulated Hungary's election system to all but guarantee a permanent Fidesz majority in parliament. With its authority sufficiently entrenched, in 2020 it moved in for the kill, effectively suspending parliament and announcing that Orbán would rule by decree in response to the COVID-19 pandemic. He was not the only 3P autocrat in the world who used the need to fight the pandemic as an excuse to concentrate power and further curtail civil liberties. Rwandan president Paul Kagame, Uganda's Yoweri Museveni, and

leaders in Tanzania, India, Turkey, South Africa, Singapore, and beyond presided over massive expansions in executive authority under
the cover of COVID-19.

During a heated public discussion on the merits and risks of eas-
ing the lockdowns and getting the economy moving again, President
Donald Trump claimed to have "absolute power" to decide, thus
overriding state governors. He was quickly rebuffed by an army of
legal scholars, political commentators, and legislators. In this case,
the constitutional guardrails prevailed, but the illiberal temptation to
ignore them was also entirely obvious.[20]

These kinds of power grabs—the unending thirst to remove blocks
on executive power and wear away at the guarantees extended to
minorities—are sometimes described as "illiberal democracy." That,
at any rate, is what Viktor Orbán calls it.[21] But a closer look at his
record shows this is a contradiction in terms. Hungary shows clearly
how, under the assault of illiberal leaders, democracy itself becomes
a mirage.

Orbán, for one, spent years on a breathtakingly broad campaign to entrench Fidesz's stranglehold on the state. Gerrymandering
was just one aspect of this; Fidesz consulted no one before halving
the number of parliamentary seats and redrawing their boundaries
alongside tried-and-true "packing and cracking" principles—North
Carolina on the Danube. But it also altered rules to make it easier for
ethnic Hungarians outside Hungary, key Fidesz supporters, to vote.

Orbán ultimately dreamed up mechanisms for malapportionment
that made American gerrymandering look tame in comparison. In
Hungary, parliamentary districts don't have to be equal in population.
And Orbán has made sure they aren't. Today, more urban districts—
which tend to go to the left—have as many as ninety thousand voters,
while in rural areas, which are Fidesz's heartland, they can have as few
as sixty thousand voters. It simply takes more Hungarians to elect an
opposition MP than a Fidesz one.

And Fidesz has gone further: in a country where the center-left
has long been divided into several competing parties, the ruling party
ended the tradition of having a second round of voting in parliamentary elections. The move allows Fidesz to win seats on pluralities

of the vote in places where it could never have won a two-round election.

Democratic-minded Hungarians might be tempted to challenge such an outcome in the courts, but naturally the courts themselves were among Fidesz's earliest targets. This mechanism will, by now, ring familiar: a new law, introduced in 2012, lowered the mandatory age of retirement for judges from seventy to sixty-two, clearing out most judges not aligned with Fidesz.

But it goes beyond that. In the Hungarian system, senior judges have to agree to the appointment of new junior judges. Cleaning out the senior reaches of the judiciary by manipulating the age of retirement cleared the way for the appointment of a whole generation of new Fidesz cronies to junior judgeships, radically remaking the country's judiciary branch. So yes, Hungarians appalled at the unfairness of the electoral system Orbán pioneered are well within their rights to bring a suit, but that suit will likely be heard by a Fidesz partisan. Pseudolaw administered by pseudojudges.

And it's here that the hollowness of the idea of "illiberal democracy" comes into sharp focus: without liberal checks and balances, there's no mechanism to ensure that elections remain competitive, free, and fair. With the ruling party manipulating the rules to put its thumb on the voting scale, and with no institutional recourse against it, illiberal democracy amounts to a sort of nonsense. Where competition is rigged, democracy is hollow.

For many of today's 3P autocrats, stealth is just an intermediate step: a messy compromise with democratic rules they despise and intend to jettison as soon as it's politically safe to do so. Viktor Orbán kept up a thin façade of democratic normality until he found he no longer needed to. So did Nicolás Maduro in Venezuela and Vladimir Putin in Russia. Brazil's Jair Bolsonaro is a similar case, as is the Philippines' Rodrigo Duterte.

Democratic norms are kept up for a time, alongside a stream of broadsides against the evils of Western liberalism. And yet these leaders always seem to find it much easier to describe what they are against— meddling EU officials, Western intellectuals, politicized NGOs, the long arm of George Soros, feminists, the LGBTQ community and those who champion its rights, progressives, secularists, Davos, the trilateral commission, Zionists, conspirators, the Foro de São Paulo, and so on—than what they are for.

When Orbán has tried to put forward a positive case for "illiberal democracy," he either falls back on empty phrases about national competitiveness or indulges in outright praise for dictatorships. And when—rarely—he makes the attempt to sketch out the principles behind his doctrine, he ends up turning to the very same language about liberty he also claims to be fighting.

On July 26, 2014, for instance, Orbán made his famous "illiberal democracy" speech at a summer camp for his followers in Băile Tușnad, Romania. The speech—billed as the most fleshed-out version of his governing philosophy—is often vague and defensive. But it sets out the key elements of illiberal democracy: "Hungarian voters expect from their leaders to figure out, forge and work out a new form of state-organization that will make the community of Hungarians competitive once again after the era of liberal state and liberal democracy, one that will of course still respect values of Christianity, freedom and human rights."

This, in its own way, is quite remarkable. Even Europe's most forthright enemy of liberalism ends up, when the chips are down, claiming respect for bedrock liberal values. Even a movement as extreme as Fidesz finds itself cloaking its ideology in a rhetorical hodgepodge that, while incoherent, draws extensively on the language of conventional liberal democracy. In a speech billed as a denunciation of liberal democracy, Viktor Orbán ends up justifying his war on checks and balances with the idea that his departures from orthodoxy are needed to safeguard "Christianity, freedom and human rights."

This kind of rhetorical incoherence isn't surprising. To live beyond the end of history is to live in a world without a coherent alternative to liberal democracy. It is a world where even committed illiberals and anti-liberals find themselves championing liberal values, justifying any departure from liberal orthodoxy as a means of delivering on liberal goals.

The era of stealthocracy is the era of anti-liberals who purposely make it difficult for a casual observer to pinpoint their illiberalism.

Shorn of any other system for explaining why their power is legitimate, today's aspiring autocrats must necessarily hide. Ultimately, they have no choice.

Tactics as brazen as Evo Morales's attempt in Bolivia to spin a tale about human rights to stay in power indefinitely are not just a product of the political backwardness of an impoverished corner of South America. In rich countries and poor ones, in fledgling democracies and established ones, the same set of tactics recur again and again in an effort to defang checks and balances and supercharge the political supremacy of 3P autocrats. It's a worldwide trend: absolute power survives, furtively, by mimicking the institutions it corrupts. Sometimes it is content to remain in that in-between space. But often it treats that space as only a way station on the path to full autocracy.

2

THE POLITICS OF FANDOM

The revenge of power rests on a paradox. On the one hand, it puts a premium on stealth; 3P power has strong incentives to hide its undemocratic ways and power-concentrating practices, especially early on. That might lead us to imagine its leaders as reclusive figures stashed away in distant palaces, happy to rule from behind a curtain. And yet this could not be further from the truth.

In fact, 3P autocrats may be careful to use pseudolaw to conceal the tricks they rely upon to obtain and retain power, but this doesn't mean they hide themselves from view. Far from it. To enable the polarization that is the second pillar of the 3P framework, they make themselves ubiquitous: omnipresent and unavoidable. More than leaders to their followers, they become stars to their fans. And just ask any avid sports fan: What fun is supporting your team without a rival team to hate?

The 3P autocrats operate a startling inversion of the twentieth-century pattern of autocracy. As immortalized in novels like Gabriel García Márquez's The Autumn of the Patriarch[1] and Ryszard Kapuściński The Emperor,[2] the traditional pattern called for an autocrat who takes pains to make himself invisible while the evidence of his limitless power is put relentlessly on display.

The old pattern was the system favored by Kim Jong Il—Kim Jong Un's father, who suffered from an extreme case of agoraphobia and who could go years without appearing in public, all the while controlling the lives of North Koreans down to their most intimate details. It was also the style of Hosni Mubarak, Egypt's ruler from 1981 to 2011, who appeared in public only at tightly controlled, formal state occasions to read wooden scripted speeches to the masses in a droning monotone, all the while keeping an iron grip over the Egyptian state.

3P autocracy reverses that equation, making the autocrat highly visible, inescapable, familiar, while carefully obscuring the mechanisms he uses to amass and wield power. While his operatives obscure the actual power grabs behind a fog of pseudolaw, the 3P leader is front and center, developing a deeply personal bond with his followers that shields him from the formal, lawful demands for accountability. Far from being in contradiction, stealth and spectacle work together to deliver the revenge of power.

But it isn't just that the new breed of autocrat revels in the limelight. Autocrats going back to Shelley's mythical Ozymandias ("Look on my Works, ye Mighty, and despair!") have always cherished admiration and sharpened the differences with their opponents.[3]

These days, though, that sharpening is different because the 3P autocrats' relationship with their followers has been transformed and has, in many cases, transitioned out of the political realm altogether. Their followers idolize them the way they idolize a sports star or a pop culture icon; they've come to act less like political followers and more like fans. The culture of fandom has run riot across a political realm ill-suited to it.

What we're describing here is a new incarnation of an age-old phenomenon. Charismatic leaders dating back to Julius Caesar and Charlemagne built cults of personality, as did more recent populists like Argentina's Juan Perón, leftists like Fidel Castro, and Fascists like Benito Mussolini. What's different now is how closely patterned today's political cults are on the entertainment values of our age.

Fans build their personal identity out of a primal identification with the stars they follow. But they also build it in opposition to—and in hatred of—"the other team." In sports, this is great fun. In politics, it sows the dangerous seeds of polarization—the second element of our 3P world.

Polarization pulls societies apart. It always has. Within the 3P framework, it is more acute, more global, digitally mediated, and widespread. It is also boosted by the intense activism of social groups that feel excluded and abused by the old order and relish their chance to take the fight to those who live on the opposite pole. Polarization solidifies the 3P autocrat's grip over his followers. A polarized polity, where supporters can be expected to fall in line automatically, allows a leader to exercise power with far fewer fetters than before. And, crucially, polarization can be sharpened unilaterally simply by heightening the rhetoric on one side of the divide and trusting the backlash on the other side to do half of the work. That's why polarization acts as such a powerful centripetal force, concentrating power that would disperse and decay in its absence.

$50 for Less than Two Hours of Work

The ad on Craigslist, the classified advertisements website, was short on detail. "$50 for less than two hours of work," it said.[4] For plenty of young actors struggling to make ends meet in pricey New York, it must have been tempting. Few could have imagined they were heading to a gig bound for the history books.

It was the afternoon of June 16, 2015. Their instructions were sparse: cheer loud on the applause lines. Nothing more.

They all likely felt a tinge of excitement, realizing they might be about to see someone famous. Most probably assumed they were there for some publicity stunt: a product launch, or maybe a slick new marketing campaign.

They weren't exactly wrong. On arrival, each was handed a T-shirt and instructed to put it on. "Trump: Make America Great Again!" the shirts read. As Donald Trump followed Melania on that now famous escalator ride down to the Trump Tower lobby, with Neil Young's "Keep On Rockin' in the Free World" blaring from the speakers, it's hard to imagine any of the extras hired for atmospherics seriously entertained the thought that they were cheering the next president of the United States.

Over the next forty-seven minutes, Donald Trump would dumbfound the world with a campaign launch speech unlike anything the country had seen before: "When was the last time you saw a Chevrolet in Tokyo . . . ? When did we beat Mexico, at the border? They're laughing at us, at our stupidity, they are not our friends, believe me. The U.S. has become a dumping ground for everybody else's problems."[5] Jumping back and forth between grand policy pronouncements, us-versus-them applause lines, and self-aggrandizing anecdotes, the speech established many of the tropes that would become the core of Trump's rhetoric.

It seemed to matter little to Trump that the ecstatic applause he was hearing was bought and paid for. He fed off it just the same. He didn't know it quite yet, but candidate Trump wouldn't need to keep spending money on rent-a-crowds for much longer.

Months after the event, the Federal Elections Commission announced that although Trump had failed to disclose the $12,000 sum paid for actors to cheer him at this event—a disclosure required by federal elections law—it would not fine the Trump campaign for the violation given the relatively small sum involved.

It's easy to forget how ridiculous it all seemed, how crass. Political experts, prominent journalists, and academics were unanimous in treating the Trump candidacy as a sideshow with no chance of success. They took it for granted that it would soon be forgotten.

Mocking his boorish boast to be worth $8 billion, for instance, *Time* magazine's Alex Altman and Charlotte Alter sneered:

> There are about eight billion reasons Trump won't be president. He was pro-choice until recently. He supported massive taxes on the ultra-rich. He has advocated tightening gun laws. He backed single-payer healthcare, a policy that conservatives abhor even more than Obamacare. His approvals are 32 points underwater in his own party, making Trump the least popular presidential candidate since at least 1980.[6]

It's not that they thought Trump wrong. It was worse than that. They thought him ridiculous.

And they were not alone.

Sophisticates knew which side of the politics/entertainment divide Donald J. Trump belonged on. They'd spent their entire professional lives among people to whom that divide was sacrosanct. The divide organized their view of politics, it kept their world together. It was a basic guardrail: the sense that the separation between politics and show business, between power and spectacle was solid, reliable, *real*.

And yet ridiculous though they may have found Donald J. Trump, the pundits just couldn't stop talking about him. News editors hungry for clicks and eyeballs in an increasingly competitive media environment quickly grasped the commercial upside of giving Trump wall-to-wall coverage. Soon everything Trump did invited a headline, a hot take, a sneering tweet. Whether it was his racist outbursts, his outrageous policy pronouncements, or his outlandish claims of huge personal wealth, Trump never bored an audience.

It was only far too late that the elite began to realize what, to Trump, must have been obvious all along: that their sneering was one of his strongest electoral assets. That his followers experienced elite scorn for him as elite scorn for *them*. That the more the elite attacked him, the stronger he got.

As Roderick Hart argued in *Trump and Us: What He Says and Why People Listen*, Trump tapped into the public's feelings along four powerful axes.[7] His persona connected with their feelings of being ignored, of being trapped, of being under siege, and he tapped into their overall weariness about politics. Over and over again, he used words denoting anger to galvanize his base—which had the additional benefit of horrifying his opponents, riling them up, and getting them to participate in the polarization strategy he so clearly needed.

He had no need to theorize any of this. Donald Trump understood the power of spectacle. He felt it in his bones. Steeped for four decades in celebrity culture and the entertainment industry, he had developed an unrivaled sixth sense for what it took to get noticed, written about, talked about, covered.

In his world, shot through with entertainment values, ratings are everything. Years later, amid the COVID-19 pandemic, he would stress-test this proposition, positively bragging about the ratings his April 2020 coronavirus briefings garnered for a period. It's a mindset that *knows* that there's no such thing as bad publicity. When he debuted on the national political stage in 2015, the political pros rolled their eyes at this upstart who thought he could transfer the methods of the entertainment world into this vastly different realm.

They were wrong. He was right.

What we didn't grasp was that as power degraded in its traditional domain, it was finding new ways to regroup elsewhere in new forms. Aspiring autocrats were responding to a changed landscape with changed strategies.

For years, celebrities seeking to trade their fame for political office took it for granted that they would have to undergo a lengthy reinvention. Their new role would demand that they step away from their former public personas and master the rules of their new trade. This wasn't impossible, but it was tricky. In the United States, figures ranging from Ronald Reagan and Arnold Schwarzenegger to comedian Al Franken and wrestler Jesse Ventura managed it. Franken, for decades one of the sharpest political satirists in America, imposed a strict no-jokes rule on himself once he became a senator. Schwarzenegger steeped himself in the minutiae of California's famously intractable public finances when he became the state's governor. Each made a conscious effort to shed their old, frivolous public persona in favor of a sober new image of the serious public policy wonk. It was the price of entry into their new careers.

Not Donald Trump. His main insight was that he could step directly into a political role without remaking himself into a "normal" politician first. Not only had the currency of celebrity become legal tender in the political realm, but the entertainment values it embodied were in the process of completely overwhelming the values of traditional politics.

America's pundit class was wholly unprepared for this reversal. They might have been better prepared if they'd spent some time in Italy in the mid-1990s.

Flashback: Milan, January 26, 1994

The stagecraft was deliberate: a slick re-creation of the look and feel of an office of state. It was no such thing. It was a private study in Silvio Berlusconi's eighteenth-century villa, just outside Milan. Seated at a large, commanding desk and broadcasting live over Italy's three main private TV networks (which, conveniently, he happened to own), Silvio Berlusconi looked gravely into the camera and spoke.

"Italy is the country I love," he intoned. "Here I have my roots, my hopes and my horizons."[8]

It was a polished speech to declare his decision to launch a political party and run for prime minister. Shamelessly leveraging Italians' storied love of soccer, Berlusconi announced he was ready to *scesa in campo*, to "come down onto the [soccer] pitch."[9] The address became immortalized as his *scesa in campo* speech.

This wasn't just any old businessperson speaking from behind that desk, though. By 1994, Silvio Berlusconi had amassed a fortune unrivaled in contemporary Italy.

A onetime cruise-ship singer who'd made good money in the 1970s as a real estate speculator in Milan, Berlusconi had made the jump from merely rich to billionaire status by establishing what amounted to a monopoly on Italy's commercial television broadcasting. Later, with cash to burn, he branched out into all sorts of industries: insurance, department stores, newspapers, financial services, magazines, books, et cetera. At the center of it all was Mediaset, his sprawling, hugely profitable TV holding company.

Mediaset thrived thanks to a legendary marketing and sales team. Fanning out across the country, Berlusconi's salespeople had perfected the art of pitching ads to midsized Italian businesses, the kinds of companies long considered too small to be a worthwhile target for advertising sales. Berlusconi found a way to sell ads on regional affiliates to the kinds of companies that had never been on Italian TV before: mom-and-pop operations selling afternoon snacks for kids, leather bags for respectable ladies, sprinklers for your lawn . . .

The ads worked. Mediaset delivered mass audiences to companies that had no other way to reach them. Why? Because Berlusconi had brilliantly spotted a market opportunity: Italy's venerable old state-owned and publicly subsidized broadcaster, RAI, was boring.

Broadcasting a long succession of high-minded but dreary shows dreamed up by intellectuals in Rome for the ennoblement of Italy's masses, RAI executives barely seemed to care that their programming was unwatchable. Italians could hardly be expected to flock to watch newscasts consisting of an anchor staring straight down at a piece of paper and droning on in monotone, or union leaders discussing the ins and outs of their collective bargaining sessions with Fiat. In fact, RAI almost went out of its way to avoid finding out whether anyone was interested in the programming they were offering: well into the 1980s, the state broadcaster had no system in place for tracking its own ratings.

Berlusconi had a much keener sense of what middle Italy wanted to see on the screen. Barred by existing legislation from setting up a nationwide operation all at once, he started to buy up small regional broadcasters in different parts of Italy and weave them together into a de facto network. He would cram each station with unabashedly lowbrow, mass-appeal programming: American series dubbed into Italian were a mainstay alongside bawdy variety shows, South American soap operas, and, of course, *Baywatch*. Lots of *Baywatch*.

It was the kind of trashy but fun programming that had been normal elsewhere for years but amounted to a media revolution in Italy. Berlusconi sensed this kind of fare could reliably deliver mass audiences to advertisers in a way no desiccated RAI documentary ever could. His remaining challenge was to build a sales team that could reach companies hungry for consumers' eyeballs and then offer to make the match.

It was not clear at the time, but Mediaset's junk TV was slowly poisoning the Italian public sphere. Decades later, Italian economists Rubén Durante, Paolo Pinotti, and Andrea Tesei looked in detail at differences in voting patterns between regions that hosted a Mediaset station early and those that could tune in to Berlusconi's behemoth only later.[10] Working from a trove of detailed data about where Mediaset expanded when, as well as granular psychometric tests measuring Italians' cognitive abilities and political preferences, the researchers found that early exposure to junk TV accounted for a substantial fraction of Berlusconi's electoral success.

But what was most jarring was *how* this result was achieved. Watching Mediaset appeared to render audiences substantially less cognitively sophisticated, as measured by the Programme for the International Assessment of Adult Competencies (PIAAC), a standardized adult literacy and numeracy test administered by the Organisation for Economic Co-operation and Development.[11] In particular, very young and very old viewers exposed to Mediaset early on turned out to be substantially less cognitively sophisticated than Italians who gained access to junk TV only later. Italians with early access to junk TV became more open to populist rhetoric, not only that coming from Mediaset's owner but also that coming from his later competitors in the Five Star Movement (on which we'll have much more to say in Chapter 6).

"Taken together," Durante and colleagues noted, "our findings support the view that exposure to entertainment television, particularly at a young age, can contribute to making individuals cognitively and culturally shallower, and ultimately more vulnerable to populist rhetoric."[12]

This empire of shallowness was staggeringly profitable, but by 1994 it was also uniquely imperiled. Never terribly fastidious about following the law, Berlusconi was being investigated on multiple tax evasion counts alongside allegations that he'd tried to bribe a judge. Faced with a dicey legal situation and hounded by aggressive investigative magistrates amid a sprawling anti-corruption investigation, he settled on an unconventional legal strategy: to stay out of jail, he would become prime minister.

Berlusconi's plan was enormously bold. He transformed his business empire, almost overnight, into a political party, Forza Italia. As Alexander Stille explains in *The Sack of Rome*, his account of that era:

> The ad executives contacted the companies that bought advertising on the Berlusconi channels. The stockbrokers and insurance agents working for Berlusconi's financial services company became cam-

paign workers and set about turning the hundreds of thousands, possibly millions, of financial clients into voters and party supporters. The personnel department of the television advertising company selected more than a hundred of the company's top ad salesmen to be candidates for the parliamentary elections. The candidates took screen tests at the television studios, were given lessons in politics, and were cross-examined to see how they would hold up under the fire of an election campaign. . . . The company's media experts, with expertise in testing TV programs, conducted focus groups to hone Berlusconi's message to appeal to the largest possible audience.[13]

It helped that by this point Berlusconi was a bona fide celebrity in his own right. His magazines and tabloids had spent years splashing showy stories of his billionaire playboy lifestyle across their front pages. He delighted in the attention and loved to pile on layer after layer of glitz and glamour. It was all terribly Trumpian, though a generation ahead. As Stille reports, in the summer of 1993, when he was assessing a jump into the political arena, Berlusconi commissioned a poll that found he had 97 percent name recognition, compared to 51 percent for Carlo Azeglio Ciampi, who was Italy's actual prime minister at the time.

Berlusconi set out to use the same approach Mediaset used to sell mortadella to grandmothers in Sorrento and dried pasta to soccer fans in Bergamo to sell parliamentary candidates to those very same people. It helped that he didn't have to go out and recruit those candidates: they already worked for him. Mediaset's regional head of sales in Tuscany, for example, was reincarnated overnight as Forza Italia's regional party chief for Tuscany, the head of a slate of parliamentary candidates in the region that, up until the week before, had been his direct reports.

It all happened with bewildering speed. Within two months of his *scesa in campo* speech, Silvio Berlusconi was prime minister of a G7 country: proof of concept for the new wave of post–Cold War outsiders. Forza Italia's strategy was unabashedly patterned on Mediaset's commercial success. At its center was a determination to keep things simple, concrete, and understandable. "Remember," Berlusconi would tell his sales-managers-turned-political-operatives, "your job is to appeal to the regular people of Italy—not to the smartest student in the class."

The appeal of simple messaging proved overwhelming. While his center-left opponents tangled themselves in knots with complex explanations of recondite fiscal policy details, Berlusconi spoke in a way anyone could understand. In one iconic TV spot, looking straight into the camera, he promised to champion "the Italy that works against the one that chatters, the Italy that produces against the Italy that wastes, the Italy that saves against the one that steals, the Italy of the people against that of the old parties, for a new Italian miracle."[14]

It was visceral, straightforward, simple in a way no political appeal had been in Italy in many decades. And it established Berlusconi— whose reputation for shady deals, ethical lapses, and personal decadence was already solidly established—as the dominant political figure in one of the world's biggest industrial powers for two decades. By the time it was all said and done, he would serve as prime minister longer than any other Italian leader since World War II, though in three separate periods between 1994 and 2011.

It worked because, like with Trump, Berlusconi's entertainment value was recognizable without anyone needing to explain it. He knew viscerally how a simple tagline in an ad could win over the masses. He didn't need consultants to help him play this game: he was its greatest practitioner. He'd seen tried-and-true marketing techniques work their magic time and again and seen his bank balance grow in tandem with them.

Watching traditional politicians try to come to terms with this upstart could be painful. Schooled in the arcane parliamentary traditions of republican Rome, they had visibly lost touch with the people they set out to lead. In debates, Berlusconi would run circles around them, delivering one focus-group-tested line after another with perfect aplomb. Nobody did it better.

In America, campaign professionals had long since grasped that you can persuade people to vote you into power with the same techniques that get them to buy this brand of canned tuna and not that one. But Silvio Berlusconi went beyond using these techniques only in the context of the campaign: he built an entirely new brand of politics around them. Having transformed Italian TV and turned it into a crassly commercial profit engine, Berlusconi did the same to the country's politics.

Berlusconi was a transitional figure rather than a fully-fledged exponent of the twenty-first-century versions of 3P leaders. But he was surely a pioneer. Berlusconi mercilessly mocked Italy's judges, painting them as engaged in a vast left-wing conspiracy against him, an honorable businessperson; he sharply denounced the nation's defects, which he claimed to have inherited from his corrupt and mediocre predecessors in government; he fiddled with the country's elections rules; and he filled the airwaves he controlled through his TV networks and the newspapers he owned with propaganda that extolled him and mocked his rivals.

Berlusconi is better seen as a forerunner, a demonstration of the way the wall separating the political sphere from the entertainment world could collapse. Berlusconi embodied a new kind of relationship between a political leader and his followers. Because more than followers, what he had were *fans*.

From Charisma to Political Fandom

Of course, Silvio Berlusconi was hardly the first politician to build a deep, personal-seeming relationship with his followers. That kind of bond is as old as politics. Aristotle described it in detail. Late in the nineteenth century, the celebrated German sociologist Max Weber identified charisma as one of the prime movers in human history.[15, 16]

But Silvio Berlusconi is not simply a highly charismatic politician. No, he is more complex than that, and understanding the way Trump's or Berlusconi's appeal differs from Max Weber's concept of charisma is important. It helps nail down what's specifically new about the practitioners of 3P power.

Weber had set out to chronicle not so much the charismatic leader but the way groups react to them and how that reaction enabled them to coalesce politically in ways otherwise impossible.

Faced with a certain type of leader, groups quickly came to ascribe to them almost supernatural qualities. These leaders struck crowds as magnetic, magic, almost divine. People would follow such leaders on adventures they wouldn't follow anyone else on. He called the *bond* between magnetic leaders and their followers "charisma," and he argued that political authority based on charisma is at the heart of rapid, historic change.

Certainly, the bond both Trump and Berlusconi created with their followers included some aspects of Weber's charisma. To their followers, both seem larger than life. But the Weberian perspective doesn't take us very far. Charisma, for Weber, was born of the direct experience of a forceful personality. But these two politicians hadn't built their myths directly or through the strength of their personalities but rather through the operation of a sprawling and sophisticated media and marketing machine.

The hold Trump and Berlusconi had over their audiences was built less on Weberian magnetism and more on a carefully cultivated publicity machine, whether in the form of *Celebrity Apprentice* and the *New York Post* or the sprawling marketing operation behind Berlusconi's business empire. The current crop of populist leaders taps into a celebrity culture that feeds on itself, as the familiarity of a name and the outrageousness of a celebrity's exploits draw people's curiosity, fascination, and, ultimately, political loyalty.

Berlusconi and Trump sought notoriety and fame for both psychological and commercial reasons—and, eventually, to build a base to support their political ambitions. Once they had become household names, the process of constantly making their personal "brand" more recognizable and known by the public became self-replicating. They knew we couldn't stand to look away—and they couldn't stand thinking we might want to. Each imposed himself as if by force on his nation's consciousness. As Trump famously put it, "When you're a star, they let you do it."[17]

Of course, charismatic authority has been remaking societies rapidly since time immemorial. But Trump and Berlusconi's charismatic bonds are manufactured in a way traditional charismatic bonds were not. Taking its cues from celebrity culture, theirs is a debased charisma emptied of genuinely political content. Instead, it is propelled by the same thirst for entertainment that saturates the rest of our culture.

This thirst for politics as just another type of entertainment has deep roots. But the most obvious is technological and goes by the name of "media convergence": the blurring of the traditional dividing lines between politics and entertainment, between the important and the trivial. Media convergence is, itself, a product of the explosion of media choices.

Dividing lines that were easy enough to patrol when there were just three networks became obsolete when there were nine hundred on cable and literally millions more online. Media saturation and the ubiquity of entertainment options have shortened people's attention spans and dramatically decreased audiences' tolerance for boredom.

This blurring of the boundaries places a whole new set of demands on leaders. Competing for the audience's mind share against a limitless expanse of distractions, politicians who can't entertain find themselves quickly tuned out. Those not gifted with good looks (as Emmanuel Macron and Justin Trudeau are) find they can make up for it with traditional entertainment chops: unpredictability, bravado, pizzazz, humor, or brawn.

The audience, for its part, responds to these leaders precisely in the same way it responds to its favorite entertainers. The leaders have an intuitive feel for this: they know they're expected to lead by amusing, to lead by riling. And they know demonizing the other is the easiest way to do that. Politics as entertainment leads inexorably to the second "P" in our 3Ps formula: polarization.

Once a new technique has established its usefulness, you can be sure it'll be copied. Politics as entertainment spreads through emulation. And in all kinds of contexts, all around the world, the performers who catch on to this trend are richly rewarded with meteoric career paths. Success breeds emulation: new entrants attempt new variants, and the explosion of communications channels puts the tools of this kind of rise within the reach of upstarts worldwide.

All around the world, outrageous public personas are becoming the new normal. In Brazil, the most voted member of the federal congress was Tiririca, a professional clown and stand-up comedian who has no discernible ideology and was probably functionally illiterate when first elected in 2010. In Guatemala, Jimmy Morales, a bawdy TV comedian running on the vaguest of platforms, won the presidency with a 67 percent landslide in 2015. In the Philippines, a former mayor, Rodrigo Duterte, set the country's political scene on fire as much by swearing in public again and again as by openly running on a pledge to institute death squads against drug dealers. In Russia, the publication of a calendar showing the president bare-chested as he fished and rode horses around the untamed Siberian wilderness set off a frenzy of excitement and launched a boom in demand for tourism in the tundra. And in Britain, Nigel Farage elevated bombast to the status of an ideology as he forced the nation's agenda to center on what were once seen as fringe views, such as the push, long seen as quixotic, to get the United Kingdom to exit the European Union. Even British prime minister Boris Johnson once hosted a satirical TV panel show on the BBC.

In a world where policy debates put everyone to sleep, the wall between policy and entertainment collapses. As politics devolves into pure spectacle, people begin to relate to their political leaders in the same way they relate to their favorite entertainers and sports stars. They cheer them on as fans, rather than engaging with them as citizens or even as political clients. The key question becomes not, "What are they doing?" but rather, "Who's winning?"

Cornel Sandvoss, professor of media and journalism at the UK's University of Huddersfield, has studied the question and concluded today's "political fans reason a lot like sports or music fans."[18] Just as a rock star crafts an identity that fans can adopt and piggyback on, Sandvoss argues, the politician's role in the era of fandom is to act as a repository of meaning, to be a vehicle for the identity of fans lacking a fully settled sense of who they are. Just like Beyoncé's fans go to her concerts to look around and recognize themselves in people who share their passion for her, political fans go to a rally to lose themselves in a crowd where they feel at home. Just like the Dallas Cowboys have earned a passionate following from people looking for groups of fellow football fans to identify with, political leadership increasingly consists of creating a space where like-minded followers can revel in the company of people who feel like kin.

None of this is entirely new: John F. Kennedy had his fans, as did Harold Wilson, François Mitterrand, Pierre Trudeau, and Margaret Thatcher. What's new is the extent to which people look at politics first and foremost as *spectacle*, as a battle where celebrities face off with each other in an antagonistic contest for supremacy. Where the line between power and spectacle vanishes completely, freedom cannot hold out for long.

According to a 2017 report in the *New York Times*, "Before taking office, Mr. Trump told top aides to think of each presidential day as an episode in a television show in which he vanquishes rivals."[19] As the first national leader with roots firmly in reality television, Donald Trump understood better than most the absolute primacy of an antagonistic story arc in creating the conditions for primary identification with a leader. He certainly wouldn't put the insight in that language, but like every successful demagogue, he has a natural instinct for it. He doesn't think it; he feels it.

Trump tapped into a preexisting trend toward treating one's political party the way one treats one's sports team. Polarization, in this sense, is less about issues and policies and much more about raw, visceral identity. Once, long ago, people pegged those identities to their social class, their religion, their community, or their ethnicity. Today, more and more, you go to the polling place for it. People no longer vote their values, much less their interests. Today, people vote their identities.

A growing body of academic research shows the way political polarization has deepened in the United States in recent decades. As any sports fan knows, half the fun comes not just from seeing your own team win but from seeing the rival team lose. In sports, the stakes of rivalry are low. But when the logic of fandom bleeds over into the political realm, they rise dramatically. Partisans come to loathe the other side more and more. Fandom, in politics, means polarization.

In some contexts, polarization is expressed with a newly militant approach to partisanship. A 2015 study by Patrick R. Miller and Pamela Johnston Conover finds that in the United States, the people most strongly motivated to vote are driven by partisan identification more than by ideological or issue preferences. Hostility to the opposing party turns out to be one of people's stronger motivators for voting.[20]

Another 2015 study by Shanto Iyengar and Sean J. Westwood suggests that in the United States, partisan affiliation is now a more powerful predictor of hostility than race. Asked to select from similar résumés, people are more likely to select an applicant from across the racial divide than a supporter of the opposing party.[21]

Francis Fukuyama agrees that "the current dysfunction and decay of the U.S. political system are related to extreme and ever-growing polarization, which has made routine governing an exercise in brinkmanship."[22] Citing research by Thomas Mann and Norman Ornstein,[23] he notes that this process has not been symmetric, with the right moving to the right much more quickly than the left moves to the left.[24] The election to the presidency of a far-right leader steeped in entertainment values has certainly accelerated the trend.

Planting Trumpian fandom onto this well-tilled soil of preexisting partisanship has yielded something new for the United States: political tribalism on a scale the country is simply not accustomed to and that, some fear, is just not compatible with its constitutional tradition. As Andrew Sullivan puts it:

> The project of American democracy—to live beyond such tribal identities, to construct a society based on the individual, to see ourselves as citizens of a people's republic, to place religion off-limits, and even in recent years to embrace a multiracial and post-religious society—was always an extremely precarious endeavor. It rested, from the beginning, on an 18th-century hope that deep divides can be bridged by a culture of compromise, and that emotion can be defeated by reason. It failed once, spectacularly, in the most brutal civil war any Western democracy has experienced in modern times. And here we are, in an equally tribal era, with a deeply divisive president who is suddenly scrambling Washington's political alignments, about to find out if we can prevent it from failing again.[25]

One indication of the dangers this trend poses lies in the fact that Russia has already begun to exploit it. Among the trove of mischief-making pieces planted by Russian trolls and disinformation accounts in the run-up to the 2016 election, there was a continual stream of fake fan material: brightly colored "Buff Bernie" materials for the "Sanderistas" alongside the more predictable memes lionizing Donald Trump. The same was true in the 2020 election.

The takeaway is that the explosion in media options and the convergence between them has simply overwhelmed the traditional boundary lines between politics and entertainment. Playing out across the entertainment era's proliferation of options—of YouTube, of nine-hundred-channel cable grids, of the geyser of stimuli on Twitter and Facebook—charisma in the information era is debased by the entertainment values of its age.

Once entertainment value and celebrity culture establish themselves at the center of a nation's politics, they are difficult to dislodge. If it's not contained early, politics as entertainment seems to metastasize, spreading into portions of the body politic not previously affected. And to see this mechanism in action, we need to go back to Italy, only one generation later.

Italy's New Breed of Populists

If you were trying to show Max Weber the strange transformation charismatic authority has undergone in the twenty-first century, you could hardly do better than to put him in a time machine and drop him 116 years into the future in the large auditorium in Rome where the popular rabble-rousing comic Beppe Grillo would give his 2007 show.[26] There, Weber would have seen a large, voluble man with a scruffy beard and a wild mane of gray hair bursting out into the audience from the moment the show began.

Beppe Grillo is a manic presence on the stage. Or rather, *off* the stage: he wastes almost no time on the actual stage prepared for him. Instead, for two and a half hours, like a man possessed, he paces up and down the auditorium where the crowd is seated, commanding a spectacle that's part comedy show, part political rally, part revival meeting.

Stalking his audience with his manic, rapid-fire delivery, Grillo drips scorn on Italy's political elite, on the West's mania for overconsumption, on consumer rip-offs, on the haplessness of the political left and the corruption of the right, ranting and raving as he grabs random audience members by the lapels—at times literally—as if to physically shake Italy out of its torpor.

Having failed to finish his studies to become an accountant, Beppe Grillo found his calling in this kind of hypercharged political comedy: a primal scream against a political class he sensed Italians uniformly despised, coupled with a visceral disgust at the usual left-right political schism. Challenged to "put up or shut up," Grillo decided to put up—specifically, he put up a political party, the Five Star Movement (known as M5S or Cinque Stelle in Italy)—and went off to contest elections.

On its very first try, in 2013, the movement took a higher share than any other political party, 25.6 percent of the vote in a splintered field. The upstarts won just 109 of 630 seats in the lower house of Italy's parliament, however, because they refused to join a coalition with any of the reviled traditional parties.

Pundits scoffed that M5S was a one-man show, that Grillo could never turn it into a real party. To prove them wrong, he pushed for a party rule barring M5S from nominating anyone with a criminal conviction. As it turns out, the move ruled out Grillo himself—he had been convicted of vehicular manslaughter back in the 1980s, after a road accident he caused had cost two of his passengers their lives. It was as though Grillo was determined to prove the Cinque Stelle could cope without him as a visible head. Sure enough, his movement confounded the doubters.

In 2016, the Five Star Movement swept to the mayor's office in Rome, electing Virginia Raggi as the Eternal City's first-ever woman mayor and taking a majority in the city council. Soon after, they came within a whisker of taking control of Sicily. Even so, some Italian pundits laughed the whole thing off—Grillo's schtick was ridiculous, merely entertainment. Anybody could see that, couldn't they? Well, couldn't they?

It turns out that no, they couldn't.

For all the differences between their leaders, there's an obvious kinship between the vibes at a Trump rally and at a Beppe Grillo rally. The crowd is there for the same kind of reason: a disgust at the elite, sure, but also something more—a thirst for drama, for the unpredictable, for *entertainment*.

Grillo's political movement wouldn't stop growing. His followers, the *grillini* (little Grillos), adhere to a confusing mismatch of an ideology—part radical environmentalism, part nativism, part heterodox economics, part anti-vaxxer hysteria. If it doesn't exactly gel into a coherent whole, that's quite all right for them: they're not in it for the coherence. They're in it for the clicks.

As a landmark investigation by Buzzfeed News and the Italian daily *La Stampa* found, the Five Stars operated a sweeping online operation that controlled a huge number of popular blogs, websites, and Facebook pages with millions of followers.[27] Often amplifying the stories produced by Russian propaganda mouthpieces like Sputnik, the sites aligned the movement closely with Moscow and even more closely with Russian-style disinformation efforts. Peddling sensationalist stories under lurid headlines, Five Star blogs like the hugely popular *TzeTze* created a conspiracy-minded information ecosystem where "they"—the elites, the Roman fat cats, the globalists in Brussels—were always out to get "you," the hardworking ordinary Italian.

It proved devastatingly effective. In March 2018, the *grillini* made the final leap into government. Their share of the vote had risen to 33 percent, and they remained the single largest party. By this time, their purist scruples about joining others in government had abated. After tortured coalition talks, M5S went into government alongside La Lega, another anti-establishment party, though this one was of the far-right variety. Together, La Lega and M5S launched one of the strangest coalition governments in recent history—a bizarre mishmash of far-right ideology and Grillo's radical clowning.

But there was a problem. Because Grillo had taken himself out of the running for office, the *grillini* were not led by him. Instead, the party elected a thirty-two-year-old activist to lead it. Luigi Di Maio had none of Beppe Grillo's magnetism. As deputy prime minister, he plainly struggled to make his mark opposite the astute leaders of La Lega.

Once the coalition was in power, La Lega's nativist populism soon outstripped the *grillini*'s iconoclastic antics, and its own television-star leader, Matteo Salvini, stepped into the fray—playing tough guy and outsider to an Italian public that reliably rewards tough guys and outsiders.

We'll have much more to say about Salvini in Chapter 6, where we discuss the nature and consequences of the anti-politics mood that swept the world. In fact, the succession of populists seems to have sent Italy tumbling into an irretrievable anti-politics spiral. For now, it is sufficient to say that Salvini's rise as one of the dominant figures in Italian politics could well cement the extinction of politics as usual in that country. A generation ago, Italian politics was among the most boring and staid in the world, with colorless career politicians of the right and left, the vast bulk of them corrupt, vying for power in elections nobody much cared for.

The trends Silvio Berlusconi launched in 1994 changed Italian public life for good. Once Italian voters had a taste for politics that shared the look and feel of show business, there was no going back. Whether it's in the form of an avowed clown like Beppe Grillo or a theatrical tough guy like Matteo Salvini, extreme positions and made-for-the-camera antics came to be the stock in trade of the political realm—just what the voting public expected.

The Tribe Chávez Built

But it's not just in the developed countries that entertainment values have colonized the political sphere. One of the most successful practitioners of politics as entertainment was Venezuela's Hugo Chávez. Chávez put the politics of fandom in the service of a full 3P strategy to grab and keep power. He used his political celebrity to create a populist political movement that thrived on polarization and reveled in post-truth.

His goal? Power for life. In this, if in little else, he succeeded—in the most literal sense possible.

This isn't the way Chávez is usually discussed. Indeed, a bit of revisionist history is in order if we're to give Chávez his due as forerunner rather than as anachronism. For most of his time in power, the world looked at Venezuela as an embarrassing throwback to a previous political era because Chávez traced his ideological roots back to the radical Cuba of the 1960s. Certainly, his rhetoric often sounded like it was coming out of some political time warp.

But to the extent Chávez had a forerunner, it was not Fidel but Silvio Berlusconi. From the Italian tycoon-cum-politician, Chávez had grasped that ideology matters less than celebrity status, and that with television you can create a world where style is substance.

The son of provincial schoolteachers, Hugo Chávez came up through the military ranks and was soon recruited to a far-left militant cell. Though he styled himself a revolutionary, his biographers later discovered that the first time he ever took a microphone onto a stage, as a young soldier, it was to emcee a beauty pageant organized by the Venezuelan army. There are shades here of Berlusconi singing on a cruise ship at the start of his career—an unmistakable sense that the persona he inhabited always came second to a psychological need to be at the center of attention.

If Milan was the forerunner, Caracas was the true site for the experiment in fusing charismatic leadership, celebrity antics, and autocratic ambition. This was a far more dangerous experiment: while Berlusconi seemed content to fatten his pocketbook and keep himself out of jail, Hugo Chávez aspired to control Venezuela permanently. And he planned to do so by leveraging his legendary knack for theatrically feeling Venezuelans' pain. The impact of the approach he pioneered is only now beginning to play itself out across the developed world.

Take Chávez's famously long-winded TV show, *Aló Presidente*. In it, the president ranged broadly, zipping back and forth between storytelling, political diatribe, singing, and fulminating against enemies real and imagined. But at its core, the theme was always the same: empathy. In each show he would chat, one-on-one, with a few of his supporters, asking about their lives, their aspirations, and their problems, and always, always feeling their pain. If Trump liked to play mogul on TV and Berlusconi portrayed himself as a heartthrob, Chávez liked to play Oprah.

His performance could be spellbinding. He'd fulminate against the rising price of chicken and then hug a woman teary-eyed over her trouble finding the money for school supplies for her children. He'd sit and listen carefully as people described their problems, learning their names and asking them questions to draw out the details of their situation.

It was during these Oprah-like moments of one-on-one bonding with his followers, more than in the ideological tirades, that Chávez shifted the basis of allegiance from the political realm to the realm of primary identification. It was moments like these that turned followers into fans, fans who, in time, would coalesce into a political tribe: people who crafted an identity out of their shared devotion to the leader.

The adulation audiences showered on their star was the raw material Chávez turned into power, power he used to dismantle the checks and balances at the heart of Venezuela's constitution.

I grew up in Venezuela, and the experience of seeing Chávez transform his fame into power and his power into celebrity marked me. Which is why, for me, the rise of Trump was baffling. I watched the circus that engulfed U.S. politics in 2016 with a horror suffused in déjà vu. The histrionics, the easy answers, the furious denunciations by a nebulous elite that woke up to the danger far too late . . . I had seen this movie before. Just never in English.

In 1998, I'd seen the rise of our own fire-breathing outsider. I'd heard the electrifying speeches. I'd seen him announce a presidential campaign that was dismissed out of hand as little more than a joke, an improbable vehicle for an impossible politician. And then I'd seen him rise and rise in the polls. I'd seen him survive controversies that ought to have done him in, that ought to have done anyone in. But they didn't.

So when Donald Trump bragged on the 2016 campaign trail about the size of his "hands,"[28] my mind shot back to the time Chávez, on national television and with all channels forced to broadcast his show, suddenly changed the subject and started talking to his wife, who, he was sure, was watching at home. It was Valentine's Day, and the president promised her that as soon as he got home later that night, she would "get what she had coming to her."[29] When Donald Trump vowed to build an infeasible 1,954-mile wall on the border with Mexico, my mind went right back to the time Chávez promised to build a gas pipeline through the Andes to Buenos Aires, 3,163 miles to the south (he never did).[30]

At times the stories get mixed up in my memory, and it becomes hard to remember who said what. Was it Trump or Chávez who called the media and the major TV networks the "four horsemen of the apocalypse"? (It was Chávez.)[31] Which one was it who once regaled his audience with a delightful story about luring his friends' wives into bed? (Trump.)[32] And what about the one of him getting diarrhea while he was live, on air, in front of the TV cameras? (Chávez.)[33] Was it Chávez or Trump who accused reporters of willful lying, of being "enemies of the people"? (Trick question: it was both.)[34] Different as Chávez and Trump were in so many obvious ways, Venezuelans who paid attention couldn't miss the overlap.

In the months that followed that Trump Tower announcement, as the Trump juggernaut gained steam, I saw the bicoastal elite progress from eye-rolling irritation to bemusement, then alarm, and finally panic—a state it's never entirely left behind. It was like watching a mirror of Venezuela from eighteen years earlier. That progression wasn't just familiar; it had been mine.

I, too, had dismissed Chávez as another populist demagogue, a clown too hapless to do any real damage. In Venezuela, too, the elites assumed that they would co-opt, capture, and control him as they had historically been able to do with other presidents. I failed to grasp the true nature of the ride I was climbing on: the way Chávez the performer would engender a legion of fans—not followers in the traditional political sense of the word but fans, who looked to him to craft their identity first and as a political leader only later. This fandom, based on charisma, set the stage for the logic of tribalism that drives polarization. In retrospect, it's all very clear.

It all began with the rise of a charismatic leader, but to leave it at that wouldn't do justice to what came next. I've seen this process play out. I know how it starts and, to my chagrin, I know how it ended in Venezuela. One of the longest democracies in the Americas became a brutal dictatorship, and one of the world's wealthiest countries became one of the poorest.

Chávez revolutionized what power meant for an audience alienated from stuffy, distant leaders with whom they could never identify. His legendary common touch cemented the cult-like devotion of millions of Venezuelans who felt, quite intimately, that they knew him.

Televised displays of intimate bonding with individual followers were the mainstay of his TV approach. But they had meaning because, in his hours-long speeches that every TV and radio station in the country was forced to carry live, Chávez wove them together into a coherent narrative. In what was part revival meeting, part history lesson, and part revolutionary harangue, Chávez pieced together an all-encompassing story that made sense of the nation's life for his listeners and gave them a sense of their place in it as well.

The rise of Chávez swept away the old systems of identifications with dizzying speed. In shifting from political party to person, the basis for Venezuelans' political identifications came to be dominated by a single, binary question: "Are you pro-Chávez or anti-Chávez?" As his followers brought an increasingly devotional flair to their fandom, detractors came to see the *chavista* movement as an existential danger to the country.

The result was an extreme polarization of Venezuelan politics. With frightening rapidity, supporters and opponents lost any sense of common belonging to a shared nation and began to treat one another as enemies. For *chavistas*, a position supported by the president was enough, on its own, for it to be accepted as true; for anti-*chavistas*, the reverse became true. Polarization and tribalism are just different aspects of the same phenomenon.

Charismatic leadership contains the seeds of its own backlash: people who aren't willing to treat a leader as superhuman or quasi-divine are naturally alarmed that others are willing to treat him that way. There's really no room in the center once this kind of dynamic takes hold: polarization forces you to choose a side.

To say Chávez was sacralized by his supporters might sound like hyperbole, but it's quite literally what happened. Immediately following his death from cancer in 2013, Chávez's figure began to be assimilated into the pantheon for Santería, the Afro-Caribbean syncretic religion millions of Venezuelans are secretly devoted to even as they outwardly describe themselves as Catholic. Chávez statuettes began to make their appearance in *santero* rites, alongside ancestral indigenous deities like Maria Lionza and historical figures turned into demigods such as Negro Primero, the slave-born lancer who, through legendary bravery and daring, rose to become the only black officer in Simón Bolívar's republican army. Like them, Chávez was destined to occupy a space somewhere between the normal and the divine, a figure of actual religious devotion.

These stories become even more telling when we examine them from Max Weber's sociological perspective. He knew that the word "charisma" derives from the Greek χάρισμα, meaning "a divine gift," a talent gifted by the gods.[35] In their ambiguous position somewhere above ordinary humankind, charismatic leaders jam the normal rules of politics. Their followers, their fans, cannot be reasoned with. Their detractors cannot compromise with them. Turbocharged by contemporary communications technology, such leaders demolish the wall dividing politics from entertainment.

Disintermediated Politics

The politics of fandom and the disappearing boundary line between politics and entertainment have major implications for the way politicians compete for power, now and into the future. The nature of political competition is in upheaval. Old political virtues have become obsolete, and the abilities that take their place will determine the kinds of leaders that will become common.

The new era devalues mastery of policy details, expertise, the ability to strike bargains and to move toward messy pragmatic compromises.

Those are the skills it takes to actually govern within the strictures of a constitutional republic. But such skills have little relevance to the new task at hand: in a political system in which the three Ps of populism, polarization, and post-truth are rampant, what counts is building and sustaining a fan base devoted enough to have your back no matter what. Fealty rules.

What Venezuelans and Italians learned two decades ago, and Americans have only started to grasp more recently, is that the skills, practices, and institutional reflexes that are necessary to sustain a democracy are startlingly fragile in the face of the threats emanating from populism, polarization, and post-truth. Debate, forbearance, compromise, tolerance, and a willingness to accept the legitimacy of an adversary's bid for power are the kinds of instincts that need to be widely shared in a political culture if democracy is to survive. But in an age of politics as entertainment, these values continually lose space to their opposites: invectives, demonization of opponents, maximalism, and intolerance.

Political parties get quickly written out of the equation. Crucial though they are for democracy, parties begin to look like nuisances when loyalties are personalized and focused on a single leader. Core party functions like articulating interests and bringing various groups together under a single platform look quaintly antiquated in a world where primary identification with the leader is what drives the followers. Political parties may survive in some form, the way vestigial wings do on flightless birds. But they increasingly act as simple adjuncts to the leader and struggle to regain their central role in governance. Needed neither to reach nor to sustain power, parties become an afterthought. Other intermediating institutions— nongovernmental organizations, professional groups, labor unions, voluntary associations—will also have to make complex institutional contortions in order to stay politically relevant.

After all, pop stars don't need any of these institutions to fill up their concerts, do they?

The havoc media convergence is wreaking on democratic politics is, arguably, just the information age's latest tech-based disruption, simply another arena where technological change has disrupted a legacy system before the implications were fully understood. If, as Marshall McLuhan famously argued, the medium is the message, it's only natural that the switchover from legacy media systems to the information explosion of the information age would bring with it a new pattern in politics.[36] To use an ugly bit of jargon, technology is *disintermediating* the political system.

Why would you need a neighborhood political boss, a state senator, or a national executive committee to connect you with a leader when you can message that leader directly on Twitter? In the internet era, these institutions have become as painfully redundant as owning a Walkman in the era of the everything-in-one smartphone.

And we're only at the beginning of this trend. While good looks and an easy screen presence have been important political assets since the dawn of the TV era, they served as valuable supplements to the traditional credentials people expected of their leaders. But what if we're moving into a new era where, rather than helpful extras, they become the whole ball game?

We are not there yet. But a new competitive dynamic is taking hold that devalues traditional credentialing in favor of media celebrity. There is no guarantee that tomorrow's charismatic leaders will balance a direct appeal to fans with traditional political abilities. What if they don't?

The 3Ps Under a Floodlight

We return to our opening paradox: the newly resurgent forms of political power are all about stealth, about hiding the operations of power under a fog of pseudolegal pretext and dissimulation. But the leaders benefiting from these strategies are anything but invisible. Highly aware of their own image, they work constantly to project themselves into their supporters' consciousness, and their personas become central to their supporters' identities.

These strands seem contradictory at first, but in fact, they are deeply intertwined in the operation of the 3P framework. Hollowing out the old institutions—legal, media, and social—that once mediated between citizens and rulers makes the new approach possible by throwing out the barriers between leaders and the instruments of power, and between leaders and their fans. Without the disintermediation of the political sphere, the 3Ps wouldn't work as effectively.

The old separation between politics and entertainment imposed its own set of guard rails: formal institutions (like laws, legislatures, and courts) and informal norms (of decorum, the "dignity of office," etc.) were highly effective ways of hemming power in. When politicians are just public servants, it's much easier for the political system to impose restraints on their behavior. The 3P autocrats' celebrity status loosens those restraints. Their fans have so much of their own identities invested in the leaders that they can't allow them to fail.

When traditional politicians break an important norm, their supporters turn on them, and their political standing suffers. But when celebrity leaders break an important norm, their fans don't turn on the leaders; they turn on the norm. In fact, they rally to the leaders, whose standing often improves, at least in the fans' eyes.

The reason is that the political supporters of yesteryear are different from today's political fans in crucial respects. Much like sports fans or music fans, political fans build their sense of identity largely through their identification with their favorite celebrities. Fans perceive attacks on the celebrities that organize their identity as attacks on them first and foremost. They defend the celebrities to defend themselves.

The language used to describe themselves gives us a clear hint of this dynamic. Beppe Grillo's followers are *grillini*, Chávez's are *chavistas*. Trump's supporters don't adopt his name as such, but they identify themselves entirely with his slogan, to the point of transforming "MAGA" from an acronym to collective noun. Salvini's fans identify him with a kind of honorific title, "Il Capitano" (the captain), while Berlusconi's call him "Il Cavaliere" (the knight), and Chávez's supporters called him "El Comandante" (the commander).

The use of these kinds of titles points again to the sacralization of power around the aspiring autocrat. In some cases, such as Chávez's, that sacralization becomes quite literal, with supporters venerating him as a demigod after death. But even when it doesn't go that far, it's clear that the kind of authority celebrity politicians wield is profoundly personal. The proof of that is how hard it is to transfer. In two of the cases we've looked at in this chapter, the celebrity at the center of a populist movement has had to bow out—Hugo Chávez, following his death in 2013, and Beppe Grillo, who opted not to participate actively in politics specifically to try to depersonalize his movement. In both cases, successor leaders have lacked the founder's easy rapport with the television camera, and the result has been a disaster for their movements. Chávez's successor, Nicolás Maduro, became one of the most hated leaders in the world after his hapless leadership accelerated Venezuela's fall into the disastrous economic vortex hatched by Hugo Chávez. And Grillo's successor at the head of the Cinque Stelle, Luigi Di Maio, soon found himself engulfed in a series of missteps that saw his movement bleed support to his coalition partners from the far-right La Lega. Not surprisingly, La Lega happened to be led by a charismatic outsider with an intense personal following, Matteo Salvini.

Salvini seemed to grasp what Di Maio never did: political followers make demands on leaders, while political fans offer them the kind of unconditional support that frees them to pursue power for their own ends. Blurring the lines between politics and entertainment isn't something these leaders do on a lark. They do it because it allows them to get away with behaviors that their more traditional rivals couldn't have dreamed of getting away with in the old world where the political and entertainment spheres were clearly separated.

Celebrity and stealth are the yin and yang of the 3P autocrats. As the old distinction between the political sphere and the entertainment sphere becomes blurred, leaders find that celebrity allows them to make plays for power that would not otherwise be tolerated. Celebrity breaks down the usual working of accountability mechanisms. It breaks down expectations about the correct ways to behave in power, multiplying the force of pseudolaw.

Or, in fewer words: power takes its revenge by embracing spectacle, even as it goes underground.

3

POWER TOOLS

Populism, polarization, and post-truth are strategies. But it takes something more concrete than organizing principles and grand strategies to make this new approach to power work. For that, today's autocrats need tools—specific psychological, communicational, technological, legal, electoral, financial, and organizational techniques to assert their power and shield themselves from the forces that constrain them.

We think of these techniques as *power tools*. They are the means through which 3P autocrats gain, wield, and maintain power. Here we get down to the brass tacks of how power has responded to the centrifugal forces that have begun to disperse and weaken it. Some of these tools are new, while others are updated versions of the tried-and-true weapons in every demagogue's arsenal; all are made doubly effective by the fragmentation of our political debates, the poisonous worldwide explosion of distrust in public institutions, and the new digital technologies that act as force multipliers of these tools.

The Power of Money

Money is power and power is money. This adage is more valid today than ever. Old-style rulers dip into their nation's coffers unrestrained by laws or institutions. Through gifts, stipends, subsidies, and preferential access to business deals—or simply through graft—they enable themselves and their families and friends to amass unfathomable fortunes. We have all seen the photos of their palaces, planes, yachts, and cars. And we have also seen how they use money as a tool to strengthen their grip on power: to keep the military happy and loyal, to buy the support of regional chieftains, to fund a vast police state and security apparatus that repress the opposition, and to ensure that journalists remain docile and tycoons content. Dictators also use their fortunes to project their power beyond their country's borders. They fund allies, co-opt foreign politicians and influencers, and buy foreign media companies and sports clubs, all while building international financial networks that serve to advance the interests of the ruling family and the nation it controls.

3P autocrats also need money to enrich themselves and their cronies. Like traditional dictators, they need the financial wherewithal to retain, cement, and extend their power. But unlike completely unaccountable dictators, 3P autocrats need to be more careful about the ways they get rich, make others rich, and use money to fortify their regime. They still do all of that but more stealthily and while being more mindful of the need to look like democrats, honest government officials, and corruption-busters.

Vladimir Putin's Russia provides an illustrative example of the use of money as a power tool. When, in 1999, Putin became president, Russia was in the grip of a wild, gangland-style constellation of oligarchs who had appropriated the bulk of the old Soviet Union's industrial, mineral, and energy wealth. The Moscow of the 1990s was shot through with frightening lawlessness, with business tycoons operating as a law unto themselves and the killings of rivals in broad daylight a frequent occurrence. The chaos of the Yeltsin years served no strategic purpose for the Kremlin, and Putin quickly realized that step one in establishing lasting control of the state would be to bring the oligarchs to heel.

In his book *Russia's Crony Capitalism: The Path from Market Economy to Kleptocracy*, Anders Aslund explains how Putin, a former KGB agent, relied on his community of spies and secret-service operatives to do precisely that.[1] From 2000 to 2003, Putin took pains to make the new pecking order clear: the rich could remain rich, could become much richer still, but only if they got clear on their political priorities. The message was conveyed without subtlety: within a few months of taking office, Putin launched a major attack on Vladimir Gusinsky, whose TV station, NTV, committed the capital sin of not merely criticizing the president but *mocking* him. Other defenestrations followed. Those who challenged the new arrangement had an alarming propensity to turn up dead in peculiar circumstances. The rest soon got the message.

Supplanting the Wild West of the Yeltsin era with a strong, hierarchical, and democratic-looking autocracy, Putin ensured that Russia's oligarchs served him first. The deal was easy to understand: stoke the Kremlin's displeasure and not only could your wealth vanish with frightening speed, but you ran the risk of being "canceled"—not in the cultural way common nowadays but in a brutal and often definitive manner. Henceforth, the oligarchs' wealth was theirs only provisionally, so long as it served the president's interests. Media could be startlingly profitable, but only so long as it actively supported the Kremlin's line across the board. Their business empires would be expected to be surrendered to the state at a second's notice, with their private ownership serving to sustain plausible deniability.

Perhaps the clearest case was that of Yevgeny Prigozhin, "Putin's chef"—the Moscow restaurateur and caterer who found himself at the head of a sprawling business thanks to his closeness with Putin. Prigozhin is best known as the putative owner of the infamous St. Petersburg–based Internet Research Agency, in effect a Kremlin asset deployed to destabilize politics worldwide and suit Putin's geopolitical interests. Prigozhin's case may be the most visible, but it is by no means unique. Prigozhin-like figures, with one foot in the legal economy and one in organized crime, seem to flourish wherever a 3P autocracy is consolidating its power.

In Venezuela, it was Colombian trucking magnate Alex Saab, who leveraged his regime contacts in Caracas into a huge personal fortune by bilking the Venezuelan state through billions of overcharges for food imports, then used his money to prop up the Maduro regime. In the Philippines, it was Dennis Uy, the Chinese Filipino son of small-town traders, whose fortune grew with dizzying speed to include everything from casinos to Ferrari dealerships to water utilities. Not surprisingly, Uy has been close personal friends with Rodrigo Duterte for twenty years. In Hungary, it was Lőrinc Mészéros, a friend of twenty years from Viktor Orbán's home village, who made the shift from construction worker to billionaire business tycoon in a short five years and was awarded enormously lucrative government contracts. And in Angola, the power of money stayed in the family as Isabel dos Santos, the daughter of longtime autocrat José Eduardo dos Santos, became a billionaire and Africa's wealthiest woman thanks to "family ties, shell companies, and inside deals."[2]

In Brazil, under the rule of the Workers Party, the country's top engineering firm, Odebrecht, was turned into a conduit for bribes to control politicians at home and abroad, with kleptocracy effectively becoming an instrument of Brazil's foreign policy.

In each of these cases, autocrats worked to both empower and control the major holders of wealth in their countries and were in no way shy about then using that wealth to bolster and sustain their own power. By the same token, the regimes were quick to punish business interests unwilling to bend to the will of the leader.

These might seem like concerns mostly for weak or endemically corrupt countries, but the big Western democracies are in no way immune. In Italy, Silvio Berlusconi blatantly exploited his private wealth to sustain his political power for decades. In the United States, the Supreme Court instituted a remarkable system of legalized payoffs to politicians through its notorious 2010 *Citizens United* decision. The ruling hatched the infamous political action committees (PACs) and opened a flood of unregulated private funding for private political campaigns. It also "fixed" the corruption problem by rendering legal the kinds of arrangements most countries treat as criminal matters. Partly as a result, the normal cost of a U.S. presidential election campaign soared past the billion-dollar mark.

In today's world, money remains what it has always been: the high road to influence, now repurposed in the service of populism, polarization, and post-truth.

The Power of Norm-Breaking

Aloof and out-of-touch elites nurture populism. Groups at the top, disconnected from the people and with dwindling popular support, create the opportunities that populists exploit. They proceed by polarizing the political sphere as much as possible, using however much truth or untruth it takes to energize, organize, and mobilize supporters. Luckily for populists, there's nothing easier than to portray an elite as aloof and out of touch. Being aloof and out of touch is a basic ingredient of what makes an elite an elite. The new breed of populists, then, can find material to work with pretty much anywhere.

Liberal democracies are based on laws and permanent institutions like parliaments and courts. Less visibly but just as crucially, they also depend on norms: the unwritten but generally accepted boundary lines that define how things are done. The outcome of slow, subtle historical processes, norms seep into the DNA of institutions over time. A norm is the sort of rule that everyone gets without anyone needing to point it out explicitly.

As E. J. Dionne, Norm Ornstein, and Thomas E. Mann explain:[3]

Political norms are defined as "a standard or pattern, especially of social behavior, that is typical or expected of a group." They are how a person is supposed to behave in a given social setting. We don't fully appreciate the power of norms until they are violated on a regular basis. And the breaching of norms often produces a cascading effect: As one person breaks with tradition and expectation, behavior previously considered inappropriate is normalized and taken up by others.

Over time, networks of norms weave together tacit but powerful understandings about what's appropriate and what's not appropriate in politics. Together, they form what political scientists Steven Levitsky and Daniel Ziblatt called "the soft guardrails of democracy"— the implicit, shared sense of "how things ought to be done" that binds together a democratic political culture.[4]

The new breed of populists finds democratic norms to be particularly inviting targets. Precisely because they're unwritten, they seem to invite a challenge. How do you call someone out for breaking a rule that isn't ever quite made explicit? Even the process of pointing out that a norm is being broken weakens it by bringing what was once tacit and unspoken out into the open, where it can be debated and attacked.

This is the paradox of norms. Unspoken rules are central to the health of democracies. But because they're unspoken, norms are ill-defined, and that makes them vulnerable. Norms are crucial but weak, and 3P autocrats know to pounce on weak restraints on their power. Better yet, flouting rules both sets you off as a different kind of leader and undermines limits that box in power, all in one go.

Donald Trump established himself as an instinctive master of this style from the very start, possibly because he genuinely never grasped the unwritten rules well enough in the first place to understand that he was breaking them. Trump's transgressions, his willingness to "go there," to do things that just aren't done, defined his approach to power. The Trump presidency was an institutional slaughterhouse of Washington's sacred cows. Time after time, he reveled in doing things everyone knows aren't done. From appointing obvious industry cronies to regulate the industries they used to represent (right up to the extreme of appointing a coal lobbyist to head the Environmental Protection Agency), openly siding with America's dictatorial adversaries above his own intelligence services, defending torch-wielding neo-Nazi protesters at the 2017 "Unite the Right" rally in Charlottesville, refusing to comply with congressional subpoenas, and refusing to commit to accepting the outcome of the 2020 presidential election, no rules seemed to be protected from the president's transgressions.

Watching this cavalcade of outrages sobered Washington's political chattering classes in a way George Packer powerfully captured:[5]

> The adults were too sophisticated to see Trump's special political talents—his instinct for every adversary's weakness, his fanatical devotion to himself, his knack for imposing his will, his sheer staying power. They also failed to appreciate the advanced decay of the Republican Party, which by 2016 was far gone in a nihilistic pursuit of power at all costs. They didn't grasp the readiness of large numbers of Americans to accept, even relish, Trump's contempt for democratic norms and basic decency. It took the arrival of such a leader to reveal how many things that had always seemed engraved in monumental stone turned out to depend on those flimsy norms, and how much the norms depended on public opinion. Their vanishing exposed the real power of the presidency. Legal precedent could be deleted with a keystroke; law enforcement's independence from the White House was optional; the separation of powers turned out to be a gentleman's agreement; transparent lies were more potent than solid facts. None of this was clear to the political class until Trump became president.

For Timothy Snyder, whose book *On Tyranny* is the standout take on the subject in our times, it is in this serial attack on democracy's soft guardrails that Russia's influence has worked most insidiously in America during Trump's term in office.[6] "A lot of the ways that our democracy is going sour already happened already in Russia," Snyder told an interviewer in 2019. "It's not just that Russia helped Mr. Trump to get elected, it's that a certain Russian way of doing politics has spread pretty widely."[7]

Other 3P autocrats have preferred a more gradual approach, one that dilutes the initial shock value of norm-breaking by spreading it out over time. You can think of this as the boiled-frog approach to norm-breaking, after the old, zoologically suspect idea that a frog dropped into boiling water will jump straight out, but one placed in lukewarm water that's gradually heated to a boil will fail to realize what's happening until it's too late. As it happens, there is increasing empirical evidence that the old adage about boiling the frog has real psychological underpinnings. As Anne Applebaum notes, citing a 2009 study in the *Journal of Experimental Psychology*, when a norm-breaking behavior is introduced gradually, people are more likely to accept it: "This happens, in part, because most people have a built-in vision of themselves as moral and honest, and that self-image is resistant to change. Once certain behaviors become 'normal,' then people stop seeing them as wrong."[8, 9]

Boiling the frog is, in itself, a form of stealth: moving gradually wears opponents out, and their cries against abuses become constant and therefore easy to tune out. Bolivia and Hungary show how this is done. Evo Morales and Viktor Orbán built much of their early appeal by flouting rules of political propriety that seemed sacrosanct to the existing elite but no longer meant anything to people outside it. In Venezuela, Hugo Chávez intuited that breaking these kinds of inside-baseball norms was a win-win for him. It's not just that ignoring rules that hemmed in their power made autocrats more powerful; that's obvious. It's that they could use the elite backlash set off by norm-breaking to cement their credibility as outsiders. As we already discussed, this is exactly what Silvio Berlusconi did in the 1990s, and Donald Trump did in the early twenty-first century.

But not all norm-breaking is of the boiled-frog variety. Some of the 3P autocrats seem to go for a different tack—call it the shock-and-awe approach to norm-breaking. Perhaps the most extreme example comes from the Philippines.

Manila, the sweltering, sprawling capital of the Philippines, may not be the kind of city you think of when you hear the word "elite," but to Filipinos, brought up in a country where a handful of Manila's old-money families have run things since anyone can remember, Manila plays very much the role in the political imagination that Brussels plays in Britain or Washington does in the United States. And nowhere is the out-of-touch Manila elite more actively resented than on the impoverished southern island of Mindanao. Home to eleven of the Philippines' twenty poorest provinces, Mindanao is also religiously and culturally different enough from the capital to feel its elite's power as almost foreign. Mindanao turned out to be the perfect breeding ground for the kind of charismatic outsider able to rally the people against the corrupt elite. And that's just what happened, in the form of the seven-term mayor of Davao City, Rodrigo Duterte.

Duterte's claim to outsider status was a carefully constructed fiction. The son of a provincial governor, Duterte literally grew up in power. He was elected deputy mayor of Davao in the 1980s, when Mindanao was known as "Little Nicaragua" because of the violent leftist insurgency that permeated the island. Alongside the Marxists were a dazzling proliferation of criminal gangs, kidnapping squads, and petty crooks that kept Davao's citizens in a state of permanent, low-level fear.

A core skill for any populist, new or old, is to identify areas where the people's common sense and the elite's common sense are in irreducible conflict. Duterte understood that the westernized elite in Manila, steeped in the culture of human rights, was aghast at the whole notion of an extrajudicial killing. But back in Davao City, his constituents were under assault by a rising wave of violence and criminality driven by small-time drug dealing. Nobody in Mindanao would mind that much if the police simply went out and killed the people dealing the drugs—in fact, constituents were clamoring for just such a move. And to Rodrigo Duterte, the howls of outrage this would raise from the Manila elite were encouraging sounds, not something to avoid.

The mayor grasped that he could build a political profile out of championing death squads—a radically simple solution to the crime problem that would, as an added benefit, clearly mark him out as different from the hated elite. Norm-breaking becomes an instrument of polarization, the second broad strategy in the 3Ps recipe. Duterte may not have owned a TV station, like Silvio Berlusconi, or a real estate empire, like Donald Trump, but he came to see a path to becoming a celebrity nonetheless by establishing himself as the guy who would champion solutions other politicians just wouldn't.

Duterte built his reputation as mayor of Davao City on his barely concealed sponsorship of what came to be known as the DDS, the Davao Death Squad. A loose confederation of hit teams run by former soldiers and police officers, the DDS was given carte blanche to take out social undesirables: street kids, small-time drug dealers, anyone who, in the mayor's view, was a menace to public order. Conservative estimates suggest that between 1998 and 2014, the DDS claimed no fewer than 1,424 lives.[10] In its straightforward brutality, the DDS incarnated an aggressive rejection of the westernized elite's devotion to due process. For a politician looking to stake out the terrain Duterte was interested in, it was a no-brainer.

Incongruously, Duterte continued to maintain he had nothing to do with the Davao Death Squads.[11] While glorifying violence broadly (he promised the fish in Manila Bay would grow fat from the corpses that would end up floating in it), he was careful never to be found giving a specific order that could be associated with a specific killing. It was a characteristic bit of populist, polarizing doublespeak: Duterte promised violence even as he distanced himself from any specific killing. It was shameless. And it worked.

In 2016, Duterte ran on an explicit promise to export the brutal practices he favored in Davao to the Philippines as a whole. Praising martial law and vowing to institute it if necessary, Rodrigo Duterte made sure no one could possibly outflank him on the tough-on-crime beat. Since his election as president in 2016, the Philippines has become a human rights catastrophe and Duterte a popular hero. Coasting on high approval ratings while the body count mounted, he wasted no chance to decry the out-of-touch elites who had pushed back against his get-tough approach to the war on drugs.

In this way, norm-breaking can also be put in the service of populism. Rodrigo Duterte built support for these brutal policies by relentlessly portraying concern for human rights as an affectation of a corrupt elite. Ordinary Filipinos' common sense is simple: if drugs are a problem, then killing all the drug dealers and addicts is an obvious solution. The elite's urge to say, "But no, but it's more complicated than that," only plays into the populist trap, portraying them as devoted to cosmopolitan abstractions rather than regular people's simple, obvious interests.

And so flouting the norm against extrajudicial killing became, in the Philippines, an instrument in the service of both polarization and populism. Daring the old elites to stand up for the rights of hated drug dealers, Duterte lured them into a trap that allowed him to portray them as the enemies of the pure people. It's a tried-and-true approach, and one that continues to pay dividends year after year.

Of course, the Philippines is an extreme example. But the Davao Death Squad shows another path whereby democracy can fall victim to the 3P autocracy. The trick is that any consensus of the elite can be characterized as corrupt. In the eyes of populists and their followers, any belief, norm, or routine shared by the elite is, by definition, suspect and therefore a prime target.

The Power of Revenge

Tapping into common people's contempt for the elite and resentment for the real or imagined abuses they have suffered is what populists have always done. Developing a sixth sense for stoking the contempt and stirring up the resentment is their superpower. The knack is to perceive, before anyone else does, what source of resentment is ripe for exploitation. Resentment of elite privilege is the preexisting condition populists are fated to mine; the trick is in knowing when and how.

But resentment is just a suppressed longing for something harder to admit: a thirst for revenge. Populists who sow seeds of resentment must be prepared to serve up revenge if their followers' appetite is to be sated.

This truth is usually too brutal to face head-on, and in normal political discussions it is usually elided. We're more comfortable with euphemism: we prefer to discuss reactionary politics, or the politics of victimhood, or the politics of economic anxiety. Underlying it all is something uglier and more visceral—too visceral for comfort but too human to ignore.

"Resentment" is one such euphemism: a polite word for the longing to hurt those you believe have wronged you. The politics of resentment are the politics of revenge.

Revenge can be physical, but it need not be. Slamming your enemies in jail and confiscating their assets can be revenge, but so can much more subtle, symbolic moves that may look tame from the outside but can be hugely resonant in a given context.

Revenge comes in all sorts of shapes and sizes. To Turkey's Recep Tayyip Erdoğan—and, more importantly, to his legions of followers—allowing women to wear the Islamic headscarf at Turkey's public universities was an act of revenge. It was a symbolically loaded rebuke to decades of strict secularism promoted by Kemal Ataturk, modern Turkey's founder. The secular part of society that Ataturk nurtured experienced Erdoğan's move as a direct, even personal attack. To Evo Morales, changing the official name of Bolivia to the Plurinational State of Bolivia was an act of symbolic revenge for hundreds of years of white domination of the indigenous population.

Populists know there are rich political spoils to be had from satisfying their fans' thirst for symbolic revenge. There's nothing new about that—demagogues since time immemorial have known there is always a constituency eager to make their enemies suffer. Surely, the Roman general who ordered Carthage razed to the ground and salt spread over the ruins wasn't doing it for strategic advantage—he was doing it to meet his soldiers' demand for vengeance.

But the twenty-first-century autocrats share an instinctive feel for how people's lust for revenge can be turned into a weapon against constraints on their power. This explains some things that are otherwise hard to make sense of: decisions whose only purpose seems to be to hurt the perceived elite. Even if those decisions do nothing for the autocrats' supporters. Even if those decisions actually hurt their supporters.

The Latin American left has long been animated by a multicentury epic narrative of oppression that gave rise to a thirst for revenge. Books such as Eduardo Galeano's *The Open Veins of Latin America* (a copy of which Hugo Chávez once famously gifted Barack Obama during a serendipitous encounter in the corridor of a presidential summit) popularized a profoundly simplified narrative of European imperial conquest and despoliation that cried out for redemption through revenge.[12] Even though decades after its publication Galeano himself came to condemn the approach in his youthful megahit, the damage had been done. 3P autocrats like Evo Morales and Hugo Chávez found a willing audience for a political line that treated the entire history of Latin America as nothing more than the story of common people's brutal victimization by a rapacious white elite . . . and they proceeded to sell themselves as the vehicles for avenging that victimhood.

. During a stroll one fine Caracas afternoon in 2010, Hugo Chávez launched his most ambitious attempt to deliver that revenge. Walking around Caracas's colonial-era central square with a camera crew in tow, Chávez theatrically asked his assistants what use a building across the street from the parliament served.

"That building is now in private hands, *mi comandante*," one of his aides said deferentially, and then added, "Some jewelry businesses now operate out of there."

"*¡Exprópiese!*" Chávez thundered. "Expropriate it!"

By the end of his short stroll, Chávez had theatrically shouted the same order—"*¡Exprópiese!*"—again and again, repeating it at each private building visible from the square, and in doing so set a course for radically altering the system of property ownership in Venezuela. In the months that followed, businesses large, medium, and small would be taken into state ownership—from sophisticated power and telecommunications companies with tens of thousands of employees to relatively small food processing plants with a few dozen employees and farms of all sizes all over Venezuela. Chávez wasted no chance to portray the expropriations as aimed at sticking it to an old, entrenched oligarchy that had been exploiting everyday Venezuelans. These were the politics of revenge put at the center of an entire governing program aimed at remaking society along revanchist lines. It was exhilarating. It was also insanely terrible policymaking that destroyed Venezuela's economy and democracy and would, within a generation, mire Chávez's ecstatic fans in one of the worst humanitarian disasters Latin America has ever seen.

For Chávez, the specific impact of a policy mattered less than its symbolic impact. To Chávez, the goal was to inscribe himself in a historical narrative as the heroic champion of the oppressed. To him, the archetype of that champion would always be Simón Bolívar, the legendary independence-war hero who drove the Spaniards from six Latin American countries and—in his telling—led a people's revolution against the elite. Chávez loved to quote a line from Chilean

Nobel Prize winner Pablo Neruda: "Bolívar awakens once every hundred years, when the people awaken."[13]

The claim, never quite uttered but never really hidden, was clear: Chávez was no normal political leader. He was a larger-than-life historical figure, a crusader sent to exact revenge for hundreds of years of accumulated grievances.

The Power of Identity

The grievances 3P autocrats address are of a particular nature. They are not the broad-based grievances of an oppressed class in the way the left-wing politics of old conceived them, nor are they the grievances against an overgrown, overweening government that the conservative right had vented for so long. Those old gripes had the ambition to *unify* large sections of society under a common cause: the economic betterment of wage workers or the increasing freedom of every citizen. They gave rise to identities that had aspirations to being universal—though of course those aspirations were never achieved.

The grievances 3P autocrats exploit are different. Rather than serving as the basis for broad and broadly inclusive identities, they configure tribes—groups of intensely loyal followers who band together under the logic of the politics of fandom. Rather than broadly inclusive distinctions, these grievances configure narrow identities that empower the logic of polarization. After all, polarization is always about us versus them, and drawing sharp boundaries between the "us" and the "them" is the key step in any polarization strategy.

You can see the beginnings of this kind of identity-for-polarization strategy as far back as Silvio Berlusconi's *scesa in campo* speech, where he drew sharp lines between the two Italies: "the Italy that works against the one that chatters, the Italy that produces against the Italy that wastes, the Italy that saves against the one that steals," and so on.[14] From the beginning, the forerunner of the 3P framework had grasped that splitting his country down the middle along emotionally charged lines could propel him to power.

As 3P strategies have been more fully developed, the power of identity to shape political battles and define the limits of what is acceptable has bloomed. From Vladimir Putin putting the Russian Orthodox Church at the center of his image of a virtuous Russianness to Hugo Chávez's creation of a newly militant "Bolivarian" identity, 3P autocrats know the key to powerfully polarizing the political sphere is to put political support for them at the center of their supporters' self-identity.

When political differences come to be identity-based, political debate shifts from being a discussion about ideas to being a conflict between incompatible visions of the good life. If my group incarnates all that is righteous, noble, and good and your group stands for all that is wrong, base, and bad, there can hardly be a civil discussion between us. I no longer need to learn how to live peacefully alongside you, despite our differences; rather, my aim is to defeat you and banish you from the political scene once and for all.

Identity is a peculiar force in the 3P autocrat's toolbox because it cuts both ways. It redefines not just the self-understanding of the autocrat's followers but also that of the autocrat's opponents. In Venezuela, to be anti-*chavista* became as much a cornerstone of regime opponents' identity as being *chavista* became to those on the other side. In Turkey, simply knowing where a person stood with regard to Erdoğan became enough to infer all kinds of things about them. In the United States, whether you were pro- or anti-Trump, self-identification came to overshadow all other political considerations. To many, not wearing a face mask during the pandemic became a signal to others of that person's political identity.

To be clear, the salience of political views in people's identities had been growing in the United States for many decades before Donald J. Trump took center stage. In 1960, just 5 percent of voters said they would be displeased if their child married someone from the opposing political party; by 2010, some 50 percent of Republicans and 30 percent of Democrats said they would be upset by such a match.[15] By 2017, though, 70 percent of Democrats were telling pollsters they could not date a Trump supporter.[16] By 2020, 83 percent of those with a very unfavorable view of Trump would refuse to date one of his supporters.[17]

Interestingly, in the United States such views have come to supplant old dividing lines that were once seen as central. In 1958, just 4 percent of Americans approved of interracial marriages. By 2020, 86 percent did.[18] This suggests a rather different interpretation of "identity politics" than the one usually bandied about. Rather than dividing over classic markers of identity such as race, Americans are increasingly sorting themselves on the basis of *political attitudes* with regard to race, with folks who identify with Donald Trump's racial attitudes forming one team and those who reject it forming the other. The intensity of ill will between the two heralds an era of ongoing political instability in the United States.

3P autocrats transform identity into power by embodying their followers' fantasies. Trump's job is to embody Trumpism—to live the dream of unlimited wealth and power his followers crave. As Francis Fukuyama has argued, leaders craft an identity that affirms the wounded dignity of their followers by living the way the followers wish they could live. That identification is always both positive (*with* the leader) and negative (*against* those the leader defines as the enemy). That's why identity politics is always the handmaiden of polarization.[19] All too often, aspiring autocrats who have a special knack for wielding identity as a tool for polarization succeed at dismantling democracies.

The Power of Skepticism

The tools the 3P autocrats use are nothing if not adaptable. They can be hitched to agendas as radical as socialist revolutions or as extreme as Filipino death squads. But the true mark of their versatility is that they need not be hitched to any ideological agenda at all.

That's the lesson of the two most successful applications of the 3P playbook in recent years: Brexit in Britain and the election of Donald Trump in the United States. These cases illustrate the new approach pushed to the limit: set up in opposition to two of the oldest and most mature democracies on earth. More to the point, they show their effectiveness not so much in the service of an agenda as in opposition to any agenda.

The tools of the 3Ps can, it turns out, be put in the service of the politics of nihilism. In some populists' hands, they can be used not so much to advance a given program as to advance the rejection of any program.

Think of Britain's traumatic experience with Brexit. It's a peculiar case because in Britain, the tools picked from the menu of options offered by populism, polarization, and post-truth were applied by committee, as it were—without having any single recognizable leader at the front of the charge. It was a diffuse, leaderless sort of new power that saw the public of a G7 country stand up to reject the organizing principle of an entire country's elite because it was beloved by that elite.

The seminal moment in the Brexit referendum came when one of the highest-ranking cabinet secretaries, Michael Gove, confronted with a long list of august organizations that had rejected Brexit, stunned his Sky interviewer with a simple answer: "The people of this country," Gove said, "have had enough of experts."[20]

Gove's official title was no less than Lord High Chancellor of the United Kingdom—an unlikely appellation for a would-be enemy of the learned elite. Here was a onetime president of the hyperexclusive Oxford Union debating club denouncing elitism and deriding expertise. But for all the shrieks of contempt from elite quarters, Gove perfectly captured the mood of deep nihilism washing over the British electorate.

After the 2016 referendum, in which 52 percent of Britons voted in favor of leaving the European Union, pollsters would find that attitudes toward experts were among the best predictors of the way Britons would vote in the Brexit referendum.[21] Those who agreed that it's wrong to rely too much on so-called experts and better to rely on ordinary people were three times as likely to favor Brexit as those who disagreed. And those who agreed that the opinions of professional people with expertise are better than relying on ordinary people were five times as likely to vote to remain in the EU as those who disagreed.[22]

Gove had latched onto an important insight, one that elsewhere I've dubbed the "paradox of trust." These days, people are increasingly unwilling to believe the insights of actual experts who have spent careers painstakingly studying a given subject. But this skepticism

that Gove was exploiting comes alongside a newfound willingness
to trust charlatans peddling easy answers to complicated questions.
Even as the words of real experts carry less and less weight in the
public sphere, the words of quacks and charlatans spread with unprecedented speed on social media. Why? Because we're irresistibly
drawn to messages that confirm our preexisting biases and flatter our
prejudices. In the hands of populists utterly indifferent to truth and
happy to exploit the paradox of trust in the service of polarization,
skepticism becomes a tool of devastating effectiveness.

The mood of deep suspicion of elite institutions, opinions, and
habits that Britain's Brexiteers had latched onto has been extensively
documented on the other side of the Atlantic as well. In his book *The
Ideas Industry*, Daniel Drezner shows how, for more than a generation, people's willingness to defer to expert opinions has cratered
throughout the West.[23] In the United States, it took a bold politician
to fully grasp the full potentiality of this moment. Where enough
voters are alienated enough from an elite, anti-intellectualism can
become a devastating ideological weapon.

In this regard, Donald J. Trump's shortcomings became his biggest asset. Take climate science. There are plenty of sophisticated
GOP politicians who are willing to cynically pretend not to understand the science of climate change. There's Representative Fred Upton of Michigan, who in 2009 sponsored green energy legislation[24]
but in 2011, hoping to ward off a primary challenge from the right,
refused to acknowledge that climate change is human-caused.[25] Or
Newt Gingrich, who a decade ago performed in thirty-second TV
ads about the need for a bipartisan approach to climate change[26] and
now denies any such phenomenon is happening at all.[27]

The feigned ignorance of an Upton or a Gingrich often isn't entirely convincing, though, because it's so obviously fake. It takes a
politician who is *genuinely unable* to understand the science of climate change to gain those voters' trust. A genuine ignoramus can
achieve things, politically, that a pretend one just can't.

Donald Trump's rejection of expert knowledge had a taste of authenticity, with deep roots in the endless expanses of his ignorance.
It works as a power tool because to the populist's mind, a stink of

suspicion clings to abstraction, to theorizing, and, in general, to a sophistication that is foreign to the pure people whose interests the populist claims to represent.

Distrust of elites bleeds into distrust of the tools the elite uses to sustain its power. Soon, hostility extends to intellectual effort of any kind, and to the institutional buttresses of that effort: universities, elite publications, research institutions, think tanks, the entire system of academic credentialing designed to certify expertise. "Burn it all down," the 3P autocrat says. "It's a trap. It works against you and your family."

As far back as 1958, Michael Young had foreseen these trends in his prescient sociological satire, *The Rise of the Meritocracy*.[28] Young imagined a dystopia where people's place in society was decided entirely on merit, with a cognitive elite sitting atop a finely stratified social system that the less meritorious came to find wholly oppressive. In the book, the poisonous atmosphere of distrust between the meritocrats and the masses they disdain builds up to a massive revolt that overthrows the entire system. The book placed the revolt in 2033.

But, outside the realm of dystopian fiction, what actually happens when a nation turns decisively against merit as an organizing principle in society? What are the consequences of reorganizing today's highly complex postindustrial societies systematically away from a reliance on expertise? Has anyone actually tried such a thing? What happens?

Here Hugo Chávez once again points the way. Chávez bolstered his populist credentials by displaying his contempt for technocrats' claim to expertise. Their reliance on technical jargon and the cold, analytic way they used to communicate looked to him like evidence that it was all a big scam. Take this passage from December 2002, lifted from one of his famous Sunday talk shows:

> Boards, meetings, reviews, because on top of it all they really know how to make your head spin. Once I called a board meeting at PDVSA [the national oil company] and came out with my head spinning. I said, "I'm going to need some sleep," because they came at me with everything: slides, projections, this, that, the other thing,

and you end up dizzy. I had to lie down, I slept about twelve hours straight, my head totally spinning. I said, "No, no more, I'm not putting up with this anymore," I want a report, so I can read first and I'll call you, one at a time, for explanations, maybe the finance chief first, and the other guy, then the other guy. But it didn't matter, you gave them orders and they weren't followed . . . Venezuela's had a state within the state . . . it was a black box, and now we're opening it and the vipers are coming out.[29]

Breaking the technocrats' grip on PDVSA became an obsession for Chávez, a project he was determined to carry out at any cost. PDVSA, the president decided, had had enough of experts. In 2020, within two decades of this style of leadership, PDVSA's oil production had fallen 90 percent, and long lines for fuel formed at gas stations throughout the country—an unimaginable outcome in one of the world's biggest and oldest oil producers.

Such catastrophes are worth it to 3P autocrats if they allow them to solidify their populist credentials. That's why the temptation to insult the technocratic elite is always hard to resist. It's difficult to believe, to take just one example, that a deliberate insult was not intended when, in 2017 as president, Donald Trump appointed onetime Texas governor Rick Perry to head the Energy Department. It was that department whose name, famously, Perry had been unable to recall in a debate four years earlier when asked which cabinet offices he proposed to eliminate. The blunder had sunk his presidential bid . . . and now here he was, asked to lead a department he'd felt such contempt for he couldn't even remember he wanted to eliminate it.

But seldom has skepticism-as-contempt been more transparently deployed than in Rex Tillerson's brief tenure as U.S. secretary of state from 2017 to 2018. Tillerson, the former CEO of oil giant Exxon-Mobil, had no government experience at all and openly disdained the expertise of the Foreign Service professionals he supposedly led. He proceeded to unleash a form of institutional vandalism that will take years, if not decades, to undo. Flouting the convention that cabinet secretaries fight to preserve their departments' budgets, Tillerson gleefully jumped onto an aggressive budget-cutting campaign that he could use as cover to purge the Foreign Service, shedding invaluable expertise accumulated over decades in one of the most prestigious parts of the U.S. government. With recruitment into the Foreign Service suspended, dozens of top posts unfilled, and the department facing draconian budget cuts, America's interface with the world was crippled by a wave of disinvestment in human capital. Together with a move, deep into the administration's lame-duck period, to weaken civil service protections insulating heads of federal agencies from political retaliation, the administration seemed intent to rid the government of its most seasoned experts.

"America has had enough of experts" seemed to be the motto favored by the Trump administration. As the premium on political loyalty to the president overshadowed all other considerations, it left not just the Department of State but the state itself weaker and less capable. The president stunned Washington by deriding even America's intelligence community, at one point comparing intelligence leaks to the practices of Nazi Germany. It's important to recognize this project for what it is: an unmistakable early warning sign of a 3P autocracy in progress, and one with terrifying echoes of even older forms of misrule. It was Hannah Arendt who first noted, back in 1951, that "totalitarianism in power invariably replaces all first-rate talents, regardless of their sympathies, with those crackpots and fools whose lack of intelligence and creativity is still the best guarantee of their loyalty."[30]

She wasn't wrong. Just right about more than she realized.

The Power of Media Control

Media constitutes one of the most powerful checks on the pretensions of would-be autocrats, which makes the taming of the press a top priority. A free media is not just enormously irritating to leaders who rely on populism, polarization, and post-truth to govern, but it is a dangerous threat to their hold on power. Free media thwarts leaders' ability to establish their narrative as the truth. Which is why a testy, adversarial, and eventually hostile relationship with the media is one of the clearest signs of looming autocracy.

Of course, autocrats have always sought to silence those who would criticize them. A generation or two ago, controlling information flows meant censorship: actual regime officials wielding a red pen in a newsroom while the political police stood ready to jail publishers, editors, and journalists who antagonized the regime. Those old, twentieth-century mechanisms of media control have hardly died out. In 2019, *New York Times* publisher A. G. Sulzberger warned that his newspaper was seeing an alarming rise in the rate at which journalists around the world were being muzzled, repressed, and jailed. "To stop journalists from exposing uncomfortable truths and holding power to account," Sulzberger wrote, "a growing number of governments have engaged in overt, sometimes violent, efforts to discredit their work and intimidate them into silence."[31] But the old mechanisms of media control are not enough to control the threat of free media in the information age.

Old-style censorship continues to be practiced in old-school dictatorships; China is the standout example, but Cuba, Russia, Ethiopia, Rwanda, Belarus, Iran, Venezuela, and many other repressive regimes continue to practice it as well. Erdoğan's Turkey, for example, is the country with the world's largest number of jailed journalists. In less autocratic regimes, the internet has rendered censorship and media repression increasingly ineffective. There are simply too many new ways to bypass the state's censorship efforts.

In the twenty-first century, the new methods of control are subtler and harder to spot. They rely more on pressure, persuasion, and cooperation than on brute force. Nowadays, censorship works via subterfuge; it is stealthy, indirect, or both.[32] Governments bribe journalists, editors, or media owners; they block or filter search results; they keep close electronic surveillance over journalists and their sources, and stealthily pressure editors to fire the most problematic ones. They control access to imports, whether newsprint or imported equipment and spare parts (for video cameras, for example), and they shut dissident media out of government economic subsidy schemes available to their pro-government competitors. Tax inspectors are constantly deployed to audit the noncompliant media companies, operations of foreign news organizations are restricted or banned outright, and editors and journalists receive stealthy suggestions about the stories that are better left untold. The security services hack online news media to disrupt them or shut them down, buy out outlets that don't toe the government line, create stealth or fake news sources, and launch lookalike sites meant to muddy muckrakers' reputations.

The tools at their disposal are endless, subtle, hard to discern, and brutally effective. They nurture an atmosphere rife with self-censorship, which in turn produces a gray area between freedom and outright coercion.

How does this work in practice? Poland offers a good example. Jarosław Kaczyński, the leader of the Law and Justice Party, announced in 2020 that his party, which had narrowly won an election, would seek to "re-Polonize" and "deconcentrate" all privately owned media. Soon thereafter, senior Polish officials confirmed that a state-owned oil company—yes, an oil company—was negotiating the purchase of twenty of the country's twenty-four regional newspapers. For those not willing to sell, Kaczyński—whom the *Washington Post* described as "a nationalist populist who crusades against immigrants and gay rights"—announced punitive laws.[33]

There are many other examples, but the cases of two broadcasters— Venezuela's RCTV in 2007 and the Philippines' ABS-CBN in 2020— are both illustrative and striking. Both were venerably old: RCTV was the oldest commercial broadcaster in Venezuela, ABS-CBN the longest-running commercial broadcaster in all Southeast Asia. Both were general-interest broadcasters, focused on entertainment programming and targeting a mass audience. Both included small but feisty news and opinion services that held the government to account and often attacked it in strong terms. They even shared a spot on the dial and a colloquial name: everyone in Venezuela called RCTV "El Canal 2," while everyone in the Philippines knew ABS-CBN as "Channel 2."

Both were shut down because their respective government regulators refused to renew their broadcast licenses. It was precisely their mass appeal that made them unacceptable to the 3P autocrats in Caracas and Manila. If a cable news network with a relatively small audience of middle-class news junkies criticizes the government, that's one thing. Broadcasters like Russia's NPR-style Ekho Moskvy, which courts a niche, highly educated, NPR-style audience, typically get hounded and harassed rather than shut down outright. But when a general-interest broadcaster beams critical content at the massive popular audience, reaching far into the country's cities and towns, it is quite another. Yet rather than being silenced by tanks and soldiers, these broadcasters were shut down with lawyers and administrative minutiae. Indeed, the governments involved steadfastly refused to acknowledge that the broadcasters had been shut down at all. Their broadcast licenses had merely been denied renewal—a pseudolegal distinction without a difference if ever there was one. Both staggered on via satellite and online, reaching a tiny fraction of the mass audiences they had once enjoyed. Each was defanged as an effective counterweight to the 3P autocrat running its country.

Or take an example from Viktor Orbán's Hungary. On the morning of October 8, 2016, the staff of *Népszabadság*, Hungary's leading broadsheet, was in for a surprise. The electronic access keys to the building and their newsroom had suddenly stopped working. Their work phones and emails also had stopped functioning. The paper, they soon came to realize, had been shut down. *Népszabadság* had become the highest-profile victim of Prime Minister Viktor Orbán's campaign against independent media. Like any good stealthocrat, Orbán had made sure to preserve plausible deniability. The newspaper was officially closed for financial reasons by its Austrian owners. It was pure coincidence, Hungarians were told, that the decision came just days after *Népszabadság* had published a series of hard-hitting corruption exposés pointing the finger directly at members of Orbán's inner circle.

Taking on an iconic brand and its most visible opponent, Orbán overreached, creating a cause célèbre that could galvanize international response. Soon, international organizations were publishing action alerts warning about the collapse of free speech in an EU member country.

The international outcry over *Népszabadság* tended to obscure what was a much broader and more systematic attempt to bring all of Hungary's media under the 3P autocrat's thumb. Starting immediately after his election in 2010, Orbán had moved aggressively to transform Hungary's state broadcaster into a propaganda organ for Fidesz, his ruling party. From that point on he set out on an aggressive campaign to neutralize critical newspapers, radio stations, and TV broadcasters throughout the country.[34] First Orbán hit them in the pocketbook, withdrawing state advertising from critical media and using the Media Council—Hungary's media regulator—to levy heavy fines against dissident media. Soon he moved to replace critical staff members altogether, largely by asking businesspeople friendly to the regime to buy meddlesome newspapers.

In August 2017, Orbán allies bought up the remaining handful of independent regional newspapers in Hungary, leaving three regime-connected businesspeople in control of every regional newspaper in the country. In previous years, Orbán's business friends had bought independent radio and TV broadcasters as well as popular online news portals. Seven years after his ascent to power, Orbán had concluded a clean sweep of independent regional media in Hungary.[35]

What's notable here is the way populists from seemingly opposing ends of the ideological spectrum converge on the same mechanisms of media control. Time was when ultimate censorship came in the form of a knock on the door from the secret police in the middle of the night. That was the twentieth-century pattern. In the twenty-first, this was replaced by tax audits, fines over recondite regulatory regulations, the withdrawal of government advertising budgets, and entreaties from mysterious "private investors" seeking an ownership stake.

And that's the story of the 3Ps autocrats' power tools writ large. Hungry for unchecked control but needing to keep a minimum of democratic credibility, leaders in vastly different contexts, even those espousing opposing ideologies, converge on the same practices for reasserting power in the face of institutions created to contain the concentration of power. They may have nothing in common ideologically, but they all intuit that ideology really has very little to do with the demands of power today. That's why they converge on the same few power tools again and again.

The Power of Emergency

Another power tool used by the 3P leaders relies on the age-old argument that in the face of a national catastrophe it is necessary to empower an emergency government. National laws in many parts of the world include emergency provisions to allow executive branches to act decisively in situations when regular legislative processes would prove too cumbersome and slow; civil unrest, foreign invasion, economic collapse, mass protests, coup attempts, and most certainly pandemics have all been cited recently as occasions for emergency rule.

As we've seen, the new breed of autocrats is forever on the hunt for ways to get around institutional checks and balances. It is not surprising, then, that autocrats of all stripes are irresistibly attracted to emergency measures. They are preexisting pseudolaws, ideally situated to be abused beyond recognition without (technically) violating any given law.

There isn't anything especially novel about this technique. The abuse of emergency legislation to unshackle the executive is a mainstay of autocratic regimes dating back generations. Fascist legal scholar Carl Schmitt noted in the 1930s that in any legal system, the ultimate power would always be the power to declare an exception. Every legal system, Schmitt reasoned, must make space for action in emergency situations. Because it is impossible for a lawmaker to foresee every potential eventuality, every legal system leaves room for ambiguity: situations that don't quite fit the framers' foresight but where decisions must be made. Some actors in the system must—by right or by might—be empowered to make those decisions and to make those exceptions. That, for Schmitt, is the ultimate fount of power—the loophole through which any and every decision can be rendered legal.[36]

In the hands of a Nazi apologist like Schmitt, this doctrine of the exception became the juridical justification for the Ermächtigungsgesetz of 1933—the Enabling Law that gave Adolf Hitler the power to legislate without the need for approval from the Reichstag, Germany's parliament. Under the Enabling Law, the exception became the norm. Emergency became permanent and eventually blossomed into the Führerprinzip, the formal doctrine that the Führer's spoken word outranked in legal status not only government policies, regulations, and practices but even written law.

Rule by exception became a mainstay of authoritarian government after the war as well, with the most notable example being Egypt, which was run under an "emergency law" that suspended basic civil liberties (including freedom of speech and habeas corpus) more or less continuously from 1967 until 2011. But countries as diverse as Argentina, Greece, India, Pakistan, Sierra Leone, Spain, and Thailand spent considerable periods under emergency law during the Cold War.

In 2008, Silvio Berlusconi pioneered the use of emergency powers to enact a populist crackdown on immigration, approving a draconian decree that allowed the government to fingerprint all ethnic Roma in the country. The measure was widely criticized as an obvious racist attack on a marginalized community. The Roma—previously known as Gypsies—had long been blamed for crime in Italy, and Berlusconi's emergency measure sidestepped guarantees against racial profiling to pick them out for additional scrutiny.

And if even fake emergencies are an irresistible temptation to autocrats, imagine how much more powerful a real emergency is. In 2020, the world got a crash course in the autocratic uses of emergency when a real emergency jumped front and center onto the world stage. The coronavirus pandemic created ample justification for expanding state power, with even the best-established democracies sharply curtailing usual freedoms to slow the spread of the virus. In Russia, this became a golden opportunity to roll out mass video surveillance on a scale never seen before, with facial recognition software attached to security cameras all around the country under the pretext of contact tracing. In Israel, the pandemic became the pretext for allowing the state to exploit gigabytes' worth of mobile phone location data, pinpointing both Israelis' and Palestinians' exact whereabouts with frightening precision.

Other countries went well beyond this in the drive to exploit the coronavirus emergency for autocratic gain. Hungary's Viktor Orbán canceled parliamentary elections and announced plans to rule by decree, issuing vague and unenforceable pledges to reverse the measures once the pandemic subsided. And China, the birthplace of the virus, unilaterally ended Hong Kong's special status under the "one country, two systems" arrangement, extending the reach of Beijing's security laws to the territory at a time when the international community was simply too distracted by the global health crisis to offer any real pushback.

In Chapter 10, we will describe in more detail the impact that the novel coronavirus pandemic had on the use and abuse of power, and how, at the same time, the virus also weakened the power of governments and leaders around the world.

The 3P Autocrat's Toolbox

It isn't any one tool that gives the 3P framework its potency but rather their simultaneity. Together, these power tools encode a repository of insights into the nature of populism, polarization, and post-truth. The autocrats who wield them know that aggrieved masses propel to power those offering not just redress but revenge. They've grasped that the people most eager to sweep them into power are the most aggrieved: those whose identities revolve around feeling victimized in their own societies. Aspiring autocrats have relearned the old insight that nothing creates a visceral bond with followers like speaking directly to a deep sense of having been wronged. And they've done so using twenty-first-century communications tools unavailable to their predecessors.

Aspiring autocrats have turned the power of skepticism into a key propellant of their political project, mining a deep vein of contempt against elite experts to shield themselves against scrutiny—turning expertise almost into a badge of shame.

And they've harnessed the power of media control, sidestepping legacy news organizations by talking to people directly, first through rallies, later on TV and online, to devastating effect. Once in power, of course, 3P autocrats often go further, turning to increasingly sophisticated methods of controlling the information people have access to.

They turn to these tools because they understand that the checks and balances that are most effective in limiting their scope of action are not those written into laws. They're written into something vaguer, more evanescent, and more pervasive: the sense of what's normal. These "soft guardrails of democracy" can't be codified, but they must be undone if aspiring autocrats are to achieve their ultimate goals. 3P autocrats know that to win they need to redefine what's normal in a democracy, to prod it, poke it, and challenge it day in and day out until it collapses. They know that until that happens, their hold on power will never be fully secure. The road to autocracy requires war on that sense of what's normal. Yes, war.

Whether they're blazing new trails or reinventing well-trodden ones, the new breed of autocrats have developed a distinctive set of techniques and tools for sidestepping checks and balances as they work to gain and maintain power. Both by breaking norms to prove their bona fides as outsiders and by sating their followers' thirst for revenge, they've learned to mobilize people's rage against elites as an instrument for their power. That means exploiting people's skepticism of experts while cutting off their access to critical reporting about themselves. And, when all else fails, it means dusting off emergency powers to circumvent the formal checks on their powers.

Each of these techniques, on its own, would be dangerous to the health of a free democracy. Deployed together, they create ample opportunities to replace a real democracy with a fake one, one that has all the trappings of the old democracy but none of its effectiveness in curbing the power of the nation's chief executive.

4

THE HUNT FOR CULPRITS

There seems to be no shortage of enthusiastic believers in the promises that populists make. In some ways, the more interesting question about them isn't why they behave the way they do, but why their followers remain so keen to believe them.

On one level the answer is obvious: because populists say what their followers want to hear. That includes feel-good promises that will be quickly ignored or, if implemented, will either be ephemeral or fall short of delivering the expected—indeed, promised—results. But at a deeper, more troubling level, the question is why the followers continue to support populists even after there is overwhelming evidence that their promises are empty, their policies a failure, and their politics bad for democracy. Why support politicians whose purpose is to stay in power as long as possible at any cost, and who are bent on concentrating power at the expense of their followers' well-being?

This is the real puzzle: not so much why autocrats are willing to do whatever is necessary to gain and retain power, but why it is so easy for demagogues and charlatans to gain followers. And behind this question lies a dark suspicion: could it be that 3P autocrats are popular because of their authoritarianism rather than despite it?

The sense that the appetite for autocratic leadership is rising is not just a matter of perception. The share of people who would like to see "a strong leader who does not have to bother with parliaments and elections" grew by 10 percentage points in the United States in two decades starting in the late 1990s, by almost 20 points in Spain and South Korea, and by 25 points in Russia and South Africa according to research carried out in 2016 by Roberto Stefan Foa and Yascha Mounk.[1] Worse, the bulk of the shift is due to changing attitudes among younger people.

What has whetted this appetite worldwide for the type of 3P leadership and policies that has ended up hurting those who supported the populists? What caused this stealthy authoritarian drift?

Did a common set of experiences across countries as diverse as Brazil, Bolivia, India, Israel, Italy, Hungary, Poland, the Philippines, Russia, Turkey, the United States, and Venezuela prime their publics for 3P leadership? What are those experiences? Are they economic? Sociological? Psychological? Technological? All four somehow? Or did this new form of stealthy autocracy spread through contagion—due to a demonstration effect pushing beyond geographic boundaries as aspiring autocrats learned from one another's success?

As we will see, political scientists, sociologists, and social psychologists have begun to converge on a set of explanations for why people's tolerance for more authoritarian governments is on the rise. In this view, common experiences of economic dislocation build up to a perception that society is changing too fast in ways that people perceive as threatening. This perception of threat activates broadly shared, but normally dormant, psychological predispositions toward authoritarianism and a preference for authoritarian leaders.

Today, those authoritarian predispositions are being activated more frequently thanks to the effects of technological hyperconnectivity. And that hyperconnectivity makes the threat implied by fast, large-scale, societal change much more potent. It gives it political depth and fosters a broad assault against the foundations of liberal societies: freedom and democratic checks and balances.

The fragmentation and degradation of the power of the nation-state is one of the biggest reasons people find their social environment threatening. Why? Because traditional power centers are increasingly constrained. In particular, nation-states—the entities that provided the building blocks of the international order for two centuries—are losing the ability to foster the economic fortunes of their societies, leaving their people hungry for increasingly radical solutions to problems traditional politicians seem unwilling to address or unable to solve. And that's a pent-up grievance that aspiring autocrats know how to stoke and exploit.

The reaction to the increasing ineffectiveness of the nation-state to provide shelter to their citizens against the mounting threats of an uncertain world is an important driver of the demand for autocratic government in the twenty-first century.

Inequality and the Corrosive Power of Dashed Expectations

Societies don't abandon democratic principles on a whim. They do so after sustained periods of dislocation, disappointment, and the deterioration of their living standards. They do so when a critical mass of citizens concludes that personal progress is an impossible dream. Once that point is reached, it is only natural then to perceive society as alien, unjust, morally adrift, and threatening.

That explains why the aspiring 3P autocrats find their ideal hunting grounds not among the poor but among the disappointed: people who've come to expect a level of material well-being and public services that they suddenly find beyond their reach.

You don't have to be poor to be disappointed about your lot in life. It is not even economic inequality, though inequality feeds the feelings of injustice that make people angry. The main problem for those who have their basic needs covered (food, a roof over their heads, some regular income, healthcare, safety) is status dissonance: the frustration that wells up when people conclude that their economic and social progress is blocked, and they are stuck in a lower rung than the one they expected to occupy in society. Status dissonance is amplified by the sense that rather than coming closer to your rightful place in society, you're falling further and further below your natural spot in the pecking order.

This experience of status dissonance ties together the outlooks of widely different people who have supported aspiring autocrats in very different contexts. The downwardly mobile schoolteacher in the Philippines, the displaced autoworker in Michigan, the unemployed young university graduate in Moscow, and the struggling construction worker in Hungary may not have much lived experience in common, but each feels the sting of disappointment from a life that doesn't live up to the expectations they had formed, to the future they had envisioned for themselves and their families. The story of the twenty-first century so far is the story of how the disappointed lash out politically, creating a series of crises that liberal political systems are ill-equipped to process fairly and respond to in a timely and effective way.

You can think of this as the "dashed expectations" model of political instability. It has been around for at least a couple of centuries. Its spiritual parent was Alexis de Tocqueville, the French chronicler of American life who back in the early nineteenth century had already pinpointed the revolutionary potential of dashed expectations and the status dissonance they engendered.[2]

This idea of dashed expectations as a prime mover in human history was fully fleshed out by the late Harvard professor Samuel Huntington in his classic 1968 book, *Political Order in Changing Societies*.[3] Standing on its head the consensus of his day, which held that countries would inevitably become more stable and democratic as they modernized and became more prosperous, Huntington persuasively argued that modernization itself is often a driver of political instability, not a solution to it.

In the mid-twentieth century, Huntington maintained, modernization gave people a powerful political voice long before developing countries' economies could give them a material stake in maintaining stability. Marshaling evidence from all around the globe, Huntington showed that both traditional agrarian societies and advanced capitalist economies were often stable, but "modernizing" countries (that is, those in transition from the former to the latter) fell prey to coups, insurrections, civil disorder, and civil war with clocklike regularity.

For Huntington, the problem was that the new technologies associated with the modernization of his day (such institutions as the labor union, the newspaper, and the political party) empowered people to make political demands that traditional political systems were not able to satisfy. He argued that modernization was prodigiously efficient at generating status dissonance on a mass scale, and that was why it brought about destabilizing political turmoil.

Fast-forward five decades. Today, the new information technologies enabling groups to organize politically—the talk radio show, affordable travel, the mobile phone, Twitter, the WhatsApp group— look much different from the ones Huntington had in mind. Huntington never intended his model to account for the breakdown of the political systems of advanced industrialized economies—he was writing about Bangladesh and Indonesia, not Italy, the United Kingdom, or the United States. Yet the mechanisms he identified resonate powerfully with the experiences of the advanced countries in the twenty-first century.

Today, new identity groups form around a burning sense of grievance. They're brought together by the very real experience of being left behind economically, disrespected culturally, and immersed in an increasingly alien-seeming, threatening society. It is these groups, propelled by status dissonance, that are creating political instability on an unprecedented scale in political systems all around the globe.

There are broad differences with the mid-twentieth-century reality Samuel Huntington examined. In his day, the world was undergoing rapid decolonization, and the Soviet Union vied with the United States for global preeminence. The flavor of political instability tended to be revolutionary: long-marginalized groups were coming to the table for the first time and demanding a share of a prosperity they had never known. Today, its flavor in higher-income countries is more often defensive: groups that have had to fight for a modicum of financial security find their positions threatened or eroded, and they demand protection. Their goal is to beat back an alien tide of change rather than to pave the way for an earthly utopia.

For all these differences, the basic insight remains: when a critical mass of people in society feel their expectations in life have been dashed, conditions soon build up to a crisis. And in today's world, those whose expectations have been dashed are able to reach out to one another and build communities of meaning in a way that had never been technologically possible before.

Economic Disempowerment in the Age of Technological Empowerment

On April 23, 2018, a young man by the name of Alek Minassian got into a rented Chevrolet Express van, drove it to downtown Toronto, and plowed it into a crowd of pedestrians, killing nine. Speaking to police after the attack, Minassian identified himself as a member of the online community of incels—short for "involuntarily celibate"— and described his action as a revenge attack against the women who had rejected his romantic advances over the years. It wasn't the first murderous attack associated with self-described incels—in 2016, a young man by the name of Elliot Rogers had shot six women in Isla Vista, California, before turning his gun on himself.

On March 15, 2019, Brenton Tarrant loaded several guns and explosives into his car and attacked the small Al Noor Mosque in Christchurch, New Zealand, killing fifty. Tarrant live-streamed the attack from a helmet-mounted camera and left behind a long, rambling, far-right manifesto aimed squarely at members of his online community of virulently Islamophobic white nationalists.

It is important to understand what specifically is new here. It certainly is not the sexual frustration of young men. Nor is it the hostility toward immigrant communities practicing an unfamiliar religion. Those are as old as time.

What is new is the way technologies now allow people like Minassian, Rogers, and Tarrant to forge new identities through online communities that validate their experiences and create a path toward radicalization for their most militant members. If they'd only had access to the technology of the twentieth century, an Alek Minassian or an Elliot Rogers might well have been driven to despair by their lack of success with women, and Brenton Tarrant might have been consumed by his loathing for Muslims, but they wouldn't have understood themselves as fellow members of a single group, a community with shared interests and resentments able to nurture the revenge fantasies of its most volatile young members.

This collision between private hatreds and internet communities of hate has proven deadly. In Toronto and Isla Vista and Christchurch, the toll was counted in innocent lives lost. And more will surely follow.

Fringe communities such as incels and white nationalists are experiencing the profound disempowerment of dashed expectations just as radical new technologies of empowerment have come onto the scene: the internet, of course, but also the broader development of an information society along with an explosion in international trade that brings millions of new products into every market and the availability of much cheaper air travel that enables much more human mobility (at least until a pandemic breaks out). We live in an era of abundance, when there is more of everything: more people, cities, nations, ideas, more products, computers, companies, medicines, NGOs, religions, terrorist groups, criminal cartels—and also more virtual communities where experiences can be reaffirmed, and new communities can come together in ways that weren't possible just a couple of decades ago.

The revolutionary changes in economics, technology, and mindsets facilitate the creation of virtual communities formed by individuals who a generation ago might never have thought their experiences made them into members of anything. Back when Huntington was writing his book on political order and the expectations gap, the sexual frustration of a young man in Canada or the animosity toward Muslims of one in New Zealand were not politically salient facts because those young men didn't create a collective identity around their experiences or views.

By massively lowering the costs of networking with others who hold them, the "more revolution" both empowers fringe views and enmeshes their proponents in communities that reject automatic deference to authority. Together with vastly increased geographic mobility, these trends contributed to the transformation that caused power to decay in the first place.

The loners of yesteryear are becoming members of collectives that can be aggressively disruptive, even dangerous. New technologies have made extreme views easily available to millions for the first time while at the same time lowering the barriers that once kept people who subscribed to those views from acting in coordination with one another. It is a combustible combination.

The postwar consensus was built on a series of unspoken understandings about the bounds of acceptable political discourse. Openly racist or authoritarian views were silenced not through state censorship but by a diffuse sense among editors that they were not respectable. All it took to police those boundaries was an editorial class educated in broadly similar institutions and sharing broadly similar values and worldviews applying broadly similar editorial criteria to a limited handful of outlets.

The system allowed considerable leeway to explore controversial new ideas, but within limits. In the second half of the twentieth century, neo-Nazis, eugenicists, and ethnonationalists did not, as a rule, find a platform on the six o'clock news or in the opinion pages of prestige newspapers. That millions of people might have wanted to read their views hardly figured into the decision.

The communications infrastructure of the twenty-first century operates in precisely the opposite way. It has developed around powerful algorithms designed to identify and cater to popular but underserved points of view. Algorithms heap rewards on those able to produce such content, directing gushers of advertising revenue at them. The communications infrastructure of the twenty-first century systematically broadens the available range of views instead of restricting it.

In the United States, a conveyor belt was established to take extreme views out of online communities and circulate them to broader and broader audiences. Extremist opinions that got their start in life in the fever swamps of the internet (unregulated message boards such as 4chan and 8chan, or lightly regulated forums like Reddit and YouTube) would get laundered for consumption by mass audiences through media outlets such as Fox News and One America News Network. Once this happened, traditional media would pick up the thread, fully normalizing the discussion of views once deemed too extreme for mass dissemination.

Similar processes took hold in many other places. In Israel, the hard-right Channel 20 gives ample airtime to extreme religious and nationalist views that often echoes with eliminationist themes as solutions to the Palestinian question. Channel 20 routinely scours Israel's far-right online media ecosystem for new contributors, such as the far-right pro-settler News 0404 website, and launders their points of view for a broader audience.

This model has proven its cross-cultural appeal. In India, President Narendra Modi's Hindu nationalist BJP government has tightly allied itself with Republic TV, a news channel anchored by Arnab Goswami, one of India's most recognizable media personalities. Launched in 2017, Republic TV hews closely to the Fox News/Channel 20 model: loud, brash, and unabashedly partisan, it trawls India's sprawling social media spaces looking for stories of outrages committed by Muslims to report. Playing continuously to a crude Hindu nationalism, it has built a mass following, and its agitators continually intimidate critics of the regime, whom it systematically slams with the term "anti-national." On Republic TV, "national" is equated with "Hindu," while "Hindu" is equated with Modi's policies. To criticize any aspect of government policy, therefore, makes you "anti-national."

As a result of these trends, aspiring autocrats find it far easier to connect with people whose views would once have been beyond the pale. Once racist and xenophobic appeals are in wide circulation and larger and larger communities have begun to sympathize with them, it becomes much easier for aspiring autocrats to claim the mantle of a cause and champion it.

Sometimes, however, this new media ecosystem can give rise to mass movements without any need for an established media organ to magnify their claims. The Gilet Jaune (Yellow Vest) protest movement that began in France in late 2018, for instance, seemed to spring fully formed from a single online petition by a motorist angry at rising fuel taxes. Week after week for months on end, the Gilets Jaunes have organized through Facebook groups to come together in numbers, wearing their high-visibility yellow vests and clashing with security forces as they put forward demands that could find no champion in organized politics. France's state and society have been rocked to the core by a message that in an earlier technological age might never have made it out of the letters-to-the-editor slush pile.

The Gilets Jaunes are one of the most dramatic demonstrations of demand for the new autocracy—but they fit neatly into a long history of previous expressions of leaderless discontent. The trend spans the globe, from Spain's Indignados movement and America's Occupy Wall Street (along with the broader Occupy movement) to the decentered mass movement for democracy in Hong Kong, the leaderless protests that rocked Chile, Ecuador, and many other Latin American countries in late 2019, and the extraordinary explosion of anger against police brutality that followed the murder of George Floyd in Minneapolis in May 2020. Each of these was the outcome of internet-enabled spontaneous organization processes that bypass traditional institutions for political participation, and each one has baffled and threatened the political elite.

Groups defending previously unspeakable views have become major power players throughout Europe, from Italy's Five Star Movement and Britain's Brexiteers to Spain's far-left Podemos and its far-right Vox movement and Germany's Alternative für Deutschland. Time and again, people whose views abhor elite opinion have banded together to create movements so powerful that the establishment is compelled to pay attention.

Yet questions remain. Why, amid the sea of views in this new world of unlimited access to every sort of opinion, were authoritarian views so often the ones that seem to win out? Why not transcendentalism, say, or radical vegetarianism? Why did the new media ecosystem pick out the messages of the 3P autocrats as winners? What made these sorts of pitches so devastatingly effective in the information age? Why, in other words, were so many willing to overlook the obvious signs of authoritarianism in these aspiring leaders' personas?

The question has it backward. The 3P autocrats became popular because of their authoritarianism, not despite it.

Inside the Authoritarian Mind

To answer these questions, we need research. Fortunately, in top universities, authoritarianism is a hot topic. Long a sleepy backwater, the academic study of authoritarianism has boomed. The reasons are hardly a mystery: the trends documented in this book—and, in particular, the election of America's most openly authoritarian president in several generations—has set off an explosion in studies, PhD dissertations, experiments, surveys, and essays.

Psychologists, sociologists, and political scientists have organized their research around a few early insights. The first is that vast numbers of people are receptive to authoritarian messaging. An increasingly well-established thread of social scientific research suggests that large numbers of people are predisposed to authoritarian politics. This is not at all the same thing as saying that people are born authoritarian. A predisposition can very well remain dormant unless and until it is coupled with an environment liable to activate it. Vast numbers of ancient hunter-gatherers may well have been predisposed toward obesity, but without easy access to foods rich in fat and sugar, few would have become obese. Similarly, people predisposed to backing autocrats will not do so unless their environment prompts them in that direction.

And what is that prompt?

Researchers have converged on an answer: the preeminent trigger able to activate authoritarian predispositions is the perception of *threat*.

Threat, in this context, must be understood not just as a physical threat, though certainly physical threat is a part of it. Sociologists typically take the concept more broadly to include threats to the moral order.

As far back as 1997, an experimental study by Stanley Feldman of Stony Brook University found that "people who value social conformity are predisposed to be intolerant but may not be intolerant without the required threat, whether it is a particular group that is threatening or a perception that social order is in danger more generally."[4]

The perception that the world around you is changing in ways you cannot predict or control feels deeply threatening to a sizable subset of any population. As Duke University researcher Christopher Johnston and his team found, ethnic change polarizes people in just this way, with those predisposed to dislike uncertainty adopting increasingly strident anti-outsider views as a response to ethnic change.[5] When coupled with economic circumstances that are precarious or deteriorating, that predisposition to equate change with threat becomes doubly potent.

Research findings are, as always, mixed, but one study, conducted ahead of the 2020 U.S. election by a team led by Michele Gelfand of the National Science Foundation, makes the link between threat perception and authoritarian voting patterns even clearer.[6] It found that the more voters were concerned about external threats, the more intolerant they became of otherness and the more supportive they were of Trump's candidacy. U.S. voters' preoccupation with threat correlated strongly with their support for policies to tighten state surveillance and control over stigmatized minorities such as monitoring mosques, creating a registry of Muslim Americans, and deporting illegal immigrants.

This is by no means a U.S.-only phenomenon. Research conducted by a team led by Diana Rieger of Ludwig-Maximilians University in Munich, Germany, shows that German students in an experimental setting were significantly more likely to be swayed by far-right propaganda if they had been previously primed to focus on threats.[7] Priming students to feel threatened also strengthened their identification with German nationality. This does not mean, of course, that foreigners are an *actual* threat—only that when they are perceived as such, that perception has political consequences. Whether in Germany, the United States, or anywhere else, ginning up people's perception of threat unlocks their authoritarian predispositions with unnerving regularity.

As Marc Hetherington and Jonathan Weiler argue in their book, *Authoritarianism and Polarization in American Politics*, professional politicians and the political class that comments on them have been polarized for some time.[8] For many decades, U.S. voters used to be relatively indifferent to the polarization of the elites. As Philip Converse of the University of Michigan established in his seminal 1964 study on the nature of belief systems in mass publics, most Americans in the early 1960s had only the haziest sense of what "conservatism" or "liberalism" meant and had little regard for the ideologies that animated the political class.[9] That finding was replicated many times in the following decades. It's only in recent decades that many regular Americans have come to fully identify ideologically. This shift can be seen clearly in the sudden rise in the number of people who tell pollsters they would disapprove of a son or daughter marrying someone who votes for the other party.

Some researchers have concluded that economic stagnation is driving more and more Americans to perceive their environment as threatening. Stagnant middle-class wages, growing inequality, and an increase in so-called deaths of despair (from addiction-related overdoses and suicide, among other causes) would, in this reading, be triggering people en masse to express authoritarian predispositions and to embrace authoritarian leadership.

In the long half century after World War II, when incomes were growing for most Americans and middle-class livelihoods were stable, the authoritarian predisposition remained dormant, and there was limited demand for what authoritarians have to sell. But when those dormant predispositions were activated, people began to look around for culprits, people to blame for their troubles. And they began to vote for leaders who will latch onto the same culprits as they do.

As Yascha Mounk notes in his book *The People vs. Democracy*, elites often make for an ideal culprit, as—in many cases—do immigrants and members of minority ethnic groups.[10] Outsiders of all kinds come to be perceived as threatening: in Turkey, the outgroup is the Kurds; in Hungary, it is Syrian refugees; in 1930s Germany, it was Jews; today in America, it is Mexicans and Muslims.

Our starting point—but, it bears repeating, not our destination—is a cold, hard look at the actual material conditions facing those who thirst for autocracy. Status dissonance often has roots firmly planted in real economic shifts. In much of the developed world, the classes have been pulling apart from one another, with the rich doing better, the very rich doing much, much better, and everyone else stagnating or falling behind. In developing countries that fall prey to the 3P autocracy, the data are often thinner on the ground, but similar dynamics are discernible.

Measures for chronic hardship aren't standardized, with different organizations and researchers applying different definitions. One such approach set out by the United Way, a U.S. charity, focuses on ALICE (asset-limited, income-constrained, employed) households. We're not talking here about the poorest people in society—ALICE households, by definition, include working people. ALICE households span a broad swath of the working and lower middle classes: childcare providers, service industry staff, call center operators, and millions more in everyday jobs.[11]

The United Way defines ALICE households as those unable to afford the basics (housing, childcare, food, transportation, and healthcare, plus taxes) on the salaries they make. Eye-popping numbers of American workers fell below this level in 2017: 38 percent of households in Connecticut, 41 percent in Ohio, 44 percent in New York. Overall, in the fifteen states where research has been conducted, 41 percent of working households had to scrimp on the basics. Research in 2016 suggested that, nationally, 34.7 million households live in such circumstances—double the official U.S. poverty rate.[12]

Another clear sign of distress is the vast number of Americans who now say they would not be able to cover a $400 unexpected expense with cash. The U.S. Federal Reserve's Survey of Household Economics and Decision Making, conducted in 2016, showed that two out of five American adults would have to borrow or sell something of value to cover such an expense.[13] A follow-up survey in 2018 confirmed the finding. Three out of five working-age adults say they are not setting aside enough money for retirement. One-quarter say they have no retirement savings at all. These figures were collected *before* the onset of the catastrophic coronavirus-induced recession of 2020.

The stagnating incomes of such households play out across people's lives in dramatic, life-altering, and, increasingly, life-ending ways. In the United States, the most dramatic manifestation has been the fast growth in deaths of despair throughout this century. Though sometimes equated in people's minds with deaths due to opiate overdoses, deaths of despair span a much wider range of causes including alcoholism, addiction to other drugs, and suicide. As Anne Case and Angus Deaton of Princeton University have shown, mortality rates from such causes grew exponentially between 1998 and 2015, with the entirety of the increase being among less well-educated people, in particular whites. Deaths of despair for this group more than doubled for men in those seventeen years and nearly quintupled among women. "Ultimately, we see our story as about the collapse of the white, high-school-educated working class after its heyday in the early 1970s, and the pathologies that accompany that decline," Case and Deaton concluded.[14]

Suicide plays perhaps an underappreciated role in increasing mortality, with the suicide rate in the United States growing by fully one-third between 1999 and 2017 to forty-seven thousand deaths yearly. Deaths from drug overdoses had also been rising gradually until 2015, when they spiked by a shocking 16 percent in a single year. But the biggest contributor to the spike in deaths of despair is alcohol. Deaths related to drinking grew by around a third between 1999 and 2014. In all, some eighty-eight thousand Americans died for reasons related to alcohol in 2017, even more than the seventy thousand who died from opiate overdoses.

Broadly similar research has been conducted in the United Kingdom, Australia, and Canada. People are not just imagining things. Economic hardship is a reality for broad swaths of the lower middle class throughout the developed world. Middle-class incomes have stagnated even as productivity rises, and while tax policies and income transfers have blunted the impact, they cannot negate it. Working-class and lower-middle-class people across the developed world have lost confidence in their ability to achieve the life that their parents enjoyed during the heyday of the postwar boom. They feel their place in the moral order is threatened because their place in the economic order is threatened.

Nor is this merely a phenomenon of the well-off West. Wherever 3P power takes hold, the pattern of economic and social dislocation

that precedes it is similar. In Russia, Vladimir Putin rose to promi-
nence after the society-wide convulsion brought on by the collapse
of the Soviet Union, when prices rose fast, standards of living were
in freefall, and there was a generalized sense that the "moral economy" of the community was under assault. In Hungary, Poland, and
the Czech Republic, standards of living did not collapse, but alarm
over an influx of unfamiliar foreigners melded together with powerful nostalgia for the lost age of "sausage socialism" (you may not be
free, but there will be a sausage in your dinner for sure) combined to
produce a powerful sense that yesteryear's certainties could no longer
be counted on.

In Venezuela, five decades of record-beating economic growth
and growth in the middle class from the 1920s to the 1970s gave
way to two decades of economic stagnation in the 1980s and 1990s
that brought social mobility to a halt, creating a pervasive sense that
the social contract between rulers and the ruled had been breached.
In the Philippines and Brazil, slowing income growth together with
perceptions of an out-of-control crime wave created an acute longing
for predictability that expressed itself in the election of some of the
most overtly authoritarian leaders in the world today.

Yet the rise of authoritarian politics and the kinds of fringe movements the internet empowers aren't just a mechanical outgrowth of
economic anxiety. The mediating factor is fear that the moral order
of society is under threat. Because people who are relatively open to
new experiences had sorted themselves into the center-left coalition,
while the threat-averse identified largely with the right, this rise in
economic insecurity translated into support for authoritarianism on
the right much more than on the center-left. In this context, cynicism
about the welfare state's ability to cushion the blows from economic
transformation builds into a kind of political nihilism: "If the state
won't help me," many people seem to feel, "let it help no one."

Samuel Huntington's Victory Lap

To Samuel Huntington's legions of admirers, there's an unmistakable
whiff of déjà vu in the air. The thesis about the revolutionary potential

of dashed expectations he rescued from Tocqueville remains as relevant today as it was a generation ago. Demand for autocracy is fed by a sense of vulnerability and threat across the fast-deindustrializing West as well as by the frustration in the global South at the sluggish pace at which living standards are rising (and in some instances they are declining). The two phenomena amount to the same problem: status dissonance as a global phenomenon.

Meanwhile, novel technologies and media landscapes create opportunities for people who feel threatened to form communities centered on ideas that wouldn't even have received a public airing a generation ago. As communications channels explode, citizen journalism becomes common, and opinions can be shared with millions, yesteryear's gatekeepers of polite opinion no longer have the power to keep authoritarian views out of circulation. In this brave new world, authoritarian messages have little trouble finding their way to ears primed to accept them. Electoral rewards are heaped on leaders willing to signal they are different by slaughtering the ideological sacred cows of yesteryear. The circle is closed, as a steady supply of autocratic leadership meets a rising demand for it.

3P leaders find their ideal hunting grounds in this specific mix of economic dislocation and technological empowerment set against the backdrop of a pervasive sense of threat. All of the ingredients for Huntington's stew are there—if in modern incarnation scarcely imaginable to his 1960s outlook.

Political order, it turns out, really is fiendishly hard to maintain in changing societies. It is as true today as it was fifty years ago. The difference is that today the pace of change is incomparably faster.

PART II

A WORLD MADE SAFE FOR AUTOCRACY

5

CORPORATE POWER: PERMANENT OR EPHEMERAL?

In few areas of life is the tug-of-war between the forces that scatter power and those that concentrate it as vividly recognizable as in the corporate world. Massive new competitive pressures exist alongside rapid concentration of power. How can those two things exist at the same time?

As the French economist Thomas Philippon has documented, increasing market dominance by a few top firms is a feature of a vast swath of industries across manufacturing, services, and even agriculture.[1] Strong corporate concentration has gone hand in hand with increasing concentration of wealth at the top of the income distribution. The coronavirus pandemic only deepened these trends. According to Bloomberg Economics, the world's top fifty companies by value added a staggering $4.5 trillion to their stock market capitalization in the course of 2020, taking their combined worth to about 28 percent of global gross domestic product. Three decades ago the equivalent figure was less than 5 percent.[2]

Yet paradoxically, these trends toward concentration coexist with far greater contestability across many markets. In industry after industry, the IT revolution would seem to have sharply reduced barriers to entry in many of these highly concentrated industries. Wasn't the internet, after all, supposed to be the cure to the concentration of corporate and political power? Wasn't that the dream of the 1990s and even as late as the Arab Spring? How did this most fearsome of centrifugal forces find itself overwhelmed by other, stealthier centripetal forces? And how does increasing concentration in markets dovetail with the trends accelerating 3P autocracy in the political realm?

Jackson Hole Versus the Tech Giants

In the first two decades of the twenty-first century, the largest tech giants—Facebook, Apple, Amazon, Microsoft, and Google—kept growing, increasing their power over the markets they dominated. Over several decades, acquisition sprees left them in control of early-stage and not-so-early-stage start-ups, allowing them to enter new business segments quickly or extinguish potential competitors before they could become serious contenders. These firms generate immense revenues and yield profits that make their founders and top executives some of the world's richest people.

Large technology companies' massive scale, huge capital reserves, alluring brands, exclusive technologies, and coveted products and services create extremely high barriers to entry for new competitors. The power that these five companies wield in the varied businesses in which they participate, their penchant for innovation, and the political influence that their money buys all make it easy to assume that their dominance is permanent. That would be a mistake. It is a view at odds with the lessons of history, the dynamics of competition, and the power shifts we have witnessed in the past three decades.

The reality is more complex. It is true that today's tech titans have amassed mind-boggling scale and a new form of corporate power. It is *also* true that such power is unlikely to last in its current and extreme form, as governments are beginning to try to rein in the giant technology companies. In this chapter, we take stock of both realities, surveying the massive scale and power of the tech giants and then explaining why that enormous power will prove hard to sustain.

It is one of the abiding ironies of our time that conspiracy theorists, when they go out looking for the shadowy confabulations where the world's future is decided, never stop to ponder the Jackson Hole Economic Symposium. Maybe the paranoid give this meeting a pass because it is not at all secret; on the contrary, it's on the record. More likely it is because the subject matter at Jackson Hole seems at first blush so esoteric and academically specialized that garden-variety conspiracy theorists can't make heads or tails of it. But make no mistake: if you went out looking for a place where an exclusive segment of the global elite meets each year to help shape the future of humanity, you could hardly do better than Jackson Hole. There, in the shadow of Wyoming's breathtaking Grand Tetons, the world's most powerful central bankers and top economists gather to discuss ideas and proposals that touch the lives of billions of people.

Organized by the U.S. Federal Reserve Bank of Kansas City, the Jackson Hole meeting allows a minuscule elite of academic macroeconomists and finance ministers to hobnob with the guardians of the world's main currencies as they think about the policies that influence the costs of borrowing money, the exchange rates among currencies, stock and bond markets, and other critical prices and institutions. If you are like most people, it's a fair bet you have never heard the names of any of the people who gather there. Yet it is a near certainty that the discussions that take place at Jackson Hole have shaped decisions that have affected your income, your mortgage and credit card payments, the costs of a vacation abroad, your retirement plan, your grocery bill, and much else besides.

At Jackson Hole, the subject is always the same: not just economics but, more precisely, *macro*economics. This is the world of large-scale, economy-wide forces: growth rates, inflation, unemployment, budget deficits, the money supply, international trade and money flows, and other key economic variables that central bankers worry about. This has traditionally been studied separately from *micro*economics, which looks instead at how firms and individuals make decisions.

Since 1936, when John Maynard Keynes published his seminal *The General Theory of Employment, Interest and Money*, a sort of invisible intellectual wall has separated these two halves of the economics profession.[3] Central bankers and finance or treasury ministers have, for the most part, felt above the concerns of the microeconomy. What this or that firm does might be of interest or concern to the firm itself, of course, but it could hardly affect the economy as a whole. Or . . . could it?

In 2018, a quiet technocratic earthquake shook the rarified world of the Jackson Hole Symposium: the macro/micro wall was breached not once but twice. The first breach came in the form of a paper presented for the conference's consideration arguing that firms such as Amazon had grown so big and so powerful that their decisions had come to have measurable macroeconomic effects. This is the kind of heresy that would normally get a first-year economics undergraduate student a failing mark on a term paper: everyone knows that single firms don't feature in macroeconomic debates. Yet here was this very heresy up for discussion at Jackson Hole.

The specific point of the paper was, as often happens in such hyper-specialized settings, technical and seemingly arcane. Written by Alberto Cavallo of Harvard Business School, the paper began by citing the increasingly common assertion that prices in advanced economies are rising less quickly than standard macroeconomic models would predict. Noting that data constraints make that point hard to prove, Cavallo said that he could nonetheless demonstrate another manifestation of what he called the "Amazon Effect."[4] The paper then put forward research showing that the pricing decisions of companies *are* being altered by online commerce of the kind Amazon dominates. For example, Amazon's technology allows it to adjust prices for millions of products throughout the day in response to forces outside its control: changes in supply, in demand, in currency prices, and so on. And Amazon's power is so vast now that competitors can no longer afford to lag in adjusting their own pricing decisions in response to those made by the tech giant. Cavallo's data showed that prices both on- and offline had begun to fluctuate more often in response to these kinds of changes. He also maintained that in the offline world, prices show a growing tendency to converge across different locations— that is, prices tended to be roughly similar regardless of where the transaction took place. These are precisely the kinds of changes one would expect if competitors were increasingly forced to follow Amazon's lead in setting prices.

The notion that prices could be so sensitive to sudden economic shocks—for example, daily shifts in foreign exchange rates turning up in prices instantly in a way that had never been possible before—was a novel one. But as Cavallo showed, this was no longer mere theory or possibility: it had become a measurable reality. Amazon's pricing strategies and its market power were augmenting the volatility of prices.

Thus, not only had the long-sacrosanct wall between macroeconomics and microeconomics been breached but, even more importantly, the actions of a single firm, Amazon, were cited to explain effects felt throughout a whole economy. In no lesser a forum than the Jackson Hole Economic Symposium, the world's most powerful economic policymakers were presented with evidence that Amazon's business practices now have macroeconomic consequences.

Cavallo's 2018 paper was the latest salvo in a heated debate among the experts about the policy implications of the tech giants' outsized power. Other researchers were already busy at work documenting the way Amazon's practices may be squeezing other retailers' margins, depressing wages for production and logistics workers, and restraining competition in a variety of markets.

Then, at a session on August 24, 2018, held in the stunning Jackson Lake Lodge, the macro/micro wall was breached *again*. This time it was by Alan B. Krueger of Princeton University, a respected and seasoned professional who, as chair of the White House's Council of Economic Advisors from 2011 to 2013, had served as the executive branch's top-ranked economist. Over lunch, Krueger showed that in the United States annual wage growth had been lagging 1–1.5 percent per year behind what economists' standard models would suggest. The reason, Krueger argued, is that labor markets have become less competitive because large, superstar firms increasingly dominate hiring conditions in any given market.[5]

The charge went far beyond the tech giants: as we shall see, there is clear evidence of increasing concentration across many industries, in particular in the United States. Krueger argued that collusion among the dwindling number of dominant employers in any market could explain why wages were rising more slowly than they ought to. He pointed out that anti-competitive employment practices had become common in large companies. Non-compete clauses, for example, have gone from rarities to boilerplate in much of the U.S. labor market, to the point that even minimum-wage sandwich-makers at the fast-food chain Jimmy John's were now expected to sign away their right to work for a competitor for two years after leaving the company.

Headlines about Jackson Hole that year were dominated by talk of the disruptive idea that a single firm's behavior could have macroeconomic consequences, and not just over competition, wages, or labor conditions. Economic theorists now had to adjust their traditional assumptions to the fact that a few corporations had gotten so large that their behavior could rock a market merely by *announcing* that they planned to enter that market. For example, on the day in 2017 when Amazon announced its intention to enter the grocery retail business with a $13.7 billion takeover of niche grocer Whole Foods, the combined market capitalization of the rest of the U.S. grocery industry declined by $32 billion.[6] Apprehension of Amazon's dominance runs deep and wide, not just among competitors both actual and potential but also among policymakers, workers, and analysts of all stripes.

Yet there is one corporate sin that cannot be pinned on Amazon: price gouging. For all its immense scale and power, it's hard to seriously accuse Amazon of overcharging consumers. Just the opposite, in fact. For much of its history, the company has been enormously aggressive in its pursuit of lower prices for its customers. Indeed, as we saw, some economists believe that its pricing strategies are holding down inflation. Driving a fierce hard bargain with suppliers and merchants, Amazon seems comfortable charging slim to no margins on many of its retail sales. What profits it makes are largely plowed back into the company to grow existing businesses, acquire other companies, and develop ambitious research and development programs in everything from robotics to artificial intelligence. Whatever the evils Amazon may be guilty of, gouging consumers is not one of them.

And this stance, it turns out, has important legal consequences. For an entire generation of legal thinkers who focused on how to contain the anti-competitive behavior of firms, prices had been the crucial variable in assessing whether firms that ought to be competing were colluding, or if they were erecting barriers that inhibited the entry of new competitors. That's why, following the publication of Robert Bork's influential *The Antitrust Paradox* in 1979, the practice of anti-trust enforcement in the United States—and, consequently, in much of the world—had become increasingly dominated by questions about prices.[7]

Bork, following the libertarian Chicago School of economics, argued that the single mechanism through which monopoly could hurt society was by allowing the monopolist to jack up prices beyond their normal level. In a normal situation, he maintained, this couldn't happen because a competitor would immediately step in to compete with the monopolist on price. Anti-trust enforcement, then, would generally be unnecessary. Only in the (rare) circumstances when a competitor could not or would not challenge the dominant firms in a specific market should the federal government step in. If government lawyers could rigorously demonstrate that a monopolist was abusing its market power to price-gouge its consumers, then—and *only* then—would courts be justified in stepping in and taking remedial action.

Bork's interpretation became the main anti-trust doctrine during the Thatcher-Reagan era of free-market reforms during the 1980s and 1990s. As it happens, Bork was right in his expectation that the standard he was setting would be hard for regulators to meet. As anti-trust enforcement cases became increasingly focused on arcane economic models trying to determine the effects of a firm on prices in a given market, government lawyers seldom managed to clear the high bars set by Bork's doctrine. Fewer mergers were blocked, court-ordered anti-trust fines and actions became far rarer, businesses in the United States consolidated and concentrated, and the blockbuster court-ordered breakup was confined to the history books. In tandem, a major shift of power from consumers, workers, and labor unions to corporations took place.

Of course, many companies welcomed Bork's 1979 interpretation of the anti-trust doctrine. If the problem with monopoly power is reduced to a question of price-gouging, digital companies famous for aggressive cost-cutting could never be at fault. Their increasing dominance in the old and new markets in which they operated could irk critics on cultural or esthetic grounds, but legally, the behemoths would be in the clear. Indeed, one critic went as far as hypothesizing that "[Amazon founder Jeff] Bezos charted the company's growth by first drawing a map of antitrust laws, and then devising routes to smoothly bypass them."[8] Ensuring that the company never priced services in ways that might have irked Bork was an easy-to-embrace strategic requirement for web-based companies, which treated prices very differently than the monopolists of yore.

Moreover, tech giants felt so comfortable in their competitive practices that initially they did not appear overly concerned by changes in the public's mood about their behavior and business model. They seemed to ignore that public attitudes toward the way they treated their users' privacy, for example, were shifting, and that such shifts in public sentiment would inevitably create political demands for regulation and governmental controls. They would soon discover that it's no use sticking to the letter of the law if your business practices are so far beyond the pale that society can no longer tolerate them.

"Facebook Is Too Big for Democracy," read a subheading in the *New York Times* a few months before the 2020 election in the United States.[9] At some point, if the practices of the tech giants come to be seen as overly abusive, society will take steps to hem them in. The need for a minimum of social legitimacy is one of the most powerful centrifugal forces operating in the business world.

Perhaps the most revealing fact about the enormous market power accumulated by the tech companies is that, in many cases, *they did away with price as the main determinant of a business transaction.* Facebook, Google, Twitter, Instagram, and others offered customers a digital barter in which the price of the transaction disappeared. "You let me know about yourself, and I will let you use my services for free" went the tacit pitch made by the tech companies who traded their goods and services for the customers' personal data. Another aphorism frequently used to describe this novel relationship between seller and buyer posits that "if you are not paying for the product, *you* are the product."

The price, of course, did not really disappear; the transaction was not free. Instead, the price is no longer expressed as a number of units of a recognizable, visible currency. Now price is expressed as an opaque, often invisible, or even unknowable volume of information about the customer's personal traits and behavior, including data about others in their world—family, friends, friends of friends, colleagues, community, and all with whom they interacted. The data, processed and refined, is then sold to advertisers by the companies able to collect it. This digital barter is profoundly asymmetric— sellers like Facebook, Instagram, and others know the resale value (to advertisers, for example) of the personal data they are gathering from customers, while the latter have no idea of the true value of the transaction. This lopsided trade has created some of the largest and most profitable companies in history.

The source of the tech giants' power, in other words, remains opaque—hidden away in the recondite phrasing of a terms-of-use document that no one reads, but which allows them to collect exquisitely fine-grained insights into millions of customers' online activities. There is a form of stealth at work here, and it is no less real for not being political.

Yet while the forces that concentrate corporate power are at work, those that disperse it are also active. As we already noted, the business model that relies on this digital barter is increasingly open to question. It is safe to assume that the anarchic, unregulated, opaque, and in some cases abusive and anti-competitive ways of the early commercial internet may not be around much longer.

As we've seen, the malign influence of artificial intelligence, social media, and other information technologies is distorting the political process of nations where democracy is still alive. But it is also already creating popular awareness of the problem and stirring demands to curb the now-common excesses. And the push toward new and more stringent regulations, while still incipient, is already underway. As of 2020, the EU was considering regulations that would allow it to exclude large tech companies from the single European market altogether.[10] Moreover, Brussels was evaluating a rating system that would allow public assessment of the companies' behavior with respect to tax compliance or the speed with which they took down illegal content. European officials were even exploring the possibility of adopting legislation that would force Big Tech to spin off certain businesses if they wanted to continue to operate inside Europe. In the United States, the Department of Justice sued Google based on what it deemed the company's market power over internet searches—which, as we know, are not really free for users.

Perhaps the biggest power-dispersing blow to the tech giants so far came in the form of a report issued by the anti-trust committee of the U.S. House of Representatives in October 2020.[11] The 449-page report was the result of sixteen months of investigation into the practices of the large technological companies and minced no words in describing what it had found:

> To put it simply, companies that once were scrappy, underdog start-ups that challenged the status quo have become the kinds of monopolies we last saw in the era of oil barons and railroad tycoons. Although these firms have delivered clear benefits to society, the dominance of Amazon, Apple, Facebook, and Google has come at a price. These firms typically run the marketplace while also competing in it—a position that enables them to write one set of rules for others, while they play by another, or to engage in a form of their own private quasi regulation that is unaccountable to anyone but themselves.

The committee made three broad recommendations: first, empower and assign more resources to those in charge of enforcing existing anti-trust rules; second, reform existing laws to give the federal government more tools to identify and battle anti-competitive practices; and third, overhaul the entire anti-trust legal framework to update it to the new realities of the digital era.

Google, Amazon, Apple, Facebook, and Microsoft strongly disagreed and assigned substantial resources to block initiatives aimed at curbing their power. This clash between the trends that foster the dilution of corporate power and those that drive its concentration will be with us for decades. While the final outcome of this clash is uncertain, it is safe to expect that the unbridled power enjoyed by big tech companies since their inception will be more constrained in the future.

In press accounts, as is natural, the credit for the U.S. House Committee's report went to the politicians who officially issued it. But in the small world of tech anti-trust, the main name associated with the report belonged not to a politician but to an improbably young lawyer who had worked with the committee. This was not the first time she had upended the world of tech anti-trust; it was the second.

Meet Lina Khan, an Improbable Trustbuster

To those who know her, Lina Khan is an unlikely revolutionary. The slight, unassuming, bookish lawyer was born in London to Pakistani parents and immigrated with her family to the United States at age eleven. She showed remarkable academic aptitude right away, and in 2017 she caused an academic commotion when, as a twenty-seven-year-old law student, she published a disruptive article in the *Yale Law Review* questioning the usefulness of Bork's anti-trust doctrine. She titled the article "Amazon's Antitrust Paradox," in a sly wink at Bork's classic 1979 book.[12]

Khan describes herself as having always been fascinated by the way large corporations wield power in U.S. society. Her interest in corporate power grew during the 2008 financial crisis. Trillion-dollar bank bailouts alongside the mass eviction of lower-income homeowners who'd seen their meager equity destroyed by the crisis sharpened her focus and gave more urgency to the questions she was researching. Yet Khan reserved the bulk of her analytical firepower not for the bankers but for the company that, in her view, had done more to accumulate power than any other: Amazon.

"Amazon's Antitrust Paradox" was a lucidly argued attack against the pillars of anti-trust law, waking the field from its decades-long Borkian and politically enabled torpor and turning it into one of the most dynamic areas of U.S. law. In the paper, Khan laid out a new rationale for anti-trust enforcement, aiming to bring this old doctrine into the internet age. She argued that the intellectual machinery of Bork's anti-trust framework fails to capture the way market power is exercised in the internet age. In the old framework, government lawyers begin by defining the contours of a single, specific market and then use sophisticated statistical techniques to quantify the dominant player's effect on prices in that market. But Amazon doesn't operate in a single market; it has expanded to cover a huge variety of product and service markets. And, very often, its low prices reflect other invisible benefits that the company derives from obtaining valuable, tradable information from its customers. In e-commerce, price as a concept is much harder to nail down than it is in offline markets.

Khan maintained that the drastically different ways in which Amazon operates render the Borkian framework not so much wrong as moot:

> In addition to being a retailer, [Amazon] is a marketing platform, a delivery and logistics network, a payment service, a credit lender, an auction house, a major book publisher, a producer of television and films, a fashion designer, a hardware manufacturer, and a leading provider of cloud server space [and computing power]. . . . For the most part, Amazon has expanded into these areas by acquiring existing firms. Involvement in multiple, related business lines means that, in many instances, Amazon's rivals are also its customers. The retailers that compete with it to sell goods may also use its delivery services, for example, and the media companies that compete with it to produce or market content may also use its platform or cloud infrastructure. At a basic level this arrangement creates conflicts of interest, given that Amazon is positioned to favor its own products over those of its competitors.

In Khan's telling, Amazon's ubiquity allows it to exercise market power without price-gouging. Rather, it exploits its multiple advantages to channel customers toward its preferred offerings in ways that are less obvious but just as powerful. Amazon, in other words, is so powerful that it can harm consumers' interests (in innovation, for example, and in a fair marketplace or their privacy) without needing to pick their pockets.

The key to understanding how this can be, Khan wrote, is to grasp that Amazon blurs what used to be a clear distinction between the provider of a good or a service and the *infrastructure* for the provision of a good or a service.

In the offline world, that distinction has been clear enough: a trucking company may provide freight services, for instance, using roads and other public infrastructure. That infrastructure will be "neutral" between different trucking companies, all of which may use the infrastructure on an equal footing. This distinction is not so clear-cut online, where much of the infrastructure for commerce is effectively in private hands. For Khan, Amazon's position is similar to what would happen if a single trucking company were to acquire the interstate highway system, enabling it to reserve certain lanes just for its own trucks. Such a company wouldn't need to price-gouge consumers to unfairly exploit its dominant position: it could offer both cheaper freight rates and faster service simply by exploiting its dual role as service provider and infrastructure owner. The arrangement would have massively anti-competitive consequences. Diversified conglomerates and vertically integrated corporations have always been a problem for anti-trust lawyers, as their activities in multiple markets may result in market practices that stifle competition. Clearly, the tech giant's consolidation and diversification are significantly more challenging for anti-trust authorities.

Crucially, Khan wrote, Amazon did not build its legal and corporate infrastructure by accident. Instead, becoming a crucial part of the infrastructure for e-commerce was baked into its corporate vision from the start. As she put it:

> Not only has Amazon integrated across select lines of business, but it has also emerged as central infrastructure for the internet economy. Reports suggest this was part of Bezos's vision from the start. According to early Amazon employees, when the CEO founded the business, "his underlying goals were not to build an online

bookstore or an online retailer, but rather a 'utility' that would become essential to commerce." In other words, Bezos's target customer was not only end-consumers but also other businesses.

Khan offered a host of examples to show how Amazon can use its infrastructure-like traits to establish dominance and then use that dominance to advantage itself across different business lines, often with anti-competitive effects. She showed, for instance, how Amazon used below-cost predatory pricing to dominate the market for ebooks and then leveraged that dominance to extract extraordinary fees from traditional publishers, ravaging their profit margins and limiting their ability to take a chance on risky book contracts.

This perverse dynamic was made worse by the fact that Amazon is also a major book publisher in its own right, meaning that when it created new rules for publishers to sell ebooks on its platform, it was effectively creating rules for its competitors that it wouldn't have to follow itself. It's as though the interstate-highway-owning trucking firm in the example set a 40-mph speed limit for competitors' trucks while allowing its own trucks to go at 75 mph.

Khan's penetrating analysis shot her to legal superstardom before she had even passed her bar exams. Suddenly in high demand across the world, she found herself consulting for foreign governments and high-powered American politicians eager to understand how to apply the new anti-trust doctrine she was helping to found. Within a few years, she was writing policy on behalf of the U.S. House of Representatives' Democratic majority. In his first hundred days in office, President Biden appointed her to lead the powerful Federal Trade Commission at the ripe old age of thirty-one. Facebook and Amazon were not happy. Both companies filed motions asking Khan to recuse herself from cases related to them.

Khan's work helped craft a vocabulary with which to describe and analyze a new reality that people had noticed but could not quite name. By explaining in clear, compelling terms how a company can hurt competition without gouging consumers on prices, Khan—along with a few like-minded officials and academics—helped create a vocabulary for twenty-first-century anti-trust enforcement.

Integration across business lines, network effect online infrastructure provision, net neutrality: a whole slew of new terms and concepts had to be put in place before the new anti-trust paradigm could be established.

In part, this is because companies like Amazon have turned traditional anti-competitive practices on their head. At the start of the twentieth century, trusts alarmed the public because they were becoming monopolies: growing rich by deploying their market power against *consumers* in markets where they were the sole seller. But what Amazon has created is not a monopoly but a monopsony: it is growing rich by deploying its power against *suppliers* in markets where it is the sole buyer. And it is the sole buyer because it owns the logistics and distribution infrastructure.

Of course, Amazon is much more than just a retailer. It is also—principally—a provider of pay-per-use computer services through its vaunted Amazon Web Services division, or AWS. This market, which accounts for the bulk of its profits, is one where it undoubtedly faces stiff competition, in particular from Microsoft, whose Azure service rivals AWS in scale and profitability, and Oracle, a second-tier (but still gigantic) tech firm. Yet even here, Amazon manages to cross-fertilize its seemingly disparate business lines, using the insights it gains from analyzing its enormous trove of internet traffic data to help position its retail, publishing, and entertainment business, and vice versa.

Traditional anti-trust doctrine, Khan grasped, is just not positioned to capture these kinds of cross-market feedback loops. Amazon's effects on competition are based on its ability to channel users' attention to the places where it can monetize them. All the disparate elements of its strategy converge on this alchemy of turning what its computers understand about your preferences into money in its bottom line. Because beyond all its other identities, Amazon is also a huge de facto advertising firm, its algorithms working overtime to turn the data you knowingly or unknowingly disclose into targeted recommendations for your consumption.

This implicit quid pro quo, the semi-knowing trade of personal data in return for alluring services, has been described as the modern commercial internet's original sin. The legitimacy of the transaction is under increasing strain because its terms are inherently opaque, and the power it allows one party to accumulate seems plainly excessive. What the tech giants face, then, is a looming legitimacy crisis, and one they do not seem well positioned to weather.

Khan wouldn't put it in these terms, but what she has established is that the nature of corporate power has morphed. After a time when hypercompetition and widespread technological disruption had seemed to disperse it, it is now concentrating once more, this time in ways that are new, stealthy, and hard to discern. Whereas the monopoly power of old had been in your face, jacking up prices for services you needed and making off with the excess profits, the new corporate giants wielded their monopsony power invisibly, behind veils of cross-cutting business lines that made their abuses hard to pin down but impossible to ignore.

Economic Power and Concentration Beyond Tech

The rise of the tech giants plays an outsized role in contemporary debates about corporate concentration, and for good reason. As the House of Representatives report amply documented, Amazon, Google, Facebook, Apple, and a few others have now insinuated themselves deeply into every aspect of our economic and even personal lives.[13] The fascination they provoke is understandable and deserved.

But there's a danger of shortsightedness here. Increasing corporate concentration is not just a story about tech. All kinds of industries face rising corporate concentration, with more and more of the market going to just the top few firms across all kinds of sectors, especially in the United States.

Thomas Philippon of NYU's Stern School of Business has chronicled the trends in detail. The facts and figures he has uncovered speak for themselves. "Since the late 1990s," Philippon wrote, "U.S. industries have become more concentrated and the profit margins of U.S. businesses have increased. At the same time productivity growth has been weak."[14]

As firms make bigger profits, they plow less of the money they make back into the business: "The ratio of after-tax corporate profits to value added has risen from an average of 7 percent from 1970 through 2002 to an average of 10 percent in the period since 2002." In plain language, this means that the portion of the firm's revenues that becomes shareholders' profits has risen a whopping 43 percent in that period. And there is more. "Firms used to reinvest about 30 cents of each dollar of profit [in their business]," Philippon wrote. "Now they only invest 20 cents on the dollar."

Philippon described this as largely a U.S. problem, finding that more aggressive anti-trust enforcement in Europe has shielded the EU from similar concentration trends. This is what he called "the great reversal": turning received wisdom on its head, he finds that the European Union has become a more competitive, less monopoly-friendly jurisdiction than the United States.

Philippon is the leader of an increasingly influential group of economists arguing that declining competition and growing market power show that something has gone badly wrong, specifically in the United States. Ufuk Akcigit of the University of Chicago finds that lessened competitive pressures are turning the U.S. economy sclerotic. In a paper he delivered at the 2020 Federal Reserve meeting at Jackson Hole, Akcigit and his colleague Sina Ates wrote:

> Business dynamism—the perpetual process of new firms forming, growing, shrinking, and dying—and the associated reallocation of factors toward more productive units is a fundamental source of aggregate productivity growth in a healthy economy. A variety of empirical regularities indicate that business dynamism in the United States has been slowing down since the 1980s, and even more strikingly, since the 2000s.[15]

A 2019 study by the Open Markets Institute shows that the combined market share of the two largest companies in any given market has grown substantially across all types of industries: home improvement, shipbuilding, private prisons, tobacco, drugstores, mattress manufacturing, craft stores, airlines, car rentals, industrial laundry, meat processing, credit ratings, truck and bus manufacturing, amusement parks, and credit cards.[16] These are just some of the sectors seeing increasing dominance by two top players since the early part of the century.

This concentration is often driven by mergers as well as by increasingly lax anti-trust enforcement by a slow-moving Federal Trade Commission. Health industries are particularly prone to these new forms of market power, with numerous specific niche services (from hearing aids and blood glucose monitors to prescription eyeglasses, dental therapies, and artificial joints) dominated by tiny numbers of firms that use regulatory hurdles to keep new entrants at bay and accumulate outsized profits as a result.

Is this what the future has in store? Not necessarily. In fact, if the past is any indication, the winners' success will prove their undoing. Corporate dominance is fleeting. In 1990, the ten largest U.S. companies in terms of market capitalization were IBM, Exxon, General Electric, AT&T, Philip Morris, General Motors, Merck, Bristol Myers Squibb, Amoco, and Dupont.[17] None of them are in the top ten anymore. Instead, the 2020 list of largest U.S. companies included Apple, Microsoft, Amazon, Alphabet, Facebook, Berkshire Hathaway, Visa, Tesla, Johnson & Johnson, and Walmart.[18]

Economic history books are strewn with the corpses of yesteryear's corporate giants. At the apex of its corporate evolution over the last century, the Standard Oil Company seemed as permanent and uncontestable as Amazon looks today. Its founder, John D. Rockefeller, was as unfathomably wealthy as Jeff Bezos has become. But things change. In 2020, ExxonMobil, the biggest of Standard Oil's successor companies, fell out of the Dow Jones index, and its market value dropped below that of Netflix, the video-streaming company. ExxonMobil was not alone in seeing its standing overtaken by the tech giants. In that year, *each* of the five largest tech companies was worth more than the seventy-six largest energy companies *combined*.[19]

Examples that point to potential upheavals and power shifts in corporate power abound. Amazon is being challenged by Walmart, the world's largest company in terms of revenues. Chinese behemoths like Alibaba not only monopolize their home market but also are making inroads elsewhere in Asia and in other continents. Fintech companies, which rely on new information technologies to disinter-mediate, automate, and make more efficient the provision of financial services, are competing head-on with the large, traditional banks.

The power wielded by the CEOs of large companies is also more brittle and ephemeral. According to the consultancy PwC, "Turnover among CEOs at the world's 2,500 largest companies soared to a re-cord high of 17.5 percent in 2018—3 percentage points higher than the 14.5 percent rate in 2017 and above what has been the norm for the last decade. . . . CEO turnover rose notably in every region in 2018 and included a large increase in Western Europe."[20] A 2018 study by Equilar, a company that collects data on boards of directors and top executives, found that "in the past five years, CEOs' transitions have become more common than they had been in the preceding five years. As a result, median tenure has fallen a full year since 2013."[21]

The centrifugal forces that fragment and weaken corporate power are an important part of a story that nonetheless highlights the immense power concentrated in a few players. New companies, tech-nologies, business models, foreign competitors, changes in consumer behavior, geopolitical rivalries, domestic politics, and global acci-dents like a pandemic or a large-scale climate accident can drastically alter the structure of the industry and trigger a power shift that weak-ens even the most solidly entrenched companies. The novel coronavi-rus pandemic that hit the world in 2020 brought entire industries to their knees, including many of the hitherto dominant players. Cruise companies, airlines, hotels, retailers, heavy machinery, and shopping malls are just some of the sectors that struggled to survive the impact of the pandemic and its aftershocks.

But as some large, iconic companies were sinking, others were booming. The pandemic created a surge in the demand for software, transportation and logistics, communications, pharmaceutical and medical devices, healthcare, and contactless technology, among many others. In some of these booming sectors, competition was fierce, whereas companies that operated behind enormous barriers to entry were shielded from competitors.

This arrangement, however, is neither stable nor permanent. In today's world, corporate domination has a short and shortening life expectancy. Popular demand to curb the power of large companies, the resulting government interventions, and continuing competition will eventually make the tech giants less dominant. They will continue to exist and control significant market shares and wield abundant power. But they will also face more constraints on what they can do with the power that they will still have. In the same fashion in which Standard Oil and the Bell System of phone companies were forced to break up, it seems very likely that today's big tech companies will be forced to exit certain markets, divest some of their offshoots, and sell off companies that they acquired to boost barriers to entry and fortify their dominance. The tech giants will continue to be large and powerful but less so than they were throughout their initial decades of existence. Companies that do not yet exist will challenge the established players and conquer a larger market share at the expense of the now dominant players. And a slew of new national champions from China, just as large in scale and as fearsomely capitalized as their American rivals, will increasingly challenge the established tech giants.

Challenger firms, foreign competition, stronger anti-trust activism, tighter regulation, and unstoppable technological innovation: such trends have constrained market leaders for generations, and it is reasonable to expect that their centrifugal effect over corporate concentration will constrain the power of these large companies.

The Political Consequences of Corporate Concentration

In the same way that economists interested in the broad trends that define the behavior and performance of a nation's economy assumed that no single company could influence the macroeconomy, political scientists preferred to focus on the broad forces shaping the political system rather than center on a single company's political influence.

Facebook and Twitter changed all that. We now know that these companies and others like them (or owned by them) can influence the way political power is acquired, used, and lost. They are not the only ones wielding such power, but surely they are some of the largest and most visible. Moreover, Fox News and Koch Industries are not web-based companies but do have politically active owners who openly pursue specific political agendas. Others, like Facebook, Twitter, Instagram, and WhatsApp, provide the platforms and massive distribution channels for the content that politically motivated actors produce. In some cases, the "politically motivated actors" are nation-states that stealthily attack their rivals, using information technologies initially developed by the private sector of these very rivals.

The best-known example of a foreign political actor who used American corporations to disseminate messages that influenced political attitudes in the United States is the Kremlin. As a 2017 report issued by the U.S. intelligence agencies concluded:

> Russian efforts to influence the 2016 US presidential election represent the most recent expression of Moscow's long standing desire to undermine the US-led liberal democratic order, but these activities demonstrated a significant escalation in directness, level of activity, and scope of effort compared to previous operations. We assess Russian President Vladimir Putin ordered an influence campaign in 2016 aimed at the US presidential election. Russia's goals were to undermine public faith in the US democratic process, denigrate Secretary Clinton, and harm her electability and potential presidency. We further assess Putin and the Russian Government developed a clear preference for President-elect Trump. We have high confidence in these judgments.[22]

The Russians are not alone in using information technologies bought (or stolen) from American companies to influence the politics of other countries. China, India, Turkey, Iran, and Taiwan are some of the most active. Not surprisingly, the United States is also a significant participant in the politically weaponized and global cyberspace.

Surely the cyberpower of the countries engaged in this global conflict would be more limited were they not enabled and facilitated by the technological power of the giants to innovate. Moreover, the impact of their technologies is amplified by their power to avoid governmental attempts to regulate their role in the dissemination of political content.

While the use of social media to influence politics in other countries takes very different forms, these interventions usually share one
common goal: sowing misinformation that deepens the polarization
that divides societies. In Chapter 8, we will return to the subject of
political polarization driven by the rise of algorithmically derived "information bubbles" that shield people from ideas they don't share. By
amplifying the most extreme and dissatisfied voices, the tech giants
have contributed to spreading an ardent and wholesale rejection of
politics.

It is to this global phenomenon—anti-politics—that we turn next.

6

ANTI-POLITICS:
THE HIGHWAY TO POPULISM

¡Que se vayan todos! Throw them all out! "All" meaning everyone who had been in power or even close to it.

That slogan didn't come out of a PowerPoint presentation by some Buenos Aires political spin doctor. In fact, it is not entirely clear where it did come from. Perhaps fed-up Argentinians read the crudely stenciled words on a wall and started shouting them at protest rallies. Or was it the other way around? There's no way to tell. At just four words, the rallying cry is too short to pin down to a specific source.

¡Que se vayan todos! became the central chant of the pot-banging protests that rocked Argentina at the end of 2001, as the nation's public finances teetered (once again) on the edge of collapse. Desperate to stem a flood of capital flight, and in a last-ditch effort to prevent an all-out financial system crash, the government had placed harsh limits on withdrawals from bank accounts. People had lost access to their savings.

Argentina has long fascinated historians of development for its unique, dystopian involution from developed country to less-developed country. Having rivaled France in per capita income at the turn of the twentieth century, Argentina has gotten poorer with each successive decade, and at the dawn of the twenty-first century it stood on the brink of disaster.

¡Que se vayan todos! became the rallying cry of a generation: a primal scream from a population that was thoroughly sick of the entire system of government that had been failing them for too long. At first glance it might seem like a retread of the old line, "Throw the rascals out!" But it is different. A rascal is lovable: the old American phrase seems to take it for granted that the new lot will be just as bad as the last.

¡Que se vayan todos! reverberates with a different kind of sentiment. Throw them all out! Dripping with contempt, it is a demand to get rid not of a government but of a governing *class*: not one party, but all parties. In its stark simplicity, *¡Que se vayan todos!* is the founding manifesto of a kind of politics that is opposed to all politics.

Spanish has had a word for this for generations: *anti-política*. It is high time the English language borrowed it. Because anti-politics long since burst its geographic boundaries and has become an animating force in public life worldwide.

It is important to be clear on what anti-politics is not. It is not just an expression of populism because populists, however wrongheaded, are in the business of proposing political solutions to political problems. It is also *not* a deep-seated frustration with the government. Frustration with the political status quo is a permanent fixture of democratic politics. Badmouthing the government is a normal, daily routine in all democracies—and more furtively in all countries, regardless of the political regime. Democracy, however, has a built-in answer for the frustrated: if you don't like the people in power, vote for different people!

That solution breaks down when revulsion broadens to encompass the political class as a whole and the entire way politics is practiced on the right, the left, and the center. It is this rejection of politics as such that we're referring to when we talk about anti-politics. It is a powerful centrifugal force that disperses the ability of old elites to govern effectively, setting the stage for new centripetal forces that aspiring autocrats can use to concentrate power once more, only this time, in their hands alone. That is why anti-politics, when it blossoms, puts a country on a highway toward populism. The reverse is also true: populism, with its emphasis on defending the people from the malignant elites, feeds anti-politics.

Arguably, there is an anti-politics moment at the source of virtually all of today's 3P autocracies. In Argentina, for instance, the *¡Que se vayan todos!* moment eventually delivered the presidency first to Nestor Kirchner, who was elected in 2003, and then to his wife, Cristina Fernández de Kirchner, who presided over the country for two terms from 2007 to 2015 (Nestor died from a heart attack in 2010); in 2019 Cristina returned to power as vice president, thus prolonging, at least in part, the reign of one half of South America's original 3P power couple.

But the trio of populism, polarization, and post-truth is not the only possible destination of anti-politics. Where aspiring autocrats fail to establish themselves in power, anti-politics can become a quasi-permanent state, the new normal for a political system as increasingly desperate voters turn to ever-more iconoclastic figures to try to deliver themselves from the miseries inflicted on them by *todos*, all of those who have hitherto been in, or close to, power.

Of course, once elected, each new set of outsiders becomes the new *todos* that needs to be ousted. It is the new status quo in need of overthrowing—and incumbents who rode the wild horse of anti-politics now find themselves challenged by the next wave of anti-politics contenders for whatever power is left to grab. Go far enough down this rabbit hole and politics and governing become permanently unstable.

Examples are proliferating worldwide. Australia—prosperous, middle-class Australia—has developed a strange sort of aversion to its own prime ministers, cycling through five of them in the six years up to 2019 as a vicious cycle of infighting took over both of its main parties, leading to a rash of intraparty coups amid mounting disgust with the entire political class. Yet perhaps because Australia is prosperous and middle class, the backstabbing involved a cast of relatively normal establishment politicians.

Poorer countries amid economic slowdowns and decimated by the COVID-19 pandemic and its economic devastation are seldom so lucky. Take, for example, the case of Brazil, the world's third-most-populous democracy. A nasty economic downturn beginning in 2014 and a long-accumulating anger over the pervasive corruption of the political elite set the country on an escalating path of anti-politics against a backdrop of constant social unrest that culminated in 2018 with the election of an unabashed, ideologically extremist leader. On its way, Brazil had one president (Dilma Roussef) impeached in 2016, two-thirds of the members of congress investigated over a sprawling mass of interlocking corruption scandals, a once immensely popular president (Luiz Inácio [Lula] da Silva) tried and briefly jailed in 2018, and his successor (Michel Temer) similarly tried on corruption charges, though a federal court in Brasilia acquitted him in May 2021, citing insufficient evidence.

The upshot of all this dizzying turmoil was the election of Jair Bolsonaro through the mother of all anti-politics campaigns: an explicit promise to govern more dictatorially. In March 2021, Lula's conviction was annulled, and he is now running for president.

Yet no country exemplifies the depth of the threat anti-politics poses better than Italy, where three decades of runaway anti-politics have yielded a kind of arms race, with parties competing to outdo one another in terms of outsider bona fides. Since 1994, Italy has undoubtedly plumbed the depths of the anti-politics vortex with special gusto. But it is not alone. In the Netherlands, Germany, Austria, Poland, Britain, and Spain, the electoral strength of anti-politics parties makes it increasingly difficult for besieged political parties of the right and left to form governments, while in Mexico, Colombia, Peru, and Brazil, the strength of anti-politics messages stands as a continual threat to the hard-won democratic advances of the previous generation.

Finally, in perhaps the most quizzical cases of all, long-standing leaders like India's Narendra Modi and Israel's Benjamin Netanyahu have managed to continually win elections by positioning themselves as vehicles for the anti-politics sentiments boiling in their respective countries—a paradoxical inversion that shows the wide range of ways a canny populist who is a long-term, professional politician can manipulate anti-politics sentiments and successfully win elections as the only candidate who can do the job of ousting politicians from politics. A good reason, as Javier Corrales has argued, to "beware of the outsider."[1]

Institutional Sclerosis: A Democratic Affliction

Anti-politics is a virus of democracies. In a dictatorship, where there is no choice of government, revulsion at the status quo normally gives rise to movements for democratic reform. In some cases, such movements achieve their goals and succeed in establishing a democratically elected government. Only once elections have become fully established and all the choices come to be seen as equally calamitous can ¡Que se vayan todos! become a rallying cry for the disaffected.

Liberal democracy is often frustrating. The inevitable delays, compromises, and half-measures inevitable in a democracy have always nurtured citizens who are unhappy with the government. Democracy is not designed to deliver permanent victories. Just the opposite, in fact. The best democratic systems specialize in messy compromises that leave everyone somewhat—but never too—disaffected and dissatisfied. Forced to come up with solutions that harmonize the interests of widely differing groups, democracy at its best is about cobbling together solutions that leave everyone grumpy but no one murderous. At its best, it is a system that demands a certain level of world-weary resignation—a clear-eyed understanding that ideal candidates don't exist, that perfect victories are never on offer, and that the system promises nothing beyond a reasonable mechanism for managing disagreement on an ongoing basis. It is an eminently reasonable system, which is another way of saying it is an endlessly unsatisfying one.

More and more, though, democracies are not at their best. Instead of messy but workable compromises, they're gripped by perpetual gridlock. Compromises, when they are found, are sometimes so minimal as to leave all sides seething in contempt. It is when this happens—when the capacity for problem-solving dips below a critical threshold—that the terrain is readied for ¡Que se vayan todos!

There is a growing body of evidence that satisfaction with democratic systems is declining not just in this or that country but among most of the consolidated democracies common in developed nations.

The University of Cambridge's Centre for the Future of Democracy has tracked views on democracy since 1995 and finds that the proportion of people in developed democracies dissatisfied with democracy climbed from 48 percent to 58 percent in 2019, the highest level ever recorded.[2]

Why are democracies struggling so mightily to come up with the governing arrangements that used to be their bread and butter? As we have seen, one important factor is the stagnation and, in some countries, decline of the living standards of the middle class. A newly empowered, better-informed, anxious, and connected middle class struggling not to backslide into poverty guarantees that democratic arrangements will be at risk.

In 1982, the noted political economist Mancur Olson proposed a controversial theory that helps explain why democratic institutions find it increasingly difficult to sustain broad-based growth.[3] He called this political malady *institutional sclerosis*. It refers to the dysfunctional, inefficient, and unjust way in which long-established democracies accumulate obstacles that hamper the government's ability to deliver public goods.

For Olson, the longer a political system sticks around without a major jolt—a war, say, or a revolution—the harder it will find it to deliver economic growth. Economic growth, he explained, has many of the features of a public good—the kind of good you can't be excluded from enjoying, even if you didn't make any effort to produce it. Cleaner air is the classic example, but the same logic applies to a broad range of public goods.

Olson made his reputation in the 1960s with a groundbreaking account of why it is fiendishly difficult to build political support for public goods such as clean air, public education, or economic growth. By their very definition, the benefits of public goods are diffuse, but the costs of providing them are concentrated in a smaller group. Also, investments in public goods yield results in the longer term, while privately produced goods and services provide quicker returns.

In the case of clean air, everyone benefits, though by an often imperceptible amount, even as a few (like owners of coal-fired power plants) bear a lot of the costs. When potential benefits would be broadly dispersed among a society and the costs would be borne by a specific group capable of organizing to defend the status quo, institutional sclerosis ensues. The benefits of clean air are a good example: clean air laws matter a little to a lot of people, but they are the driving factor for only a tiny handful of voters. By contrast, policies that make the air dirtier—relaxing environmental standards, say—can put a sudden windfall in a small number of pockets, and those who stand to benefit will find it easy to organize politically to secure those windfalls.

That's why in the United States the coal lobby is powerful, lavishly funded, well connected, and extremely effective, even though just 0.03 percent of the U.S. workforce is directly employed in the coal industry. Small numbers, counterintuitively, are an advantage in political fights where intensity of feeling and willingness to devote resources to the fight are the key to victory. As a result of this asymmetry between diffuse beneficiaries and concentrated cost-payers, Olson explained, air will often be dirtier than it should be in a democracy, dirtier than society would want it to be.

The problem goes far beyond clean air. Economic growth itself, Olson argued, shares some key features of a public good. From his vantage point in 1982, he could plausibly say that growth benefits everyone a little, while many policies that hinder economic growth have benefits that are concentrated on just a few players. Special-interest groups that receive concentrated benefits from those policies will have an easier time organizing politically to lobby for them than the much larger groups that receive diffuse benefits from growth.

In the decades since, one premise of Olson's approach has come to look dated. In the 1960s and 1970s, it made sense to argue that economic growth helps everyone a little but no one a lot. That truism has been losing currency ever since. Starting in the 1980s, the economic fortunes of the elite became even more uncoupled from everyone else's. First in America and Britain, and later and more slowly throughout the rest of the developed world, the wealthiest households came to capture more of the benefits from economic growth, growing their share of national wealth even as most people saw incomes and wealth stagnate.

Olson's basic insight still holds: in established democracies, policies that concentrate the wins in a few hands and spread the losses across many have a built-in advantage, regardless of whether the overall wins outweigh the overall losses. By the same token, policies that threaten to impose losses on a few people even as they spread wins across society have a structural disadvantage—even when they're good from a society-wide point of view.

Olson's insight on institutional sclerosis sheds light on several interesting political and economic phenomena. Take, for example, "regulatory capture," the situation in which industries, through lobbying and political contributions, are able to exert enormous influence over the regulatory agencies supposed to look over them. This is sometimes seen as a purely American disease, but it shouldn't be. In all mature democracies, well-organized interest groups increasingly "own" the decision-making processes in the issue areas of concern to them. It is well-known that it is impossible for the European Union, for instance, to make significant changes to its agricultural policies without the approval of European agribusiness. Mining interests in Australia, telecoms in Canada, and cement firms in Japan have all perfected the dark arts of regulatory capture, becoming by far the predominant voice in policy debates in their area. Wall Street, Hollywood, and Silicon Valley are not just geographical locations; they are also home to the headquarters of some of the companies with the tightest grip on their regulators.

In the United States, more former lobbyists were appointed to cabinet-level posts during the first three years of the Trump presidency than during George W. Bush and Barack Obama's combined sixteen years in office. An analysis from ProPublica and Columbia Journalism Investigations found that at the halfway point of President Trump's term, his administration had hired one lobbyist for every fourteen political appointments made, onboarding 281 lobbyists to critically influential positions.[4]

The list of countries in which lobbyists for private interest have become makers of public policy could be expanded nearly indefinitely. In each case, special interests benefit handsomely by keeping in policies that impose almost unnoticeable costs over huge numbers of people in those countries. A tiny increase in the price of sugar may be unnoticeable to most consumers who buy sugar, but it can increase by hundreds of millions of dollars the profits of the companies that dominate that market. The inability to contain regulatory capture is institutional sclerosis, pure and simple.

Olson's argument needs an update. Today, sclerosis does not make itself felt in the form of low economic growth. Instead, as income inequality deepens, growth itself has become one of those policies that benefits a few people a lot and many people hardly at all. That doesn't mean sclerosis is not real; on the contrary, it is more dominant than ever. Hemmed in by more areas of policy that have been captured by industry interests, today's democracies find it increasingly hard to find adequate responses to the demands of the voters. That's a recipe for the kind of resentment that builds gradually and then boils over all at once.

Institutional sclerosis thrives on secrecy, on opacity, on the cover afforded by complexity and obscurity. Lobbyists work in silence, protected by the fact that their aim is to shape obscure rules of interest to only a few people. Politicians who support their interests never trumpet their support: they, too, move furtively to subvert the interests of the majority. Any one of the thousands of small, routine bureaucratic and administrative decisions involved might seem inconsequential, but together they're anything *but* inconsequential. Together, they conspire to shut out broad swaths of the population from the place in the pecking order they think ought to be theirs. This frustration sometimes expresses itself in support for authoritarianism; other times it comes out as a visceral disgust with the entire system, the *¡Que se vayan todos!* energy that fuels anti-politics the world over.

Worse, at the same time that sclerosis eats away at the power of the state from below, other trends do the same from above. Italy's case of anti-politics is so extreme that it perfectly illustrates this global trend.

Italy's Anti-Politics Death Spiral

Italians' contempt for their rulers is so old and so entrenched that it is now virtually a part of the national identity, like pasta and soccer. Some might trace the origins of this contempt to antiquity—after all, just twenty of ancient Rome's seventy-two emperors died of natural causes, with the vast bulk of the rest meeting grisly, violent deaths.

In modern times, Italy became the butt of jokes for its famously short-lived governments (fifty-two cycled in and out of power from 1946 to 1993—about one per year on average). But Italy's politics began to succumb to all-out anti-politics in the early 1990s, when a sprawling anti-corruption investigation known as "Mani Pulite" (clean hands) swept through the political class, ensnaring pretty much everyone who was anyone.

Day after day, from 1992 to 1994, Italians saw a shocking procession of perp walks on the evening news as mayors, members of parliament, bankers, ministers, officials, business leaders, and VIPs of every sort were put on trial for a never-ending list of corruption crimes. Mani Pulite was most notable for its bipartisanship: as one major thrust of the investigation was revealing that the longtime Socialist Party leader Bettino Craxi ran what amounted to a racketeering organization out of his ornate Roman office, another branch was pursuing so many figures within the center-right Christian Democrats that the party had to be dissolved. The left and the right, it was easy for Italians to conclude, were exactly the same: an incorrigible bunch of crooks.

It was the shock of Mani Pulite that laid the groundwork for the initial rise of Silvio Berlusconi described in Chapter 2. But then a funny thing happened: over the course of several years, Berlusconi revealed himself to be not only exactly as venal as his predecessors but exactly as incompetent, too. Long-standing problems with the way Italy was governed went unaddressed for two decades as Berlusconi took turns in power with the remnants of a gray center-left that could not inspire, could not reform, and could not lead. Political gridlock was the deeply entrenched norm that made it impossible for Italian leaders to make any fundamental decisions.

For years, polite opinion in Rome and Milan remained convinced Berlusconi would turn out to be a temporary blip. His manifest failures, the never-ending eccentricities, the tax fraud convictions, the racist outbursts, and the sex scandals made him seem like an aberration—a strange but short-lived departure from normal political life led by dour politicians in dark suits. But it didn't work out that way. Berlusconi's lackluster performance in office left economic growth in Italy in the late 1990s and early 2000s more anemic than anywhere else in Western Europe. And sagging living standards are fuel to the anti-politics fires.

To be sure, Italians fed up with the Berlusconi circus did vote in governments of the mushy center-left twice—first in 2005 and again in 2013—but rather than heralding a return to normal politics, these governments served as a living, breathing demonstration of Olson's ideas about institutional sclerosis. Take the surprisingly divisive question of whether Italians ought to be able to buy acetaminophen (sold in the United States under the brand name Tylenol) at the supermarket. Bizarre though it may sound, this question brought governments of the center-left nearly to their knees on more than one occasion. The proposal was part of a broader set of reforms aimed at liberalizing occupational markets and removing barriers to competition that helped a handful of Italians at the expense of the many. Olson had hypothesized that this was precisely the kind of policies where democracies would underdeliver.

The Tylenol example may sound odd and arcane, but it is quite instructive. Shortly after World War II, Italian pharmacists had been granted monopoly rights to sell all kinds of medicines—even the sorts of simple, over-the-counter drugs people all over the world are used to buying at a corner store. Foreign tourists fighting off a sightseeing-induced headache in Florence or Venice discovered that only a licensed pharmacist could accommodate them. And if a little bit too much *tagliatelle al ragù* left you with a case of heartburn after the pharmacies' usual closing times, well, you were just out of luck.

To pharmacists, the monopoly was enormously valuable. Not only did it allow them to sell medicines like aspirin and antacids at much higher prices than their counterparts around Europe, but it guaranteed a steady supply of foot traffic into their storefronts, where customers could be enticed to buy other things as well.

A powerful special interest group, the Ordine Nazionale dei Farmacisti (National Order of Pharmacists), fought bitterly to block reforms that would allow medicines of any kind to be sold outside a pharmacy setting. They banded together with other groups fighting equally hard to prevent commonsense reforms in their realms that would benefit the great bulk of Italians while making a few well-organized insiders worse off. It took a draining, two-decade-long fight to reform protections for pharmacists, with acetaminophen making its triumphant entry into Italian supermarkets only in 2012. Fights like this one sapped the political capital governments needed to pursue more consequential reforms.

Key among these interest groups were the labor unions—still powerful in Italy, and doubly so when the left was in power, due to the long-standing intertwining of the two. Proposals to reform Italy's famously rigid labor laws sparked prolonged and costly strikes and bitter protests on the street, forcing center-left governments to water down their reform proposals again and again. Italy became a laboratory case of sclerosis: pinging back and forth endlessly between a populist center right uninterested in reform and a center left unable to deliver it.

One early and inevitable casualty was the government's credibility. Investors concluded that if the government—any government—lacked the power to get Tylenol into gas stations, it was also too weak to overhaul the Italian state's stifling regulations and bloated finances. Italy's debt-to-GDP ratio continued to climb ever higher, reaching a head-spinning 130 percent in the mid-2010s, meaning Italy's public debt was equivalent to everything everyone in the country produced in fifteen and a half months.[5]

It surely didn't help that the Italian elite was—and continues to be—a heavy user of offshore tax havens and enthusiastic about tax evasion. In 2015, a think tank associated with Confindustria, the Italian Industrial Chamber of Commerce, estimated that Italians were underpaying taxes by a whopping 122 billion euros.[6] If that money could be collected, Italy's gargantuan debt would be paid off in less than eight years. But if that was an unrealistic goal before the economic consequences of COVID-19 sank most economies, it became a complete impossibility given the economic aftershocks of the pandemic.

Together with political sclerosis, this tax-evasion-fueled debt broke the historic bargain between the Italian state and Italian citizens. With so much money allocated to just paying off bondholders, not enough was left over for public investment. Capital flight, tax avoidance, tax evasion, and paltry economic growth fed chronic government deficits. And with the political system unable to overhaul an economy riddled with privileges and inefficiencies of the kinds that kept Italian pharmacists happy, millions of Italians saw their standard of living not only stagnate but substantially decline. Between 1990 and 2010, Italian household income declined by a quarter, from just over $40,000 per year to just over $30,000, according to research by the Pew Research Center.[7] It is little wonder a bitter cynicism took a deep hold of Italy's public sphere.

Desperate to be delivered from this malaise, fed-up Italians became easy prey for a long succession of populist hucksters happy to pin the blame for all their troubles on someone else. Recriminations flooded the political sphere, sharpening polarization and blurring the lines between reasoned argument and overheated harangue. To regular people, the intensity of the fighting itself became a huge turn-off, leading to the kind of "a pox on both their houses" sentiment that anti-politics thrives on.

It all made for a poisonous kind of politics. Italian voters, frustrated with the left and disgusted by the right, didn't go off and throw their support behind a more traditional figure. Just the opposite: once they'd had a taste for anti-politics, they kept demanding something stronger. By 2018, the political mood had soured so much that populist promises, deeply polarizing public discourses, and blatant lies—the 3Ps—reached levels not seen before in Italy. All this would lead to a kind of *reductio ad absurdum* of European anti-politics.

Rather than coalescing around a single anti-system firebrand, Italians split themselves between a baffling proliferation of political extremists. In the March 2018 general election, more than 4.3 percent of Italian voters (1.4 million of them) turned out to vote for Brothers of Italy, the postwar reboot of Benito Mussolini's original Fascist Party, which in one way was the original anti-politics option. Another 14 percent (4.6 million) voted for Silvio Berlusconi, still on the ballot at the age of eighty-one and, remarkably, still making anti-politics noises after more than a decade as prime minister.[8]

But the biggest vote haul in right-wing politics went to La Lega—a strange populist beast that had recently switched from peddling the contempt northern Italians feel for their compatriots from the south to banking on the contempt all Italians feel for foreigners.

La Lega had been born as the Northern League (La Lega Nord), a regional party based in Italy's better-off, more developed north that leaned hard into the racially tinged contempt people in Milan and Turin felt for what they perceived to be backward, welfare-leeching Sicilians and Calabrians. In its first decade, the party vacillated between outright separatism and fiscal austerity.

At one point, La Lega championed a fanciful plan to create a new republic north of the River Po, to be called Padania. When that idea lost steam, La Lega embraced more moderate demands for increased "fiscal federalism," a dog whistle signaling a plan to stop spending northern tax dollars on programs that benefit the south. The Northern League established itself as a successful protest movement, often obtaining over a third of the vote in the wealthy towns and suburbs of Milan, Turin, and Venice, where resentment of fiscal transfers to the south ran deep.

But the limits of this strategy were clear all along: Padania was often seen more as a quixotic side project than a realistic separatist proposal, and the party's regionalism meant it could never hope to form a government nationwide. It took the visionary leadership of a new party boss, Matteo Salvini, to realize that contempt for southerners was the little game; he could win big by ditching its regional focus and running on nativism on a national, pan-Italian basis.

Starting in 2016, Salvini launched an audacious movement to rebrand his party into a nationwide far-right party. He ditched the word "Nord" from the party's original name, rebranding it as just La Lega, and hardened the party's line against a whole host of outside threats. Immigrants were the first target, with La Lega taking an uncompromising stance against refugee resettlement. In this they were clearly inspired by Donald Trump, whose 2016 campaign for the U.S. presidency Salvini had openly backed.

But it went beyond that. The old Lega Nord had often painted the north as the more genteel and civilized part of Italy, a natural fit with the European Union's values and institutions. Yet Salvini sensed that the anti-politics mood would reward a hard line against all things European, including the currency itself, and he committed the party to the most aggressively Euroskeptic program of any major party inside the eurozone. Salvini railed against continental elites in one breath and against the refugees they wanted to force Italy to resettle in the next. This approach instantly made him the de facto leader of Italy's right wing.

Even more baffling was La Lega's success in the south, the region whose inhabitants La Lega openly disdained. A party that just a few years earlier had distinguished itself for its nasty, borderline racist contempt for *terroni*—the slur of choice for southerners—was suddenly electing members of parliament all over the south of Italy.

On the island of Lampedusa, Italy's southernmost province, just off the coast of North Africa, where many boat people disembarked, La Lega scored an astonishing 15 percent of the vote. In Calabria, the tip of the toe in the Italian boot, it came close to 10 percent—a seemingly unthinkable figure for a party long defined by its venomous disdain for Calabrians. Altogether, nearly a million southern Italians voted for La Lega in elections held in early 2018.

Thanks to those southern votes, Salvini displaced Berlusconi as the titular head of Italy's right-wing coalition, which was now wholly dominated by La Lega and second only to the Five Stars, both parties nurtured by anti-politics. Out of the 12 million Italians who voted for one of the four parties in the right-wing coalition in March 2018, less than half a million did so for the last remaining "establishment" center-right party: the latest incarnation of the long moribund Christian Democrats, the party that had dominated Italy for decades after World War II. Surprisingly, Christian Democrats received less than half of the votes nationwide that La Lega obtained in the south alone.

And yet this motley crew of Berlusconists, neo-Fascists, and far-right erstwhile northern separatists wasn't even the biggest anti-politics story of the Italian election. That distinction went to Beppe Grillo, whom we first met in Chapter 2, and to the baffling, impossible-to-categorize populist insurgency he founded, the Five Star Movement.

Attempts to label M5S along the familiar left-right axis are doomed from the start. The party represents a collision of views, positions, and sensibilities seldom seen under the same roof elsewhere. Radical environmentalism is one ingredient, as are an unbridled contempt for Italy's corrupt political elite, an admiration for Vladimir Putin, deep loathing for the European Union, and hard-line absolutism on consumer protection and anti-fraud legislation, all seasoned with a dash of anti-vaxxer sentiment and unabashed sympathy for Hugo Chávez.

This strange mishmash shaped the party's platform more than any internal deliberative process. In fact, the movement's rise had to do less with policy statements and more with Grillo's bad-boy, nonconformist image and with the movement's expert use of the internet as both an organizing platform and offensive weapon against its detractors. The party's platform appears designed specifically for the purpose of not fitting anywhere on the left-right axis, reflecting Grillo's absolute determination not to be lumped with either the traditional left or the right.

It was also a novel take on anti-politics: the rejection of the usual political categories was baked into the Five Stars platform. And it worked. In March 2018, Grillo's iconoclastic strategy made M5S the largest party in Italy, with over 10 million votes and 227 seats in parliament. But M5S didn't have anything like an outright majority, and Grillo's determination never to cut a deal with any other party left Italy essentially ungovernable, as no workable coalition could clear the 50 percent threshold to form a government.

Months of tortured negotiations followed, as Five Stars explored the ultimate strength of their no-deals-with-anyone credo. The centrality of anti-Berlusconi feeling in the Five Stars support base ruled out any coalition that included Forza Italia, Berlusconi's party, but it took weeks of talks to persuade the rest of the right to consider a coalition.

In fact, Five Stars was caught between aspects of the 3P framework that are incompatible in the Italian context. Grillo's populism ruled out deals with the corrupt elite, but Italy's voting system made such deals inevitable for a party seeking power.

What resulted was an initially unthinkable coalition of La Lega and M5S: a bizarre hybrid, half far-right, half centrist, whose politics overlapped basically nowhere except in a vague anti-politics rage against all elites: financial, national, European, medical. Contempt for anyone who actually knew what they were doing was, in the end, the only agent binding together the government of the world's eighth-largest economy.

The size of Italy's economy and its already outsized public debt made it especially important that it keep within the strict anti-deficit rules that constrain countries using the euro. Unlike Greece's tiny economy, Italy's was big enough to bring Europe's single currency down with it if its politicians went on an unimpeded borrowing binge. But La Lega and the Five Stars viewed rules preventing it from borrowing too much as technocratic straitjackets designed by hated, out-of-touch eurocrats to prevent them from growing Italy's economy the old-fashioned way: by spending much more (M5S's priority) and taxing much less (La Lega's).

Ultimately, Salvini overreached. Trying to set off an election he believed La Lega was poised to win outright, he brought down his own government by withholding parliamentary support. Fearing impending electoral doom, the Five Stars pivoted to form a coalition with people who, arguably, made even more bizarre bedfellows for them: the cushy, establishment center-left Democratic Party. For the *grillini,* who had built a political identity chiefly out of chafing contempt for mainstream politics, sharing a cabinet with the Democrats—the most establishmentarian of Italian parties—was a hard-to-swallow requirement. For the Democrats, who had spent years warning of the perils of Five Stars–style populism, joining this parade of freaks around the cabinet table was similarly incomprehensible—a surrender of foundational values.

Little by little, Italy's constitutional rules forced all its parties to embarrass themselves as they pursued deals they'd long vowed never to consider. The deal-making further alienated and angered Italian voters, who continued looking for more and more outlandish outsiders to "send Rome a message." It is an anti-politics spiral incarnate.

Italy today serves as the clearest warning sign yet to those who imagine that the defeat of one populist outsider will naturally result in a return to political normalcy. In Italy, populism, fiscal disarray, and institutional sclerosis fed back on one another in a vicious cycle that brought the country's political mainstream further and further away from the normal. The last few years have seen the bizarre sight of a comedian and a far-right rabble-rouser attempting to negotiate the finer points of a governing pact before turning on each other and giving way to an even less natural coalition. Normal is a thing of the past.

Italy's story neatly illustrates how anti-politics has become the highway to populism. Disgust with the corruption revealed by the Mani Pulite investigations launched Italians on a chase for the true champions of the "pure people" willing to do battle against the corrupt elite. But that hunt proved elusive, sending Italy down increasingly perilous political paths. As political conflict sharpened and polarization widened, Italian voters found themselves "speed-dating" ever-more outlandish outsiders, who bent and warped the truth in their search for votes. The age of anti-politics turned the Italian political system into the mythical ouroboros, a snake that eats its own tail.

The Italian lesson has been stark: there is nothing "natural" about political normalcy. No automatic mechanism guarantees that the failure of populist parties will herald a return to politics as we used to know it. Just the opposite, in fact. Countries can become entrenched deeper and deeper in a pattern of protest voting that brings an increasingly stranger cast of characters to the corridors of power, making stability and good government a distant memory.

Italy showed what this trend would look like if taken to its wildest extremes. But it was no isolated case. All around Europe, countries that not so long ago were dominated by parties of the moderate center right and center left came to face the rise of a wild proliferation of newcomers on the far right, on the far left, and in the center. The decline of major parties became a decisive phenomenon in much of continental Europe after the Brexit referendum. In Austria, the far-right Freedom Party joined the government in coalition then caused its collapse after it was shown to be willing to sell contracts to Russian interests. In Germany, the Netherlands, and Spain, the far right began to crowd out space in the political center, which made the usual coalitions needed to form governments in those countries increasingly hard to put together. In France, long-established parties went into sharp decline as well. Neither the center-right Republicans nor the center-left Socialist Party broke into double digits in the 2019 European elections, and both together failed to top 15 percent. With the bottom falling out of the center, politics in all these countries came to look more like an all-out battle between ideological extremes than like a genteel negotiation between fellow members of the establishment. It's not surprising because polarization has always fed on the collapse of the center.

That 2019 European Parliament election saw a nadir for Britain's two major parties, which garnered a combined 22 percent. In part, this was because the Labour Party had undergone a bizarre transformation under the far-left leadership of Jeremy Corbyn and could scarcely be considered a traditional party of the center anymore. Even then, the two together were outperformed by an anti-politics pro-Brexit outfit led by Nigel Farage, which garnered 30 percent of the vote, much of it coming from people willing to pay any price to rip Britain out of the EU—even, it seems, if that price is the destruction of England's union with Scotland and Northern Ireland.

Farage's success finally forced the Conservatives to bow to the inevitable and elect their own populist rabble-rouser to party leadership lest they be outflanked on the right. Boris Johnson "saved" the venerable old British Conservative Party but at the cost of turning it into a populist vehicle.

Much of this decay can be traced back to the 2016 referendum that saw Britain vote to leave the European Union. Brexit will be remembered as the distillation of the anti-politics spirit in an advanced Western country. The storm of exaggerations, distortions, untruths, and lies at the core of the Leave campaign left a permanent imprint in British politics, creating a poisonous climate of distrust between partisans and alienating the broad middle of a British electorate racked by "Brexit fatigue." The escalating multiyear political crisis that followed turned, in time, into a kind of anti-politics auction, with British politicians fighting to outdo one another's radicalism in proposing increasingly reckless and economically destructive ways to undo the ties between Britain and the EU.

Born out of a poisonous climate of distrust toward the European

Union, the Brexit process reverted back onto Britain, manifesting itself as a collapse in trust in the governing class in London. The stifling logic of ¡Que se vayan todos! worked itself out as parallel purges of moderates, with the Corbynite left cleansing the Labor Party of centrists while the hard Brexiteers around Boris Johnson purged moderates from the Conservative Party's ranks. The contrast with France was instructive: rather than leaving the traditional parties to vote for anti-politics outfits, the British turned their traditional parties into vehicles for anti-politics.

Even in the rare country where the traditional parties still manage to win elections, the sudden ascent of radical political groups forces the incumbents to make concessions and try to join the anti-politics bandwagon. In Spain, for example, the PSOE, a center-left socialist party, still won several elections, but none yielded enough votes to produce a majority that could form a government. In 2019, the PSOE made an alliance with the far-left Unidos Podemos, a group whose Marxist radicalism places it closer to the politics of Venezuela's dictator Nicolás Maduro than those of Scandinavian social democracy. This alarmed the center right and the right, which saw their fears of a slide toward the autocratic left materializing before their eyes. The tone of political conflict escalated alarmingly, with the right accusing the left of hostility to the concept of Spain itself, while the left brooded darkly about the right's crypto-fascist Franquista leanings.

But Spain's center right was unable to mount a credible alternative because it was bleeding votes to its right flank, to the nativist, anti-immigrant newcomers from Vox, a newly created party whose surprising electoral performance proved that half a century after the end of the Franco dictatorship, Spaniards aren't as averse to extreme reactionary politics as people once assumed. And even as centrifugal forces push Spaniards to the extremes nationally, a poisonous battle over Catalonia's independence pits Madrid against Barcelona in an emotionally charged battle that has seen regional leaders in Catalonia jailed for sedition. The crisis was too tempting a target for foreign adversaries, which saw it as an invitation to meddling. With Russian hackers actively stoking the divisions in Spanish society, online disinformation exploded, creating a pervasive climate of post-truth. In

Spain, no one knows what is true except for one thing: the other side is evil.

It's sobering to think that even in the midst of all this, Spain was doing relatively well by European standards—and *far* better than some countries of the global south, where anti-politics run amok has pushed people into despair, leading them to elect some of the most extreme and troublesome leaders of recent times.

From Anti-Politics to Tropical Extremism

Institutional sclerosis and disempowered national governments seem to be a surefire recipe for sending countries into the anti-politics death spiral, but the most destructive cases come in countries that share three other features: runaway corruption, widespread crime, and a bad economy. Here, the demand for anti-politics sometimes intersects with a yearning for authoritarian leaders, leading to the election of some of the most disquieting 3P leaders of the twenty-first century.

We've already seen how frustration over the Philippine government's inability to come to terms with low-level crime fueled demands for the radical, blood-soaked anti-politics of Rodrigo Duterte. But an even more disquieting case of tropical fascism came in Brazil, where the chaotic failure of the entire political system gave rise to a groundswell of support for an extremist with positions that are radical even in politically reckless Latin America.

Brazilian politics has been marked by a peculiar combination of endemic corruption and comparatively strong judicial institutions. Fernando Collor de Mello, Brazil's second democratically elected president after the fall of its 1960s-era dictatorship, was ousted amid a corruption scandal two years into his term. In 2016, President Dilma Rousseff was removed from office following her impeachment. In the early years of this century, the Brazilian congress housed troves of deputies facing indictment for corruption and other crimes. (To be clear, the culture of kickbacks may not actually be more prevalent in Brazil than in the rest of Latin America, but because its investigative judges are powerful and independent, that corruption ends up seeing the light of day more often.) The result has been a political scene continually roiled by high-profile investigations. First there was the *mensalão* scandal, where political operators of President Lula da Silva's party were found to be paying regular monthly bribes to "opposition" members of Congress to support the government's agenda. But that scandal, and many from the same era, paled in comparison with what was to come: the sprawling, massively complex, multinational festival of corruption that came to light in 2014, when Brazilian federal investigators asked themselves how on earth one particular car wash in Brasilia could be doing the volume of business it was allegedly doing. The Lava Jato car wash was soon revealed to be a money-laundering front for Odebrecht, a giant Brazilian engineering firm, which used it to funnel multimillion-dollar payments to politicians and ministers in more than a dozen countries in Latin America and Africa: kickbacks for approving Odebrecht's bids to take on large infrastructure projects including dams, airports, bridges, rail lines, and more.

The byzantine ins and outs of the Lava Jato scandal have echoes of Italy's Mani Pulite investigations of the early 1990s, in that they engulfed the entire political class. As investigators pulled on this one loose thread—a car wash that was obviously being used to launder money, *Breaking Bad* style—they came to uncover a tangle of kickback schemes involving the nation's biggest construction firm that ensnared dozens of members of Brazil's power elite, including all six of its living former presidents. And just like in Italy, the scandal created the perfect conditions for the politics of populism, polarization, and post-truth.

But unlike Mani Pulite, Brazil's Lava Jato scandal was born internationally, involving politicians in almost two dozen countries. It did deep damage to the region's democracies, in part, because it coincided with a brutal, years-long recession stemming from the collapse of global commodity prices in 2014. Latin Americans found themselves reading one dispiriting story of public wrongdoing in the newspaper after another at a time when millions were losing their jobs and the purchasing power of salaries was falling. Their expectations for economic advancement were being dashed at the same time they were hearing lurid tales of officials lining their pockets: a uniquely corrosive combination. The spirit of *¡Que se vayan todos!* would not take long to be felt.

Brazil's longer-term economic underperformance owes much to the severe sclerosis in its political system. A retirement system designed to curry favor with voters at the expense of common sense allowed millions of public employees to retire on full pensions while still in their forties or early fifties. Expansively drafted pension plans designed to protect widowed people from destitution in old age gave rise to what Brazilians smirkingly call the "Viagra effect"—male pensioners in their seventies marrying women many decades younger, who become entitled to continue receiving their husbands' full benefits even after they died. On top of that, rigid labor laws discouraged investment, job creation, and growth. It all added up to chronic deficits and a mounting pile of public debt, which soaked up money that ought to have gone to public investment. Analysts of the left, right, and center understood the problems and concurred on the broad outlines of a solution. But politicians held hostage to the kinds of special interests Mancur Olson had identified were paralyzed: textbook sclerosis kept Brazil loyally wedded to a policy regime everyone could see was damaging its people's futures.

When a political system remains this dysfunctional for many years, voters will naturally begin to look for radical change. And they turned to a populist uniquely positioned to channel the seething contempt Brazilians had been nursing for their leaders for a generation: Jair Bolsonaro.

Whatever one might say about Bolsonaro's authoritarianism, one can never call it stealth. Rather than dog-whistling, Bolsonaro shouts his nostalgia for dictatorship from the rafters. An ineffectual long-time member of congress following an army career of little note, he had cornered the market on the kind of rhetorical bomb-throwing that, to Brazil's establishment, made him seem little more than a clown. Viciously contemptuous of every progressive cause, from gay rights to the conservation of the Amazon, he openly pined for a return to the kind of unaccountable, strong-arm regime Brazil had under the military in the 1960s and 1970s.

It is easy to see why the parallel with Donald Trump is often made: both share an unfailing instinct for saying the most incendiary thing possible at any given moment, and both have led executive branches routinely seen as chaotic, with sky-high personnel turnover and unending Twitter drama on offer. Yet Bolsonaro is a different kind of leader than Trump: an actual evangelical Christian, he really does hate the targets of his tirades, rather than pretending to hate them for electoral gain as Trump so often did. And, improbably, he's managed to win some momentous early policy battles on, among other things, pension reform.

Jair Bolsonaro is the greatest example of Latin America's newest wave of leaders who gain power and govern exploiting the opportunities created by the 3Ps. Propelled by rampant anti-politics in the context of collapsing trust in political institutions, he shares the polarizing instinct of every successful new autocrat this century. The trends that drove his ascent to power long preceded him, of course, but it was his genius for mobilizing the disaffected that ensured his political success. And despite a shambolic administration long on conflict and short on results, he has consolidated a dedicated following among those most disaffected with politics as usual: Brazil's anti-politics grassroots.

Is There a Way Out of Anti-Politics?

"¡Que se vayan todos!" is a cry heard around the world. The forces of anti-politics are on the move globally. As once-formidable political parties implode and improvise, untested radicals rise to power, and the realization is starting to dawn that this is no temporary blip, no mere holiday from normal politics. As Italians found out, once the public develops a taste for anti-politics, it seems to get hooked, demanding more and stronger doses of the same thing just to feel normal. Anti-politics is the necessary precondition for more anti-politics.

Some countries seem to get stuck in a cycle of anti-politics. According to the Mexican newspaper *El Universal*, of the forty-two presidents who governed Guatemala, El Salvador, Honduras, Nicaragua, Costa Rica, and Panama between 1990 and 2018, nineteen spent at least some time in prison after their term ended.[9] As I argued in *El País*:

> In South America, Peru makes a fascinating case study. President Pedro Pablo Kuczysnki was forced to resign in 2018 and was then sentenced to three years of house arrest. Former President Ollanta Humala was also imprisoned, as was his wife, Nadine Heredia. Alejandro Toledo spent years in U.S. federal prison while his extradition to Peru was processed. His wife, Eliane Karp, is wanted on an arrest warrant and is staying abroad. Keiko Fujimori, the leader of the opposition, has been sentenced to three years of house arrest, while her father, former President Alberto Fujimori, continues to serve a 25-year sentence. Prison would have likely been the fate of twice President Alan Garcia, had he not turned a gun on himself when the police arrived at his house to arrest him.[10]

When Peruvians shout *¡Que se vayan todos!*, they don't just mean that the powerful should relinquish their power. They want them out of sight forever.

Is there a way out of this impasse? Can political systems regain a sense of normality after they've been bitten by the anti-politics bug? Or are they doomed to a future of escalating anti-politics, with each upstart simply setting a new standard for radicalism the next challenger will have to try to outdo?

The record is not encouraging. While the spread of anti-politics has been slowed and blunted in some places, it has seldom been reversed. The Italians did manage to reject Silvio Berlusconi in the polls a couple of times, but rather than heralding a return to normal politics, these episodes are remembered as interludes in a record of deepening anti-politics. In Argentina, the place where the phrase *¡Que se vayan todos!* was born, Mauricio Macri managed a short-lived break from Peronism from 2015 to 2019, but his failure to stem Argentina's secular economic decline marked his term as a mere pause between bouts of Peronism.

In fact, the one case where the anti-politics death spiral was well and truly stopped was in Thailand, after the tumultuous period of Thaksin and Yingluck Shinawatra, a brother-and-sister duo who rose to the prime minister's office on classic anti-politics themes. Following eight years of escalating conflict, street protests, and unprecedented polarization, the cycle was ended by a military coup. The putsch brought in a long-lasting military dictatorship more closely resembling the old autocracies of the twentieth century than the new ones of the twenty-first.

¡Que se vayan todos! indeed—only, in this case, chiefly to jail.

It is not a way out of anti-politics anyone could actively want. Yet in many places these days, it seems to be the only one on offer. Even then, it hasn't entirely succeeded. In 2020, a new outbreak of raucous street protests rocked Bangkok, with young Thais openly calling for the reform of the monarchy, a once unthinkable apostasy in a country where insulting the king is a criminal offense. The accession of an eccentric and, in the eyes of many, megalomaniacal new monarch—King Phrabat Somdet Phra Paramendra Ramadhibodi Srisinra Maha Vajiralongkorn Mahisara Bhumibol Rajavarangkura Kitisirisumburna Adulyadej Sayamindradhipeshra Rajavarodom Borommanat Pobitra Phra Vajira Klao Chao Yu Hua, to give him his official title, or just King Rama X for intimates—has politicized what many saw as the last above-the-fray institution in the nation. Anti-politics spares no country.

In reality, the paths that lead away from anti-politics and back toward a normal democratic political consensus are still to be blazed. Once the state has been hollowed out both from the bottom (by falling prey to institutional sclerosis) and from the top (by handing power over to global financial markets, supranational institutions, and capital housed in offshore shelters), voters hardly have a good reason to return to the fold of normal politics once more.

Once faith in institutions has been corroded, rebuilding consensus politics requires a skill set no one seems to have discovered yet. Withering contempt for institutions and elites metastasizes. Once this dynamic is in place, alas, the most likely next step is into outright kakistocracy: rule by the very worst a society has to offer.

This is why, in its own way, anti-politics is one of the most dangerous threats facing contemporary democracy. Anti-politics is a powerful centrifugal force: it destroys the basis of democratic politics, creating the spaces aspiring autocrats take over. That's why its perils are systemic, because anti-politics eats away at society's capacity to make decisions together, to work out differences in a calm and institutional way, and to build structures that include everyone. Anti-politics leaves behind a political sphere that can only be governed by imposition. In that sense, its corrosiveness on institutions has few parallels.

Societies in the grip of anti-politics often find that they can no longer agree on a shared set of objective facts. This is a trend amplified and energized by the third P: post-truth.

7

POWER AFTER TRUTH

The 3Ps at the center of our tale were not created equal. The first two, populism and polarization, have long histories and have been amply documented by scholars dating back to antiquity. Post-truth is different: a frontal attack on our shared sense of reality that catches us unaware and, therefore, unprepared.

We instinctively "get" populism and polarization in a way we don't get post-truth. Why? First, because we find it hard to differentiate mere untruth from post-truth, which is a fundamentally different concept. Second, because a long tradition in the Western world connects the kind of nihilism at the heart of post-truth with totalitarian regimes unashamed to trample on freedom of speech. Post-truth in the context of democracies is a new and frightening phenomenon.

Politicians lie. They have lied since time immemorial. Even the old story about George Washington and the cherry tree—America's most cherished encomium to truth-telling—was a whopper concocted by Mason Locke Weems, a sales-obsessed itinerant pamphleteer out to cash in on the good general's name: eighteenth-century Infowars.[1] Spin and messaging, half-truths and deceptions are as much a part of the democratic process as judicial review and periodic elections.

At the outset, it is important to be clear about what we mean by post-truth and how it is different from simple political fibbing. Jay Rosen captured this newness well, tweeting, "Phrases like 'rewriting history' and 'muddying the waters' do not convey what is under-way. It is an attempt to prevent Americans from understanding what happened to them through the strategic use of confusion."[2] It is this strategic use of confusion that makes post-truth much darker than the run-of-the-mill mendaciousness of the powerful. It is not about the spread of this lie or that lie but about destroying the possibility of truth in public life.

By shaking our shared sense of reality, post-truth elevates popu-lism and polarization from a normal kind of political nuisance into something different and more fundamental: an existential threat to the continuity of free governments and free societies. As Alan Rus-bridger, the former editor in chief of the British newspaper *The Guardian*, put it:

> A society that cannot agree on a factual basis for discussion or decision-making cannot progress. There can be no laws, no votes, no government, no science, no democracy without a shared under-standing of what's true and what is not. Of course, a commonly agreed basis of facts is only the beginning. Societies with no inde-pendent source of challenge or scrutiny are also not to be envied.[3]

Post-truth has been defined by the *Collins English Dictionary* as "the disappearance of shared objective standards for truth."[4] It is a condition that arises in public life when the dividing line between facts and knowledge, on one side, and belief and opinion, on the other, withers away, or at least when they are used interchangeably so often that the dividing line between them is no longer widely agreed upon. Unlike lying, post-truth is not an individual moral failing. It is not a personal fault of a given public figure. It is a fea-ture of the communications infrastructure of politics and power in today's world.

To philosophers, the slow unraveling of a shared sense of reality had long been seen as a problem of hard-core dictatorships. Much of our thinking about the problem comes in books about Nazi Germany or Soviet Russia. Philosopher Hannah Arendt famously argued that "the ideal subject of totalitarian rule is not the convinced Nazi or the convinced Communist, but people for whom the distinction between fact and fiction and the distinction between true and false no longer exist."[5]

Arendt, who barely survived the Holocaust after fleeing occupied Paris on a fake American visa, concluded that only the ruthless boot of a totalitarian regime could bring about such a nightmarish outcome. But the most successful among the 3P autocrats have grasped that the absolute explosion of information and media, online, and off, creates unprecedented opportunities for deception, manipulation, and control. Nowadays, they don't require old-fashioned censorship or tight control of what messages can reach the people. Rather, they rely on just the opposite: strategies centered on exhausting people with an all-out deluge of information that overwhelms their critical filters through sheer volume. Machine-aided targeting of messages based on the recipient's beliefs, prejudices, and preferences amplifies the impacts of those messages in unprecedented ways.

3P autocrats have learned to wage this kind of warfare by exploiting the defining characteristics of today's information architecture: its radical openness, the sharply curtailed role it reserves for information gatekeepers, and an ever-more permeable membrane separating "prestige" press outlets from the ungoverned wilds of the digital public sphere.

The most celebrated case is Russian interference in American elections, but the phenomenon goes far beyond that. For one thing, Russia meddled in elections and politics far and wide, not just in the United States. For another, deliberate disinformation online is quickly becoming a standard part of the political arsenal used by politicians across the globe. Post-truth, today, is everywhere.

The Age of Active Measures: Putin's Empire of Doubt

To understand how post-truth grew into a defining force for contemporary society, we need to go back to its origins in the Soviet Union.

In 1923, the Soviets created the Special Disinformation Office. The new office was a personal initiative of Joseph Stalin's, and its mission was "to spread false and misleading information, often of the slanderous sort."[6]

That Vladimir Putin, the unquestioned master of disinformation in the twenty-first century, turns out to be a former KGB operative should come as no surprise. Long before the rise of the internet, the Soviets had expanded the mission of the Disinformation Office and had already perfected the use of "active measures": an information-war strategy centered on deploying false information to destabilize democratic opponents in the context of the Cold War.

The Soviets spent decades developing a sophisticated array of tools aimed at planting stories in Western media specifically for the purpose of undermining the credibility of Western institutions. The stories Soviet operatives concocted are easy to spot as the forerunners of today's fake news. Nearly always, they sought to exploit fault lines in the societies they targeted and deepen the existing rifts or create new ones. And while many of them fell flat—try as they might, the KGB couldn't get anyone to believe the CIA was somehow behind the mass suicide at Jonestown in 1979 (the episode that bequeathed us "drinking the Kool-Aid" as an expression)—the Soviets understood this was a numbers game: not every theory would catch on, but a few of them did, and some had success beyond their creators' wildest dreams.

A select few of them linger on to this day as often-debunked (and just as often repeated) conspiracy theories, if not outright urban legends. Few today realize that when you hear your old uncle argue adamantly that the moon landings were a hoax, you're hearing the faint reverberation of a Soviet active-measures campaign launched decades ago for strategic advantage in the Cold War: for Moscow, the loss of face that came with losing the race to the moon was a serious setback in the quest for global prestige, and spreading rumors that the Americans had faked the landing was the Soviet Union's attempt to reduce the U.S. strategic public relations payoff that came from winning the race. If you've ever found yourself parrying the arguments of someone convinced that water fluoridation is part of a mind-control experiment by the United States government, or that the HIV virus was developed as part of a U.S. biological weapons program, or that the CIA was somehow involved in the plot to assassinate John F. Kennedy, you have personal experience of being ensnared by KGB active measures.

The main problem for Soviet disinformation was always the same: the gatekeepers. In the 1960s or 1970s, planting a false story involved fooling professional journalists and editors, news professionals trained specifically to sort out fact from fiction. To have a chance of success, disinformation operations needed to be relatively expensive affairs, elaborate hoaxes that required the sort of prolonged and substantial investment that only a superpower could easily afford. Documents had to be forged by hand, then dangled by human agents in front of skeptical editors with the power to decide if the text was publishable. Witnesses might have to be produced and coached. A lot could go wrong, and even if the operation was successful, there was no guarantee that the resulting story would have the impact intended. Operatives could work for months on an active measure that yielded a single story in a single publication that failed to be picked up and amplified by others. Expensive failures were common, successes rare.

Take, for instance, the Soviet active-measures campaign against Senator Henry "Scoop" Jackson. In 1976, the leading anti-Soviet campaigner in the U.S. Senate's Democratic caucus announced his candidacy for the presidency. A veteran senator from Washington State and a dyed-in-the-wool anti-communist, Jackson was at one point the front-runner for the Democratic nomination to challenge President Gerald Ford. His candidacy set alarm bells ringing in the Kremlin, and soon the KGB was tasked with ensuring that Jackson could not win.

The active-measures campaign the KGB thought up was relatively crude. A series of forged documents, purported to have originated in the FBI, were sent anonymously to a series of national news outlets as well as to some publications of the then small and deeply stigmatized gay press and to rival Democratic candidates' campaigns. The documents alleged Jackson was a secret homosexual and a member of an underground gay sex club.[7] Reporters did indeed investigate the smear, but the stories couldn't be verified and were quickly dismissed both by the mainstream press and by the small gay publishers that, the Soviets had hoped, would slam Jackson for keeping his homosexuality secret. Even though this was a priority project to the Kremlin and considerable resources were devoted to it, the campaign fell flat, having no discernable impact on the race. In time, Jackson would lose the nomination to Jimmy Carter, then a little-known governor of the state of Georgia. In this case, the KGB's active-measures campaign against Jackson was only one minor reason among the many behind Jackson's failure to secure his party's nomination.

But imagine how the Scoop Jackson story might have played out if 2.5 billion people had been on social media back in 1976 like they are today. Simply seeding the story in a fringe online publication would be enough to get the ball rolling. From there, made-up stories of Jackson's perversions could probably have been induced to go viral on Twitter with minimal expense. Editors in the same quality publications that rejected the hoax in 1976 would likely have been forced to cover, if not the story, then at least the online chatter about the story.

Once the story was being talked about in the quality press, that very fact would give rise to a second wave of stories in the fringe press and on social media precisely about the fact that the establishment press was now covering it up. In parallel, a Twitter bot army might have been mobilized to target LGBTQ activists to put further pressure on Jackson. Facebook groups for this purpose might have been created, rallying the left around the story as well as the right. By the end, hundreds of hours might be devoted to discussing the question on cable news. And all of this could've been achieved for a fraction of the cost of the failed 1976 campaign.

Around the same time the Scoop Jackson active-measures operation was unfolding, a twenty-four-year-old recruit was undergoing initial training at the 401st KGB School in Okhta, in what was then Leningrad. Vladimir Vladimirovich Putin had dreamed of becoming an intelligence officer since he was a teenager, raised on Soviet propaganda tales of KGB agents' heroic derring-do on behalf of the dictatorship of the proletariat. Over the next fifteen years—five of which were served in Dresden in what was then communist East Germany—Putin would become a KGB man through and through. Unsurprisingly, next to nothing is known about the detail of the work he did as a Soviet spy, but what we do know is that the KGB of his day spent enormous resources on active measures. By the time he retired with the rank of lieutenant colonel in 1990, Vladimir Vladimirovich had absorbed the lessons well.

There is strong evidence to suggest that Putin's rise to the top of the Russian state nine years later was itself built on one of the most audacious, ruthless, and blood-drenched active measures ever recorded. Starting on August 31, 1999, Russia was hit by a strange wave of terror attacks. Over a period of seventeen days, large bombs detonated in a Moscow shopping mall and then in four separate high-rise apartment buildings (the first in Buynaksk in Dagestan, then two in Moscow four days apart, and finally a large truck bomb outside a nine-story residential building in the city of Volgodonsk).[8] The bombs went off at night, maximizing the number of civilian casualties. In total some three hundred people were killed and over a thousand injured. After a cursory investigation, Vladimir Putin, then Russia's prime minister, blamed Chechen separatists and used the incidents as a casus belli to justify a brutal war to subdue the restive, Muslim-majority republic.

But there were serious inconsistencies with the official explanation. The biggest was that while four attacks succeeded, three others were foiled by neighbors in the hypervigilant climate that followed the first bombs. In one foiled plot, in the city of Ryazan, the perpetrators were apprehended. They were carrying identification cards issued by the FSB, the KGB's successor agency.

The authorities had no coherent response to this development. After initially praising Ryazan's people for their vigilance against the Chechen terrorists, the FSB changed tack when its operatives were implicated, describing the entire incident as a security exercise. Over the following years, calls for an independent investigation of the bombings were systematically blocked, and Russians who questioned the official story blaming the Chechens were ruthlessly persecuted.

The most famous and most dogged of these, journalist Anna Polit-kovskaya and former agent Alexander Litvinenko, were both mur-dered. Independent inquiries of these assassinations have pointed to the involvement of Russia's security apparatus.

Today, the consensus among independent Russia experts is that the apartment bombings were orchestrated by the FSB to consoli-date Vladimir Putin's ascent to power. The bombings appear to have been a peculiar hybrid: both a false-flag operation designed to pin the blame for the terrorist attack on an innocent party and a murderous type of active measure, with control of the Russian state at stake. What cannot be disputed is that the wave of nationalist fervor that followed the apartment bombings and Putin's war on Chechen sepa-ratism led to his undisputed control of Russia.

The 1999 apartment bombings should make the nature of Vladi-mir Putin's character abundantly clear. From the perspective of some-one willing to undertake active measures at this scale, the internet becomes first and foremost a vast force multiplier. The radical open-ness of the new information ecosystem solves basically all the prob-lems that made those early Soviet campaigns relatively ineffective, and all at a fraction of the cost. An old KGB hand on Facebook or Twitter is a kid in a candy shop.

The best-known active measure undertaken in recent years was the successful effort to influence the 2016 U.S. election. It was nota-ble for combining the old tropes of Soviet disinformation with the tools of the internet age. But its notoriety has overshadowed the re-ality that it was simply the latest in a very long line of Russian online active-measures campaigns.

Michael McFaul, an Obama-era U.S. ambassador to Russia, re-counts what it was like to have been personally picked out as the focus for one such disinformation campaign:

> On the night of the [Russian] presidential election on March 4, 2012, a fake Twitter account that looked identical to mine tweeted out criticisms of the electoral procedures even before voting had ended. The Russian media went crazy, as did some Russian govern-ment officials, accusing me of blatantly interfering in the electoral

process. This stunt was so well executed that it took us a while at the embassy to realize what was happening. Even I initially thought that one of my staff members had gone rogue, sending out tweets on my behalf. We eventually figured it out—the fake account was using a capital letter I in place of a lowercase L in the name associated with my Twitter handle, @McFaul (@McFauI looks so similar). We eventually explained the origin of the spurious tweets, but only after a few hours of hysterical news coverage.[9]

It was a vintage KGB active measure: cynically deployed to destroy any possibility of a U.S.-Russia rapprochement. It was, McFaul would later reflect, "the smear that killed the reset"—the Obama administration's abortive attempt to patch up bilateral relations with Russia—making it an active-measures operation with real-world diplomatic consequences. For Russia, manufacturing reality is a tool of statecraft.

The speed and efficacy of online active measures encouraged the Russians to try bolder gambits. Consider the dueling demonstrations that hit downtown Houston's Travis Street at noon on May 21, 2016. On one side of the street, around a hundred conservative demonstrators rallied to "stop the Islamification of Texas." Across from them, a counterprotest by the United Muslims of America rallied to "save Islamic knowledge." The scene was tense, with insults hurled in both directions. Both protests, later investigations made clear, resulted from a Russian active-measures campaign.

The operation on Travis Street was likely scored as a failure back in St. Petersburg, where the Internet Research Agency—Putin's seemingly arm's-length active-measures shop—had planned it all. Ideally, the dueling protests would have escalated to violence, drawing mainstream media attention and fueling the polarization and discord that were the Kremlin's goals. It didn't happen this time, but then the operation had consumed little in terms of resources. Unveiling in 2017 an investigation into the incident, the chairman of the U.S. Senate Select Committee on Intelligence, Sen. Richard Burr (R-NC), estimated it cost the Kremlin as little as $200 in Facebook ads to orchestrate the whole thing. With the cost of failure so low, the Internet

Research Agency could afford a kind of probabilistic approach to active measures. Like an oil prospector happy to dig a hundred wells even if ninety-nine of them come up dry, the Russians calculated they could try everything, fail 99 percent of the time, and still win big in the end.[10]

They were not wrong.

Like the Soviet disinformation campaigns of the Cold War, what the Russians needed for an active measure to succeed was for it to get picked up in respectable media. The fragmented media ecosystem of the internet age makes this path much easier to traverse. A story could begin on the outer fringes of social media, and if enough people shared it, it would be picked up by a newly invigorated far-right media ecosystem centered on Breitbart or any other major online spreader of disinformation. From there it might be picked up by a more mainstream conservative outlet like Fox News. Often, the rest of the media had little choice but to follow suit. The result is the constant muddying of the difference between different types of news, with the entire range from serious journalism to outright disinformation becoming increasingly difficult for readers to pick apart. As we will see, with the advent of "deepfake" technology, which allows an existing image or video to be replaced with someone else's likeness, the digital version of active measures has become a terrifying new strategic threat.

Princeton University professor Melissa M. Lee described this sort of approach as "subversive statecraft"—identifying subversion as a low-cost alternative to traditional military force.[11] In this view, new forms of digitally enabled subversion create a gray zone between outright offensive military action and mere propaganda. It is a gray zone that Western policymakers still have to figure out how to navigate.

Researchers at the RAND Corporation described the new approach as a "firehose of falsehood" because of its two distinctive features: the "high numbers of channels and messages and a shameless willingness to disseminate partial truths or outright fictions." They noted that today's Russian propaganda "is also rapid, continuous, repetitive and, crucially, . . . it lacks commitment to consistency." Russian propaganda happily contradicts itself from one day to the next because its goal is not to be believed but to be repeated and, in that way, to obfuscate and confuse while disrupting the dissemination of truthful reporting.[12]

To implement its firehose of falsehood, the Internet Research Agency relied heavily on bot armies to amplify the impact of online disinformation. A bot army is "a group of computers, infected with malign programs via the internet, that can be controlled remotely to, for example, mount denial-of-service attacks."[13] They are, without a doubt, a formidable weapon of post-truth. But there are dangers to overstating the impact of these bot armies.

Bot armies did little beyond helping along a process that many internet users are only too happy to help along. Sinan Aral, a professor at the MIT Sloan School of Management, found that human users are around 70 percent more likely to retweet false news stories than true stories on Twitter. It takes a true story around six times longer, on average, to reach fifteen hundred Twitter users compared to a false story. Falsehoods are retweeted more widely than true statements at every depth of a tweet cascade (an unbroken chain of tweets).[14, 15]

The study proposes a troubling explanation for this finding: we're suckers for novelty. Rather than a bias in favor of the false, what human people display is a bias in favor of the unexpected, shocking, and new. Of course, false news is much more often unexpected, shocking, and surprising than real news. Released from the humdrum necessity of checking for accuracy, the fantasist disinformation peddlers are liberated to produce stories so shocking and compelling, they tickle all our shared triggers.

An old newsroom joke is to label certain stories "too good to check." That is, they are so perfect in their current form that it seems a shame to check their accuracy and, all too predictably, find out that the real story is not nearly as compelling and shareable as the initial report. To professional editors, "too good to check" is a joke. In serious publications they will, of course, check. They must do so. The stories that a serious fact-checking process yields are very often less exciting—and less shareable—than they would have been without the checking.

For disinformation practitioners, on the other hand, "too good to check" is a mission statement, a critical edge allowing them to craft stories people can't resist sharing. The internet's radical openness and the diminished role of information gatekeepers become critical advantages, allowing them to operate with a degree of freedom previously unimaginable. With the practices and institutions that protected society from disinformation in tatters, practitioners of the dark arts of post-truth find themselves kicking penalty shots without a goalkeeper to stand in the way.

To make matters even more confusing, active-measures-style propaganda techniques have a way of colonizing mainstream information spaces as well. In the United States, for instance, the local six o'clock broadcast news was long seen as a haven of "straight" reporting, but new players like Sinclair Media have strategically bought up local TV stations throughout the country and now produce a TV product that looks like the standard news but is in fact aggressively partisan in its coverage. Sinclair appears to see its mission chiefly as spreading Republican Party talking points—a pattern that repeats itself when populism, polarization, and post-truth reign free.

In Venezuela, shady figures presumed to be furtively associated with the ruling party bought up *El Universal*, the nation's oldest establishment broadsheet newspaper, as well as Globovision, its main twenty-four-hour news network, and swiftly transformed them into regime mouthpieces. They took care not to alter the look and feel of either product: the typeface and layout in *El Universal* stayed the same, as did the theme music, logo, and many of the journalists on Globovision. For anyone outside a very small, politically savvy elite, it was easy to miss it. But the content gradually changed until both became difficult to distinguish from other regime propaganda outlets.

Similar stories are found in Egypt, Hungary, India, Indonesia, Montenegro, Nigeria, Pakistan, Poland, Russia, Serbia, Tanzania, Tunisia, Turkey, and Uganda, among others. The stealthy morphing of media companies from independent to governmental mouthpieces has become a common sight in stealthily autocratic regimes. In each case, propaganda is suited out in the outer garb of traditional journalism, yielding a product carefully calibrated to baffle and confuse its audience into submission.

Elections to the European parliament in 2019 saw social media giants playing whack-a-mole, struggling to shut down fake news pages as quickly as fakers could put them up. In just one month, May of that year, Facebook shut down twenty-seven pages, with 2 million Polish followers between them, for sharing blatantly fake content that was "anti-Semitic, anti-Islam, anti-migrant, anti-LGBT and anti-feminist."[16] A week earlier in Italy, it had shut down twenty-three mostly pro-government pages, counting a total of almost 2.5 million followers between them, for spreading fake news and anti-immigrant content.[17] In April, it had been seventeen pages from Spain, with 1.4 million followers.[18]

Any event that polarizes and divides democratic societies becomes an opportunity for propaganda, and the COVID-19 pandemic was no exception. In mid-2020, researchers at the Oxford Internet Institute found that news and information from Chinese, Iranian, Russian, and Turkish state-backed outlets actively spread disinformation about the crisis to French-, German-, and Spanish-speaking social media users.[19] Each country's propaganda organs emphasized a different type of disinformation, with Chinese and Turkish outlets more focused on burnishing their own country's role in fighting the virus, while Russian and Iranian outlets sought to stir the pot, sowing active discord in recipient societies and spreading conspiracy theories about the pandemic, many aimed specifically at Latin American audiences. Whatever the goal of the disinformation, content from state-backed propaganda outlets consistently achieved "higher average engagement per article than information from prominent news sources such as *Le Monde, Der Spiegel,* and *El País.*"[20]

In many of these countries, the traditional media is still there trying to compete with these purveyors of disinformation. But they compete with a critical disadvantage. Real journalism that hews to traditional standards for accuracy and verification can never match disinformation along one critical axis: novelty. And, as noted, our brains are wired to seek out novel information.

The result is a sort of journalistic dysfunction that makes bad information systematically drive out the good. And if the situation is dire in the public sphere, it is even worse in the ambiguous, quasi-private domain of dark social.

The Darkness at the Heart of WhatsApp

While open social media platforms like Twitter and Instagram dominate the conversation in the developed countries, a different type of platform is surging in popularity elsewhere. In India, Nigeria, Mexico, and Indonesia—to name just a few countries—disinformation increasingly travels in the form of sharable content that at best stretches the truth and more often just openly falsifies it for political advantage as it's passed around through private messaging networks.

The king of these so-called dark social networks, the Facebook-owned texting platform WhatsApp, has proven explosively popular and impossible to control across the developing world, thanks to its powerful combination of end-to-end encryption (which prevents even Facebook itself from knowing what content it is used to transmit) and the unbeatable price tag of "free."

For a sense of how damaging falsehoods can be on these platforms, look at India. Starting in 2017, a spate of rumors of child-abduction rings began circulating around WhatsApp networks in India, setting off a moral panic that soon turned into a spasm of mob lynchings as scared groups of villagers rounded up people they suspected to be behind the kidnappings. No evidence that any child had been abducted ever surfaced—and yet the rumors seemed impossible to control. Many of the villagers sharing them had limited literacy and little to no access to alternative sources of information that might have warned them that the rumors were false.

The cost of India's child-abduction panic was counted in dead bodies. By the middle of 2018, more than fifty separate attacks arising from the panic had been logged, with forty-six people killed. The rumors would flare up in one area, set off a spate of attacks, and then die down only to resurface days or weeks later somewhere else, sometimes hundreds of miles away. The authorities were visibly at a loss for how to react.[21] In June 2018, the government of India's

Tripura state shut down internet service for all its 3.7 million people for a week following one attack—a desperate attempt to stem the flood of rumors.[22] Facebook eventually limited the number of times a piece of content could be shared through the WhatsApp platform to try to slow the spread of disinformation.

The child-abduction panic was not politically motivated. Instead, it appears to have spread organically as scared parents tried to help one another protect their children. It served as proof of concept, though, for how powerful dark social messaging could prove in the Indian context. By the time India's mammoth 2019 national elections, in which over 600 million people voted, came around, the terrain was fertile for an explosion in fake news.[23]

One story disseminated on WhatsApp claimed that Rahul Gandhi, the leader of the Congress Party, would pay large sums of money to the families of suicide bombers who had attacked Indian soldiers in Kashmir.[24] Another—a perennial favorite—claimed that his mother, Sonia Gandhi, is richer than the queen of England.[25] And in a country where political Hinduism is strong and cows literally sacred, allegations of beef-eating shared online marred the election prospects of dozens of politicians.[26] Much—though by no means all—of the disinformation appeared to be generated by an aggressive campaign conducted by the ruling Hindu nationalist BJP to mobilize voters around their religious identity by painting the opposition Congress Party as pro-Muslim, pro-Pakistani, and insufficiently Hindu.[27] It worked, with the BJP prime minister coasting to an unexpectedly comfortable landslide reelection.

WhatsApp allows people to identify recipients through their photo and makes it easy to send short recorded messages (called "voice notes"), thus sidestepping the literacy barrier altogether, turning it into the first social media platform to gain a mass following among illiterate people. According to *The Economist*, a voice note claiming that Nigeria's Atiku Abubakar, a top presidential contender, had been endorsed by the "Association of Nigerian Gay Men" went viral.[28] No such association exists in what remains a deeply homophobic country, but gay slurs of this kind are among the most enduring and damaging of slurs in most of the world.

WhatsApp's design makes it impossible to say exactly how many people received the message, but the story stuck and may have contributed to Abubakar's defeat by Muhammadu Buhari. Another false rumor held that Buhari, a Muslim, was actively plotting to kill Nigerian Christians. How is an illiterate villager whose main source of news is WhatsApp supposed to distinguish the truth from the lies?

In Mexico, fake news mills aimed at social media were a key part of the 2018 presidential campaign. One analysis by Mexican data privacy NGO Artículo 12 found some three thousand separate websites actively being used to generate and disseminate fake or tendentious news stories during the campaign.[29] Some 55 percent of active Twitter accounts backing the ruling party's candidate were found to be bots (computer programs that simulate humans on social media), many dedicated to spreading fake news. Some apparently well-orchestrated campaigns appeared designed more to sow confusion and chaos than to benefit any given political party. In early 2017, for instance, amid rising social tensions and nationwide protests against the recent rise in fuel prices, an army of around 1,500 bot accounts began to position an alarming hashtag, #SaqueaUnWalmart, or #GoLootAWalmart, sending people scurrying to hunker down at home for safety as rumors spread of mass disorder.[30] Seventy-nine stores were looted in the following days, none of them Walmarts. It remains unclear who launched the campaign or to what end.

Indonesia's 2019 presidential elections showed just how ugly things can get when dark social media is used to stoke ethnic tension in a politically volatile environment. The main opposition candidate, Prabowo Subianto, centered much of his campaigns on appeals to Muslim solidarity coupled with claims that the incumbent, President Joko Widodo, was in the pocket of Chinese interests.[31] It is an incendiary claim because ethnic tensions between indigenous Indonesians and the powerful ethnic Chinese minority, which is disproportionally represented in the country's trading elite, have long been a fault line in the Muslim-majority country. Videos circulating on WhatsApp claimed President Widodo was planning to ban the Muslim call to prayer as well as the wearing of Islamic headscarves in public.[32] Disinformation flowed in the other direction, too, with one viral disinformation video claiming Prabowo was planning to legalize gay marriage.[33] Stories like these became commonplace, even routine. It is impossible to monitor all of the disinformation shared online, of course, but one official report by the Indonesian Ministry for Communications and Information documented at least seven hundred separate election-related hoaxes in the run-up to the vote.[34]

Things spiraled out of control directly after the April 2019 vote. By May, the authorities went as far as to shut down access to Facebook and WhatsApp after riots spread through Jakarta soon after a closely fought presidential election. Directly after Widodo was elected, conspiracy theories spread through Indonesia's dark social networks about secret Chinese soldiers posing as riot police or cops shooting protesters as they prayed at mosques, setting off rioting in poorer Muslim neighborhoods that left at least eight dead and seven hundred injured. Rioters chanted "Kick the Chinese out!" and "Beware of foreigners!" as they rampaged through Jakarta in what can only be described as an anti-Chinese pogrom.

These episodes show that fear, uncertainty, and doubt—FUD, as the trio is called—have an especially easy time spreading through dark media channels. If, as Marshall McLuhan argued all those years ago, "the medium is the message," then the message contained in dark social is clear: FUD wins, and the more of it the better.[35]

This novel media landscape, where the boundary between different kinds of news is blurred, is uniquely suited to a simple strategy: flooding the zone. Simply generating such a volume of messages—many false, nearly all deceptive—and bringing them to people through unregulated (and unregulatable) channels makes disinformation functionally impossible to beat back. Even the best-educated, most sophisticated media consumers struggle to tell truth from lies in this environment—who among us hasn't hit the share button only to be alerted, minutes later, that we have unwittingly aided disinformation along? If such educated media users can't figure this out, what hope is there for the villagers of Tripura state and the slum-dwellers of Jakarta?

And dark social is just one part of this radically new information ecosystem, firmly anchored in post-truth—the third of the 3Ps—

and marked by an explosion in communications channels that relies on the internet and other technologies. Together, these technologies sideline traditional gatekeepers and systematically blur the difference between different types of news. As the costs of reaching more and more people through more channels fall, the guideposts that used to reliably inform people of which stories could be trusted and which could not vanish. In this new world, simply cranking out FUD-based messages at a big enough scale to overwhelm an audience becomes a winning strategy—far superior, in cost-benefit terms, to the dull work of painstakingly convincing an audience on the basis of reasoned argument.

Beyond FUD: Ridicule as Weapon

But it is not only developing countries that are prone to the peculiar politics of post-truth, and FUD (fear, uncertainty, and doubt) is not the only way of leveraging revolutionary communications technologies and putting them at the service of confusion and conflict. In some of the world's most consolidated and longest-established democracies, 3P leaders have discovered how ridicule can be deployed both online and off to devastating effect.

To see this mechanism at work, we must cast our minds back to the mid-1990s. At the time, European fruit and vegetable wholesalers had a problem. Though a grand European single market had been declared in 1993, implementation remained spotty. Take the lowly banana: different European countries had different rules for grading and classifying wholesale bananas. Most had one top grade for bananas deemed suitable for retail sale and one or two lower grades for bruised or misshapen fruit that might still be good for making different kinds of processed banana products—juices, baby food, baked goods. But the classification scheme in Belgium didn't quite match the one in France, which was different from the one in Italy, which in turn was incompatible with the one in Britain. A wholesaler buying bananas in Africa would need to sort a shipment four times to meet the different classification standards in each country. Wouldn't it make sense to have a single, Europe-wide system for classifying bananas so grocers and wholesalers with operations in different countries didn't have to keep juggling these different codes? The needless proliferation of slightly conflicting banana regulations was, after all, precisely the kind of wasteful market friction the Single European Act was designed to prevent.

This is how European Commission regulation 2257/94 was born.[36] On September 16, 1994, the commission set out a simple, three-tier classification system for bananas designed to harmonize the old hodgepodge of national regulations. Bananas intended for retail sale, the regulations set out, should be "free from abnormal curvature," and for them to be sold to grocers as top grade ("extra") they should be free from defects in shape as well. Of course, lower-grade (and lower-priced) bananas could be traded even if their shapes weren't standard—but only if they were marked as such. This was harmonization in action—the kind of nitty-gritty regulatory standard-setting that, methodically carried out across thousands of product markets, added up to a grand idea: turning all of Europe into a single market.

If on September 15, 1994, you had walked into the Brussels offices where European Commission officials were finalizing the language on the bananas directive and tried to warn them they were about to make a potentially catastrophic blunder, they would have assumed you were joking. The instrument they were working on was not just obscure; it was routine and seemingly unobjectionable. Regulation 2257/94 didn't ban anyone from selling anything: in fact, it didn't create new rules at all. All it did was simplify and streamline the different sets of rules that already existed. The notion that this dry technical document could turn out to be of any interest at all to anyone beyond a few hundred grocery, shipping, and wholesaling professionals actively involved in the international trade in tropical fruit would have struck them as . . . well, bananas.

And yet the regulation would become a cause célèbre and an early test case in the dynamics of post-truth. Britain's tabloid press was already heavily invested in a campaign that used the term "Brussels" as a stand-in for an out-of-touch, meddlesome bureaucratic elite. With its layers of bureaucracy, its fetish for codification, its continental legalism, and its sheer *Frenchness*, the European Union might as well have been hatched in a laboratory for genetically engineering the perfect British populist foil. Fleet Street—the home of Britain's raucous tabloid press—was an early forerunner in the hunt for viral fake news, only back in the 1990s this took the form of a race to juice up newspaper sales.

The moral panic Britain's tabloids went on to unleash over "Bendy Bananas" would become the template for an unending stream of stories poking fun at European bean counters. "Now They've Really Gone Bananas" headlined *The Sun*, the mass-circulation daily owned by Rupert Murdoch, the legendary, card-carrying Euroskeptic. The subhead? "Euro Bosses Ban Too Bendy Ones."[37] The *Daily Mirror*, *Daily Express*, and *Daily Mail* all jumped on the bendy banana bandwagon. For a while, it seemed impossible to sell a tabloid newspaper in Britain unless it contained at least one alarming story about the banana regulation.

None of it was true, of course. Alongside the more respectable parts of the British press ("Putting the Banana Story Straight" was one sober-minded headline in *The Independent* on September 21, 1994),[38] European officials drove themselves half-crazy trying to beat back the bendy banana myth. But even back in 1994, a virally irresistible headline traveled much faster and established itself in the public consciousness much more firmly than any fact-checked story could. Somehow, the sight of sober, serious-minded European mandarins in fine suits explaining their stance on the curvature of bananas made them seem only more ridiculous.

In time, "barmy Brussels bureaucrats" stories became a kind of journalistic genre unto themselves, with the EU's continual production of directives and regulations providing a never-ending stream of material for creative British hacks trying to write the next viral story. Among the most energetic peddlers of these stories was the ambitious young Brussels bureau chief for *The Telegraph*, a right-wing broadsheet. His name was Boris Johnson.

Having had a hit with the bendy bananas myth, the tabloid press was soon on the lookout for other produce-curvature stories. Soon it alighted on its next campaign: Europe's supposed ban on bendy cucumbers. Again, a regulation approved with the needs of shippers and wholesalers in mind became the center of a populist press furor. (Bendy cucumbers were never banned, but a European directive did establish that excessively curved cucumbers have to be labeled and packed separately for wholesaling purposes.)[39]

A whole host of similar "Euromyth" stories followed, each more preposterous than the one before. At least five hundred of them ended up published in one form or another in Britain's Euroskeptic press. We know the figure because the European Commission, in one more doomed attempt to push back, ended up collecting all of them on one website, the better to try to debunk them.[40]

Among the headlines featured:

- New European Rules Forbid Butchers Giving Dog Bones
- EU Rules Demand Organic Fish Farms Must Treat Any Signs of Illness Using Homeopathy
- EU Officials Want Control of Your Candles
- [Your] 21-Gun Salutes Are Just Too Loud, Brussels Tells the Royal Artillery
- EC to Ban Ploughman's Sandwiches
- Church Bells are Silenced by Fear of EU Law
- Warning Signs Are to Be Put on Mountains to Let Climbers Know They Are High Up
- EC to Standardize Coffin Sizes
- Food Outlets Will Have to Offer Condiments in Sachets Rather than in Bottles or Squeezy Tubes
- Circus Performer Must Walk Tightrope in Hard Hat, Says Brussels
- EU Could Ban Orchestras from Using Cow Gut for Strings

It is easy to see why these sorts of stories made newspapers money: they were sharable content *avant la lettre*. Boris Johnson turned stories like these into a personal specialty, cranking out story after story that stoked Euroskeptic fires despite having little to no basis in fact. The Europe of Johnson's imagination would impose a single standardized condom size. It would ban recycling tea bags. It would ban shrimp-cocktail-flavored snacks. It would ban small children from blowing up rubber balloons. None of the claims withstood scrutiny. It didn't matter: the stories had already put Johnson on a path that, in 2019, would end at 10 Downing Street as he became the post-truth prime minister.

The European Commission tried different ways to hit back at the nonsensical stories—some replies are serious and technocratic, others curt, some almost pleading, a few just sarcastic. Faced with outright nonsense, the commission at times just gave itself permission to pun. The commission called one over-the-top story about a purely made-up directive to force cows to wear diapers on Alpine slopes "udder nonsense."[41]

Still, European officials struggled to counter the corrosive effects of stories like these. Anybody who's been taunted in a schoolyard knows there's no simple way to counter ridicule. It matters not at all that very few of the stories turn out to be entirely true, and none are remotely fair. EU-bashing stories were devastatingly effective in portraying the EU's Brussels headquarters as a place where an illegitimate elite leveraged complexity as a weapon against the pure British public. This was raw, unadulterated populism and another concrete example used by its practitioners to show how the long-suffering people need the protection of the valiant 3P leaders.

To read these stories is to get a sense for the political potency of ridicule as a technique for dismantling truth. Their staying power defied repeated debunking. As late as the 2016 Brexit referendum, more than twenty years after the story was originally circulated and shown to be wildly deceptive, Boris Johnson was still riding that hobbyhorse. "It is absolutely crazy that the EU is telling us how powerful our vacuum cleaners have got to be, what shape our bananas have got to be, and all that kind of thing," he told an interviewer just a few weeks before the vote.[42]

Some hoped that the weight of responsibility associated with becoming prime minister of a nuclear power might chastise Johnson, summoning once more the bookish Oxford intellectual he had been in his youth. No such luck. On the eve of his election as leader of Britain's Conservative Party—and, consequently, as prime minister—Johnson stood in front of a cheering crowd holding up a kipper (a smoked fish), saying he'd spoken to a trader from the Isle of Man who had griped loudly about European regulation destroying his profit margins by forcing him to ship his kippers on "pillows of ice." "Pointless, pointless, expensive, environmentally damaging," he thundered, before adding with a flourish, "We will bring the kippers back. It is not a red herring."[43] None of it was true. European regulations say exactly nothing about pillows of ice or about kippers. The Isle of Man is not part of the European Union . . . or even of the United Kingdom (it is a "crown dependency"). None of it mattered. Telling tall tales about European regulations had gotten Johnson this far, and he was not about to stop.

Still, it wasn't Boris Johnson who brought Britain out of the EU—it was the hardened feeling that the Brussels elite and London's plutocrats were abysmally detached from the pure people's common sense that created the conditions for Britain's divorce from Europe. That feeling was stitched together out of two decades' worth of stories ridiculing EU rules based on systematic disinformation. And they didn't even need the internet to pull it off.

But while these post-truth tactics were possible in the pre-internet era, they depended on newspapers, magazines, or radio and TV to disseminate their messages widely. Not anymore. The internet has made all its users spreaders of information. Some of these users reach a few close friends and relatives. Others reach millions. Some are humans and others are bots. The great majority of the messages are anodyne, while others are part of an effort to obtain and retain power or to weaken a rival.

Enough has been written about Donald Trump's pathological penchant for untruth. According to fact-checkers for the *Washington Post*, by the end of his term in office, President Trump publicly made 30,573 statements that were either misleading or simply false.[44] As Chris Cillizza, a CNN reporter, pointed out, that meant that the president of the United States, lied in public more often than the average person washes their hands.[45] But just as important to Trump's post-truth strategy is the systematic use of ridicule to belittle and humiliate opponents: from "low-energy Jeb," "Li'l Marco," and "Crooked Hillary" to Elizabeth "Pocahontas" Warren and "Sleepy Joe" Biden, Trump displayed an instinctive feel for bullying and for the political potency of humiliation. Ridicule, it turns out, is a crucial complement to fear, uncertainty, and doubt.

In each of these cases, post-truth is about the rejection of complexity, nuance, and reason. It is about the unembarrassed embrace of manipulation as a governing technique. It is about the systematic exploitation of people's preexisting biases—whether it is Nigerian Christians' distrust of gay people, Indian Hindus' animus toward Muslims, Indonesians' hostility to the Chinese, or English distaste for all things continental. It is about exploiting the collapse of the old boundaries between real news and propaganda for cynical short-term gain. It is premised on the uncomfortable reality that an emotionally fulfilling lie is much more likely to be believed than an emotionally unfulfilling truth. And as the cost of disseminating lies declines, it becomes easy to overwhelm audiences with massive numbers of fraudulent messages. This is how truth fades away, and its role in public life is colonized by clashing sets of incompatible tribal certainties.

The Revenge of a Dangerous Idea

The idea that nothing is ultimately true has a long history. In the 1970s and 1980s, a small band of far-left campus intellectuals led by radical French sociologist Michel Foucault began to argue that knowledge was an elite construct: a fiction like any other fiction, created by the powerful so they can exercise their power.[46] "Knowledge," Foucault famously quipped, "is not for knowing: knowledge is for cutting." In this poststructuralist view, reality is a sophisticated fiction—an arbitrary construction pieced together by the powerful to justify and perpetuate their domination over everyone else.

Couched in the turgid, impenetrable language of the postmodern academy, the theories of this gaggle of elite intellectuals were extremely unlikely to go viral. They were intended to drive social scientific debate and intellectual exploration—and their proponents were animated by the abstract hope that if this ideology of truth could be dismantled, the deadly hold of a predatory elite over the workers could be eased. In the hands of sociologists like Bruno Latour, this idea was extended to science and the radical contention that scientific facts themselves do not exist "out there" in the world but are merely constructed artifacts of human thought.[47]

The twenty-first century is proving Foucault and Latour right—though not in a way they could have anticipated or would have welcomed. Rather than aiding the radical liberation of the downtrodden, the rise of post-truth is enabling the establishment of stealthocracies all around the world. Everywhere from the villages of Nigeria to the White House driveway, "alternative facts" are being used to consolidate the grip on power of 3P rulers interested in wielding power unaccountably and permanently.

As David Frum shows in his book *Trumpocracy*, this poststructuralist mindset that dismisses truth as nothing more than a social construct was, in fact, one of the central organizing principles of the Trump administration. The barrage of half-truths, deceptions, exaggerations, misstatements, untruths, and outright lies pouring out of the White House might have been unsettling to many Americans, but it was uncomfortably familiar to people all around the world with long experience of coping with autocracies built on the 3P framework. As the White House deepened its campaign of lies, dissident Russians, Venezuelans, Turks, Hungarians, Iranians, Argentinians, Indians, Filipinos, Nigerians, Algerians, and Nicaraguans all looked knowingly at their American brethren as if to say, "See what we've been dealing with for all these years?"[48] In each of these countries, the rise of a new type of autocrat coincided with the collapse of the public sphere as a place for reasoned debate about public affairs.

Foucault's dangerous idea was in for a turbulent second life. Let out into the wild, it would switch sides, becoming weaponized by the most retrograde forces in society intent on cementing their hold on power. In the 3P autocrats' hands, the social construction of truth transformed into the era of "alternative facts" and "fake news": an era when the powerful recognized no restraints at all when it came to deploying FUD from the very top.

By 2017, things had gotten far enough out of control that even some of the original proponents of the social construction of science school were having second thoughts. In an interview that sent shockwaves through the French academy, Bruno Latour argued that intellectuals should help "regain some of the authority of science." Like Pandora looking ruefully at the pandemonium she had set loose by opening her box, Latour pivoted to a conventional defense of science against constructed falsehood: "We are indeed at war. This war is run by a mix of big corporations and some scientists who deny climate change. They have a strong interest in the issue and a large influence on the population."[49]

Too little, too late.

Deepfakes and Frequent Lies

Most sobering in this discussion is the realization that we've only scratched the surface in terms of post-truth's potential to destabilize democratic public spheres. The types of manipulations and distortions we've experienced so far, profound though they've been, could pale in comparison to a future in which ever-cheaper, more accessible, and more powerful disinformation tools are set free on the internet with dangerous consequences.

The most attention so far has been focused on the prospect of "deepfakes." Using artificial intelligence and other currently available technology, it is possible—and, increasingly, easy—to produce fully realistic video of events that never took place. After starting with pornographic videos purporting to show celebrities engaged in sexual activities that never took place, deepfakes then began percolating into the public consciousness and the public sphere as a uniquely disruptive technology in the service of post-truth.

Deepfakes have already turned on its head the presumption of authenticity that was long attached to video evidence; now that is a quaint relic of a bygone era. And we've seen only the beginning.

Developed democracies with still-functioning legacy gatekeeper institutions (newspapers, serious broadcast news, etc.) will see their resilience tested. Yet they stand some chance as governments and consumers become more aware of the dangers posed by deepfakes. More serious is the situation in developing democracies with weaker (or nonexistent) legacy gatekeepers and lower levels of public trust in general. It is sobering to realize that the politicians who become targets of deepfake attacks would probably be right if they calculate they'd be better served by retaliating with their own deepfakes against opponents than by setting off on a futile attempt to set the record straight.

Once a technology spreads, it is hard to tame it or contain its diffusion. While some forms of deepfakes will continue to be part of the dirty tricks used by overly ambitious and irresponsible politicians and their advisers, new technologies will help limit their impact. In 2020, for example, Microsoft launched its Video Authenticator, a software that analyzes videos and photos and provides a score indicating the chances that the images have been manipulated using artificial intelligence. The company also launched a technology that will allow creators to certify that their content is authentic and inform users that deepfake technology has not been used.[50] It is safe to assume that as deepfakes become more popular and more dangerous, the demand for technologies that neutralize them will also mount.

And it is not just deepfakes. It is also the normalization of lying. With alarming regularity, aspiring autocrats across the globe alight on similar solutions to the problem of restoring some efficacy to their power. Obliterating truth has become too common an approach.

The mendacity revolution is at the core of the 3P autocrats' challenge to the status quo. That so many of its core practices have their roots in the practice of Soviet-era propaganda gives us a disquieting hint as to the nature of the challenge and the autocratic core of its practitioners. Yet it is important to grasp not only what is the same but also what has changed in the shift toward an internet-based information architecture. When media channels were few and tightly controlled by professional gatekeepers, autocrats used to fear facts and work feverishly to conceal them. Today, as we've seen, they practice "censorship through noise"—using a firehose of falsehood to drown out the truth in a miasma of uncertainty. Donald Trump learned the lesson, and his barrage of tweets became an important factor in American politics.

As the Ukrainian-born British journalist and author Peter Pomerantsev put it in his book *This Is Not Propaganda: Adventures in the War Against Reality*, this has led to a frightening sense that the truth has lost its purchase on reality somehow:

> During glasnost, it seemed that the truth would set everybody free. Facts seemed possessed of power; dictators seemed so afraid of facts that they suppressed them. But something has gone drastically wrong; We have access to more information and evidence than ever, but facts seem to have lost their power.[51]

The disinformation techniques perfected over the Cold War era now look as crude and unsophisticated as the special effects in a 1970s sci-fi movie. The state of the art has advanced immeasurably since then, and the information ecosystem has as well, giving practitioners troubling advantages over their competitors. In a one-on-one fight for viewers' eyeballs, fake news beats real news every single time. And we can only guess at the technologies that in a couple of decades will make today's fake news look as unsophisticated as the Soviet active measures of the 1970s seem to us now.

8

MAFIA STATES, CRIMINAL GOVERNMENTS

The dark history of the twentieth century made it clear what the natural endpoint of old-power autocracy was. When taken to its extremes, authoritarianism in the twentieth century led to the totalitarian state: all-powerful central behemoths that controlled all aspects of people's public and private lives, such as the ones built by Adolf Hitler, Joseph Stalin, Mao Zedong, and Fidel Castro.

But what is the endpoint of a world of populism, polarization, and post-truth? Left to its own devices and developed to its furthest consequences, where does 3P power lead? In this chapter, we will explore how the thuggery that is the cornerstone of the new power gives rise to a criminal takeover of the state, subtly twisting the government into a sprawling criminal conspiracy centered on the predatory extraction of profits from society. The proceeds of this strategy fill the rulers' pockets and those of their cronies and are used to buy the necessary political support at home and overseas.

This process is gradual. At first, 3P leaders merely transgress some of the established norms of public propriety—Donald Trump overcharging the Secret Service to stay at his hotels, say, or

Viktor Orbán building a lavish soccer stadium in his hometown. If these initial transgressions are successful, the autocrats' goals rapidly escalate, and what ensues is an all-out effort to neuter laws, norms, habits, and institutions designed to contain malfeasance. Successfully weakening or altogether eliminating the existing guardrails against crime cements the autocrats' power and confirms that transgression pays. Rather than trying to build old-style dictatorships, autocrats progressively hollow out the state as an impartial arbiter of the law and turn it into their ally in strip-mining society for profit.

Many confuse the shady business deals widely used nowadays by the 3P autocrats with corruption. But corruption centers on practices that augment a person or a group's wealth. This is different in that criminal enterprises are used as an appendix of the state.

Writing in 2020 in the journal *Foreign Affairs*, Philip Zelikow, Eric Edelman, Kristofer Harrison, and Celeste Ward Gventer recognize that while graft has always existed, it has acquired a renewed potency. What is new, they write,

> is the transformation of corruption into an instrument of national strategy. In recent years, a number of countries—China and Russia, in particular—have found ways to take the kind of corruption that was previously a mere feature of their own political systems and transform it into a weapon on the global stage. Countries have done this before, but never on the scale seen today. The result has been a subtle but significant shift in international politics. Rivalries between states have generally been fought over ideologies, spheres of influence, and national interests; side payments of one kind or another were just one tactic among many. Those side payments, however, have become core instruments of national strategy, leveraged to gain specific policy outcomes and to condition the wider political environment in targeted countries. This weaponized corruption relies on a specific form of asymmetry. Although any government can hire covert agents or bribe officials elsewhere, the relative openness and freedom of democratic countries make them

particularly vulnerable to this kind of malign influence—and their nondemocratic enemies have figured out how to exploit that weakness.[1]

Corruption implies a normal state beset here and there by breaches of propriety and ethics. Corruption implies a departure from the normal state of things. But in the criminal states hatched by autocrats, appropriating public funds to private ends or promoting unfathomably profitable deals that are illegal in nature and whose profit is available to the rulers and cronies has become the normal state of things. Just think about the conglomerate of "private oligarchs" that controls Russia's riches and that exists at the Kremlin's—and Vladimir Putin's—behest.

Some will see this as a return to the kind of state systems that dominated the global landscape four centuries ago, what political scientists call the "patrimonial state." Throughout history, controlling the state has meant putting its resources to use for the ruler's personal ends. The Great Pyramid at Giza and the Taj Mahal were not built for public purposes, unless you see the interests of the pharaoh or the raja as entirely indistinguishable from those of the state.

This is a situation that modern democracies thought they had left behind. Modern states were supposed to replace this kind of personalist rule with rational bureaucracies that administered the public's wealth in the public's interest. Which is not to say that they weren't corrupted now and then by unscrupulous politicians in cahoots with "private" business leaders, but just to note that the overall direction of travel was clear. And many imagined it to be irreversible.

Democratic backsliding, lubricated by populism, polarization, and post-truth, often involves a return to a kind of twenty-first-century patrimonialism, what scholars often refer to as "neopatrimonialism." As Francis Fukuyama has argued, the decay of the modern bureaucratic state is typically marked by backsliding into this kind of structure.[2] Starting out from some version of rational bureaucracy, 3P leaders attempt to turn back the clock, re-creating the personalist rule of antiquity in the era of Twitter and artificial intelligence. Left to their own devices, they will reverse decades or even centuries of progress toward building an open society where power is constrained by a panoply of checks and balances and they will work to turn the state into a sprawling criminal conspiracy instead. Instead of building a state to protect their citizens from the mafia, they morph the state into a mafia-like organization designed to take over the nation's most precious assets and control of the most valuable businesses and transfer them to their families and cronies.

The criminalized political regimes built on a 3P-foundation are fundamentally unlike the old-style dictatorships of the twentieth century. The dour, austere police states of a Francisco Franco or an Augusto Pinochet are of relatively little interest to most twenty-first-century autocrats. Instead, the final destination is the mafia state: a predatory system designed to allow its leaders maximum latitude to enrich themselves with impunity and to turn the firepower of the state against anyone who threatens them militarily, electorally, or commercially.

The State's Gangland Roots

Charles Tilly, a Columbia University sociologist, persuasively argued that all states have a mafia-like origin.[3] He was not alone in holding this view. In the academy, theories of state formation are at pains to stress that the state is not a reaction against lawlessness but rather a codification of lawlessness: states form because racketeers have an interest in making their extortion more stable and more sustainable.

In his influential 1982 article "Warmaking and Statemaking as Organized Crime," Tilly argued that "governments often constitute the largest current threats to the livelihoods of their own citizens." They operate in essentially the same ways as racketeers. Citing historian Frederic Lane, Tilly argued that, like racketeers, governments are in the business of "selling protection . . . whether people want it or not." Extracting taxes from their subjects allows them to fund enough armed forces to hold off rivals, both foreign and domestic. At its root, the state-maker's occupation is different from that of the racketeer's only in scale, not in principle. "In this model," Tilly wrote, "predation, coercion, piracy, banditry and racketeering share a home with their upright cousins in responsible government."

This rather dismal view of the state's origin has a long lineage. It traces its history back to Machiavelli's sixteenth-century paeans to thuggery in government[4] and to Thomas Hobbes's *Leviathan*, a 1651 treatise on the rational need for a power able to suppress any challenge to it in order to sustain a stable social order.[5] For a more contemporary take, Mancur Olson's later work, contrasting the logic of the "roving bandit" with the logic of the "stationary bandit," provides a useful analytical perspective. In Olson's view, in the absence of government authority, the vacuum is always filled by ambitious people who seize the opportunity to become "roving bandits," traveling from one territory to the next stealing, looting, and pillaging.[6] As long as they are on the move, bandits' incentives are depressingly simple: just grab as much loot as possible using however much violence is required. But imagine one especially successful bandit who tires of life on horseback and decides to settle down in one spot. The moment he hangs up his spurs and becomes a "stationary bandit," his incentives change decisively. Just stealing as much as he can from the people he now rules over will soon prove self-defeating: they'll all starve to death and produce no more wealth he can steal from them. Once rooted to a single spot, a bandit finds reason to offer a mix of protection and despoliation: protection from other, still-roving bandits, who now become a threat to him, and despoliation in the form of regular extortion payments that, in polite circles, come to be described as "taxation."

For Olson, the stationary bandit, interested only in exploiting those he rules for his personal pleasure, inevitably starts to provide some of the services of a state. He does this not because he is benevolent but because he is cunning. His personal interests push him to monopolize violence in the territory he rules, keep invaders out, and collect taxes that may be onerous but never so high as to put at risk the livelihoods of his subjects (who now double as his tax base).

As his power matures, he will need to establish relations with other stationary bandits in neighboring territories (thus diplomacy is born), and he'll want to hand over the fruits of his effort to his children (which is how the seeds of hereditary monarchy are sown). States, this view goes, form naturally not out of any considered agreement between freely contracting individuals but rather out of the very worst human proclivities: a will to pillage and dominate.

In time, successful kingdoms will grow larger and more complex. As they do, they often find they host more than one stationary bandit: dukes and earls will want to run their own protection rackets, though on a smaller scale. The challenge, then, becomes how to organize these various enterprises such that the racketeers don't tread on one another's toes and open conflict doesn't break out among them. The goal of these early states was to keep the peace between the lords, allowing them to extract rents and privileges from the peasants without stumbling into destructive feuds and wars between one another. Just like every mafia needs a *capo di tutti capi* (boss of all bosses) to keep the captains from gunning each other down, the early state develops not to serve the people but to be sure they can be exploited with relative stability.

The miracle of modernity is precisely that this early predatory state evolved over a period of about four hundred years into peaceful, modern democracies where the law protects all people equally. At least in theory.

How Mafia Values Are Reconquering States

All over the world, from Russia and Hungary to Venezuela, Nicaragua, Turkey, and, shockingly, the United States, new elites have slammed the brakes on the kind of modern order the Dutch Republic and Britain's Glorious Revolution first pioneered. In its place, they're building the modern mafia state: vast criminal enterprises headquartered in the presidential palace.

This is one important facet of what Fukuyama has called "political decay"—an ever-present danger for advanced polities. For Fukuyama, the transition from a patrimonial state (where the ruler's assets are indistinguishable from those of the state) to a modern state (where citizens are treated impersonally and equally) is always precarious and liable to backsliding—what he described as the "repatrimonialization" of the state. As a state is repatrimonialized, it regresses several hundred years and devotes itself once more to making sure only the rulers' friends have access to truly great wealth.[7]

One useful way to think about this is to think about *rents* in the sense economists use the word—benefits that accrue not from the creation of value to society but through political power. Originated by Gordon Tullock in 1967,[8] the term was popularized in 1974 through the work of economist Anne Krueger,[9] who explained why societies that focused more on the distribution of spoils than on the creation of value would ultimately stagnate and fail. Mafia states are single-mindedly focused on the creation and distribution of rents—in this case the benefits attaching to proximity to political power—and on the exclusion of the politically disloyal from access to rents.

That a renewed focus on rents would be a telltale sign of a collapsing democracy is by now widely accepted. In *Why Nations Fail: The Origins of Power, Prosperity and Poverty*, Daron Acemoglu and James Robinson noted that incumbent elites typically feel threatened by political systems that permit the failure of large businesses that underperform, the kind of "creative destruction" that scholars since Joseph Schumpeter in the 1950s have seen as the crux of capitalism's remarkable ability to repair and renew itself.[10] These elites would often prefer to replace that unstable system with one that leverages state power to guarantee them stability at the top. Nations fail when those able to produce wealth lose faith in the state's impartiality and begin to realize the fruits of their labor are likely to be plundered and transferred to the politically connected—something that is virtually a mission statement for the mafia state.

An early, incomplete case study of this trend came in Italy, where Silvio Berlusconi showed it could strike even at the heart of a G7 industrial power. Berlusconi barely bothered to conceal that he saw the prime minister's chair as part passport to riches, part get-out-of-jail-free card, and part the nation's top executive. Starting in 1994, he seemingly reveled in the dizzying conflicts of interest generated by his dual role as both owner of most of Italy's private media and, as head of government, ultimate decision-maker for all public broadcasting. He aggressively pursued policy options designed to enrich him, including quite brazen moves to weaken anti-trust regulations that limited the profitability of his finance and insurance industry holdings. Yet Berlusconi's unwillingness (or inability) to fully entrench himself as an autocrat limited the impact of such measures: when all was said and done, he found himself out of power and convicted on a host of tax fraud charges, staying out of jail purely through a combination of his advanced age, legal maneuvering, and Italy's quirky statute of limitations.

Berlusconi's seedy machinations—which included alleged payments for protection for a top Sicilian Mafia capo—were certainly embarrassing for Italians. But though he abused his power for personal gain, it would be an exaggeration to argue that Berlusconi turned the Italian state into a full-fledged criminal organization. His vision was more limited and the impact of his dirty tricks more circumscribed. Italy's chronic chaos also made it more difficult to install and run the highly centralized governance required by a mafia-like organization. While Berlusconi showed the extent to which a populist with a flair for show business could corrupt the state, he fell well short of transforming it into a criminal enterprise.

The mafia states built by the more autocratic 3P leaders are far more ambitious. These new autocrats often take power in countries that have made at least some progress toward building a political system that has some of the trappings of a democracy. Once they gain power, they start to work to reverse the process. They undermine the institutions that sustain the limited, incipient democracy using the tools we have discussed in previous chapters. Given enough time and leeway, they metamorphose the state into a criminal organization.

The paradigmatic example remains Russia. It is, after all, the country for which a nameless U.S. diplomat coined the term "mafia state" some years ago—as revealed in a WikiLeaks memo.[11] Vladimir Putin has proceeded further down the road of gangsterization than any of the other practitioners of the 3P framework—and the mafia state operating out of the Kremlin now destabilizes countries worldwide, from Mexico to Poland, from Kosovo to Spain.

Yet Russia wasn't always a mafia state. For all its immense—indeed, genocidal—faults, the Soviet Union had at least created the appearance of socialist meritocracy: any Soviet citizen who was ideologically docile and adroit at managing the petty politics of the workplace could rise quite far along the hierarchies of party, army, and state on the basis of talent. The post-Soviet chaos of the 1990s gave an opening to the world's most successful practitioner of the 3P power. Over the following two decades Vladimir Putin would ruthlessly erase any memory of Russia's fledgling attempt at openness to create the world's most ambitious, ruthless, and effective mafia state.

The origins of the Russian mafia state are well understood. It owes its origins to the birth of Russia out of the rubble of the Soviet Union: an economic calamity and a social catastrophe. In an atmosphere of pervasive lawlessness and macroeconomic chaos, and under pressure from the United States and Europe to liberalize and quickly create a market economy, Russia launched what might have been the largest transfer of ownership from public to private hands in the history of the world. But rather than spawning a Thatcherite Shangri-La of empowered citizen-owners, the process was quickly hijacked by a small cadre of well-connected players, often little more than street hustlers who had mastered the art of exploiting personal connections for profit. In successive rounds of thinly rigged privatization proceedings, they appropriated the Soviet Union's industrial heritage, winning control of state assets for a minuscule fraction of their true worth. In a little over ten years, the process made Russia one of the world's most unequal countries.

Soviet assets were looted with a brazenness and on a scale that remains difficult to fathom. Case studies abound. Take Boris Berezovsky, one of the most notorious of these politically connected players. He went from low-key software engineer to one of Russia's most powerful oligarchs within a few years. Using his experience producing software for Soviet car factories, Berezovsky took over a network of car dealers that, in time, effectively seized control of the mammoth Avtovaz car company, able to produce 740,000 Lada-branded cars per year. Berezovsky concocted a mechanism to essentially appropriate Avtovaz's profits without taking actual ownership of the company, letting its own balance sheet get loaded down with debts that became liabilities of the Russian government. Through a complex series of offshore companies and key allies placed in Avtovaz's upper management, Berezovsky managed to consistently buy Ladas at less than their production cost and resell them at gross margins topping 50 percent—about ten times the global norm. It was an insanely profitable arrangement made possible only by the connivance of the Russian state and the automotive sector. And Berezovsky extended this approach to other parts of the Russian economy, from Russia's flag-carrier airline, Aeroflot, and the oil industry to television and aluminum. At times it felt easier to list the sectors of the economy in which Berezovsky wasn't involved than those he had a hand in. One of his biographers concluded that "no man profited more from Russia's slide into the abyss."[12]

In the gangland atmosphere of Russian capitalism in the 1990s, there was no shortage of rivals looking to muscle in one or more of the extremely profitable business territories Berezovsky had carved out for himself—culminating in a number of assassination attempts against the oligarch, one of which involved a car bomb that killed the driver of his armored Mercedes and left him seriously injured.

With succulent profits to be made at each step, members of the small, charmed circle of Kremlin-connected insiders found themselves sitting atop billion-dollar fortunes in just a few years. But with more business disputes being settled via the gun (or the car bomb), none of them could feel entirely secure in their position. What the oligarchs needed more than anything was protection: a final arbiter able to settle disputes between them. In Sicily, they would have said they needed a *capo di tutti capi*. In Russia, his name was Vladimir Putin.

Putin's rise to the top of the Russian state fits with uncanny precision the logic set out in Tilly's framework of state-making as akin to organized crime. As Ruth May, a specialist in contemporary Russia, has written:

> The twenty or so oligarchs in Putin's Russia do not get access to powerful people in government because of their wealth, as is the case, say, with many billionaire political donors in America, but rather the reverse: Russian oligarchs get access to obscene amounts

of wealth because of their affinity with those most powerful in government. Men become oligarchs in Russia (there are no women oligarchs) because they are loyal to the only person in government who matters: Vladimir Putin.[13]

Through this handful of chosen oligarchs, Putin has managed to turn the old Soviet system, where anyone willing to toe the party line was able to climb the hierarchy of power, into a mafia state. In the system Putin built, a handful of insiders monopolize access to wealth and privilege . . . safely. The Soviet system was anything but a liberal paradise, but after the death of Stalin it provided avenues to a degree of material well-being and security for anyone willing to be a good loyal communist. Putin's mafia state, by contrast, reserves security and extraordinary wealth for a minuscule elite that answers directly to him alone.

The outcome of Russia's crash privatization drive of the 1990s is a strange hybrid. An economy that's technically in private hands is in fact a criminal appendage of the state. The entire Russian economy is, for all intents and purposes, beholden to the dictator. Putin can make or break an oligarch with a single phone call, a power he has been willing to display to show other tycoons what can happen to those who lose the boss's trust.

Boris Berezovsky's story shows the system at work in all its brutal effectiveness. Having amassed billions of dollars through shady business practices, he made the fatal mistake of criticizing Putin's move to amend the Russian constitution to give the president the power to dismiss elected governors. He voted against the reform and resigned his seat in the Duma, Russia's parliament. Beginning in late 2000, Berezovsky-owned media outlets began attacking Putin on a variety of fronts. The boss could not let this stand, and he did not. An escalating feud followed, but there was little doubt who would come out on top.

By 2006, Boris Berezovsky had been forced to sell all his Russian assets and flee to a gilded exile in London. He ended up bankrupt, dodging multiple assassination plots, and suffering from clinical depression before, it appears, committing suicide in 2013. In a pathetic coda to a peripatetic life, one of his final acts was to send a letter to Vladimir Putin begging to be allowed back into Russia and apologizing for his "mistakes."

The type of order Vladimir Putin had created in Russia relied on oligarchs' unquestioning acquiescence to his dictates. For Putin, destroying Boris Berezovsky was not an act of vengeance, at least not primarily. Being seen to have destroyed Berezovsky was, rather, an act of statecraft: an exercise in power necessary to guarantee the stability of the overall arrangement. Which is why it wouldn't really be precise to call the state-economy complex Putin leads "corrupt." Criminality and racketeering aren't departures from the norm: they are a central feature of the system that Putin built.

Mafia States: Beyond "Corruption"

The Russian case illustrates the problem with using the language of "corruption" to describe the maladies of mafia states. Corruption—even when it is widespread—implies departure from the norm. Mafia states do something different. They go beyond merely condoning criminal arrangements. Instead, they forcibly take them over, incorporating criminality into the structure of the state. Indeed, they turn crime into a tool of statecraft—projecting power through criminal means in a move that Philip Zelikow and his colleagues dubbed "strategic corruption."[14]

The way criminal networks can be used strategically to secure and exercise power is clearly seen in narcostates: mafia states specializing in drug trafficking. In Venezuela, what began as a few corrupt military officials turning a blind eye to drug trafficking in return for kickbacks ended up with a state takeover of drug-trafficking routes through the country. As the award-winning Brazilian journalist Leonardo Coutinho has reported, for instance, the Venezuelan diplomatic service became a cheap and secure international distribution channel for drugs. According to the Bolivian pilot who personally flew dozens of such missions, hundreds of kilos of cocaine were regularly flown in diplomatic pouches protected by international law from inspection or control by government officials. The parcels would be flown weekly from Bolivia to Venezuela and, at times, onward to Havana: a three-nation mafia-state confederacy conspiring to put the resources of the state in the service of big-time drug trafficking in exchange for huge profits for those running the nation.[15]

But the melding of the Venezuelan state and criminal organization goes beyond drug trafficking. In Guayana, Venezuela's southeastern mining region, military officials have long been deeply involved in the notoriously violent, dangerous, and exploitative business of illegal gold mining. "Keeping order" in the vast, thinly inhabited, gold-rich jungle regions has always been a bloody business. In recent years, local military officials have increasingly turned over the whole distasteful task to criminal groups. At first these were often local prison gangs, with military officials effectively outsourcing controls of the mines to them. Prison gang lords would pay a kind of licensing fee to the military for the rights to keep order at specific mining sites. In the mines, ruthless violence would be meted out to ensure that harshly exploited miners turn over all the gold they mine to the prison gangs. Massacres of miners suspected of holding back some of the mined gold were common, and the region is so remote the killings were often never reported. Meanwhile, the army officers sitting at the top of the system got ferried from one expensive restaurant to the next aboard luxury SUVs.

Later, when conflict between rival prison gang lords threatened the stability of the arrangement, the military turned increasingly to the ELN, a Colombian guerrilla group, to control the mines—adding a further layer of "criminal management" to the chain. In ELN-controlled mining camps, all aspects of everyday life are run for the profit of ELN. From grocery stores, pool halls, and restaurants to brothels and health clinics, every business is either run directly by ELN operatives or pays protection money (known as "vaccines") to them. Failure to be vaccinated, as everyone knows, can be harmful to your health.

There is no prospect of Nicolás Maduro's investigative police or the courts doing much to clamp down on such arrangements. A key distinguishing mark of a mafia state is the way the investigative functions of the state are taken over by criminal elements and come to act as key enablers of the system. This is a key reason that, paradoxically, mafia states are rarely struck by corruption scandals. It normally takes a measure of prosecutorial power to propel a story of wrongdoing into a sustained public scandal. The normal progression of criminal proceedings, from investigation to indictment to trial, lends a structure around which journalists can produce a series of stories that, together, make up a scandal. Where investigators resolutely refuse to investigate, it is rare for stories of wrongdoing to escalate to the level of scandal.

While budding mafia states always set out to create a small oligarchy of reliably loyal connected businessmen, Hungary's Viktor Orbán distinguishes himself for the forthrightness with which he pursues this objective. In Hungary, putting Orbán's preferred cadre of connected businessmen on the receiving end of the economy's most lucrative lines of business is an explicit policy goal—empowering Hungarian national capital. Orbán speaks with startling frankness about this, openly describing how he has sought to create a layer of connected businesspeople who owe every part of their substantial fortunes to him and of the need to pick out committed nationalists for the role. That the mechanisms these "Hungarian national capitalists" use to enrich themselves would be considered criminal anywhere else is not mentioned in Orbán's propaganda but is entirely clear to anyone who cares to look closely at their wealth and its origins.

A March 2018 investigation by Reuters underlines the startlingly brazen modus operandi.[16] Under European Union rules, the EU—an organization that Orbán virulently attacks on an almost daily basis—is committed to providing billions of euros in development assistance to the less-developed regions within the union. In Hungary, hundreds of millions in EU aid was earmarked to develop tourism infrastructure in Keszthely, a derelict resort town on the southern tip of Lake Balaton, the largest body of water in central Europe. In the months before the announcement was made, however, a slew of oligarchs close to Orbán began buying up run-down lakeside hotels in Keszthely at fire-sale prices—properties that would multiply in value once the foreign aid funds coming from Europe were invested in highways, electricity, sanitation, parks, and other enhancements. The contracts to implement those public works would, predictably, end up in the same businesspeople's pockets. Viktor Orbán has perfected the art of railing against the EU all morning and stuffing EU money into his cronies' pockets all afternoon. And the corruption in Keszthely is no exception: according to the independent Corruption Research Center Budapest, 90 percent of the total revenue from EU-funded public procurement contracts in Hungary now ends up under the control of Orbán allies, with cost overruns that can be two to ten times the size of the original budget estimates.[17]

So far, this is pretty humdrum—no different from hundreds of corrupt arrangements the world over. Dmitry Firtash's $3 billion grabbing of Russian gas assets under Kremlin sponsorship comes to mind, as do any number of other corrupt deals the world over. The mafia element comes in when you realize the people enriched by these arrangements are central to keeping the government in power. Like any good mafia boss, Orbán expects his captains to kick some of the loot they make upstairs in the form of favors that solidify the boss's grip on power. In return, he provides blanket immunity from prosecution, enabled by his iron grip over the nation's courts and prosecutors.

Following the Russian model, Orbán's cronies then act as proxies to expand Orbán's power: funding his campaigns and buying up regional newspapers to ensure they never criticize the prime minister. In 2018, a dozen independent media owners handed control of over four hundred news websites, newspapers, TV channels, and radio stations to the Central European Press and Media Foundation, a front group controlled by Orbán's allies.[18] Recently, Orbán's cronies have expanded their scope of action, buying up news outlets in the rest of eastern Europe to expand Orbán's ideological reach beyond Hungary's borders. The entire arrangement works as a finely tuned machine for extracting rents from Hungarian and European taxpayers illicitly and ensuring the impunity of the enablers and the stability of the ultimate boss. In this, as in so much else, Viktor Orbán is Vladimir Putin's star pupil.

Illicit: Has Today's World Become a Safer Place for Large, Transnational Criminal Cartels?

Full-fledged mafia states in the Venezuelan mold are extreme phenomena. Countries that develop a rule-of-law-based state rarely revert to the kinds of criminal enterprises at the root of the state. Yet the rise of mafia states has made life immeasurably easier for transnational criminal cartels, which now find permanent safe harbors inside states run by their own.

Partly as a result, we are living in a sort of golden age for transnational crime networks. Mexican drug cartels are increasingly powerful, sourcing a wider array of narcotics into increasingly sophisticated trafficking and distribution networks. In North Africa and the Balkans, criminal gangs specialized in smuggling everything from cigarettes to people find growing business opportunities in a porous, unevenly patrolled European border. Lightly governed, semi-recognized territories from Abkhazia and South Ossetia (Georgia) to Transnistria (Moldova) to Kosovo (Serbia) have found that their twilight status both inside and outside the international system makes them valuable weapons-trafficking hubs. And traditional dictatorships from Myanmar to North Korea find that their state status allows them to pursue everything from currency counterfeiting to methamphetamine production with levels of impunity unavailable to nonstate actors.

Recent years have seen a sharp rise in concern over globalization "going into reverse" as a result of trade frictions between the United States and China, European disunion, and the sense that consensus around multilateralism, free trade, and global integration has frayed. Surely the coronavirus pandemic has slowed down the international travel of people and products. Yet in the criminal underworld, globalization continues full speed ahead, aided by underlying structural changes that have accelerated the mobility of people, data, ideas, and capital. And where various strands of the story we have been telling begin to intertwine, things become dangerous.

The Iranian theocracy, for example, maintains active links with criminal proxy organizations. Hezbollah, its Lebanese proxy, is known to be active in weapons and drug trafficking, terrorist-financing operations, money laundering, and a host of other illegal activities. Hezbollah has found a convenient safe haven in Venezuela, where a long-standing Levantine Arab community allows operatives to blend in with the locals. Of course, the Venezuelan narcostate finds plenty of room for collaboration with Hezbollah.

Transnational criminal networks are inherently tricky to detect. They allow collaboration across geographies and criminal enterprises that may be difficult to discover and have knock-on consequences that can be difficult if not impossible to foresee. The route to smuggle cigarettes today may be used to move illegal immigrants tomorrow, terrorists next week, and surface-to-air missiles next year. Once the procedures are in place, the right palms greased, and the relationships cemented, the businessperson's natural propensity to diversify, turning from one business opportunity to the next, takes hold, and the future becomes impossible to predict.

At the far end of populism, polarization, and post-truth lies an international system littered with actors that see lawlessness as the normal condition of humankind, actors only too happy to traffic anything and everything for profit. The notion that free societies can learn to coexist side by side with a proliferation of mafia states is likely to prove a mirage. Lawlessness anywhere is a threat to security everywhere.

Barbarians Inside the Gates: The Russification of Interpol

Transnational criminal networks have an advantage over their adversaries in traditional law enforcement because they're precisely that: transnational. In a world of formally segmented national jurisdictions, their ability to move people, contraband, and money easily across porous borders leaves the patchwork of national police authorities perpetually playing catch-up. National law enforcement bodies find it awkward to coordinate across borders, and this friction is baked into the business models of the most successful criminal syndicates. Transnationalization comes with its own risks: as Odebrecht found out, the more jurisdictions you are corrupting, the more places you may be exposed. Mafia syndicates are always safest when they stay rooted in countries where the authorities have been bought and paid for. Yet the really big money will always attract adventurers willing to take big risks.

The main international body charged with redressing this balance, Interpol, has been understaffed and under-resourced practically since its inception. At its best—and Interpol is rarely at its best—it is meant to act as a clearinghouse for sensitive information between national police bodies. But in mafia states, those national police bodies are often deeply involved in criminal activities themselves, meaning that any information national authorities hand to Interpol has a fairly good chance of filtering back to the people it is meant to target. There's no way around the fact that when you are sharing information through Interpol you are sharing it with the criminals who govern Russia, Hungary, Bulgaria, Montenegro, Burma, Equatorial Guinea, Venezuela, and every other mafia state in between.

As a result, few serious investigators trust Interpol. They are understandably reluctant to share their best information with a body widely assumed to leak like a sieve. The presence at the higher levels of Interpol of official representatives of nation-states run by criminalized governments severely undermines the effectiveness of the one global body designed to take up the fight against transnational criminal networks.

But it is not just that mafia states stand to benefit from access to the information shared through Interpol. It is that the world's premier mafia state, Russia, has waged a multiyear campaign to turn Interpol on its head, using it as an instrument to extend the reach of Putin's power beyond Russia's borders.

For years, the top Russian official in Interpol, Aleksandr V. Prokopchuk, has been using his access to the organization to harass Kremlin critics around the world. Using Interpol's "red notice" system—something akin to an international arrest warrant—he has continually sought to get Russian dissidents jailed wherever they travel. For American businessperson-turned-anti-Putin-activist Bill Browder, dodging Interpol red notices has become something of a way of life, with the organization having waved through red notices against him "dozens of times" in his estimation.[19]

Most of the countries where Browder travels know the background and disregard the politically motivated red notices against him. But not all. In May 2018, Browder live-tweeted his arrest in Spain at the hands of officials who saw his identity flagged in an Interpol database. While the Spanish quickly caught on to their mistake and freed Browder, Russia's campaign against him has undermined the credibility of the red notice system, turning what might have been one of the most useful deterrents to international crime and turning Interpol into something of a joke for many in law enforcement.

Later in 2018, in what must be counted among the Kremlin's most daring international operations of recent years, Russia lobbied hard to have Prokopchuk elected Interpol president and amassed nearly enough support to carry it out. Only a last-minute campaign by Browder and a rear-guard diplomatic push from Western allies prevented his elevation. But only just: Prokopchuk was named Interpol vice president instead.

In practice, the presidency of Interpol is a largely ceremonial post. But the Prokopchuk nomination served a valuable signaling role. The circus that surrounded his nomination further eroded the trust that law enforcement agencies worldwide had in Interpol. And a malfunctioning Interpol is a highly desirable outcome for the world's mafia states.

9

THE 3P AUTOCRATS GO GLOBAL

3P practitioners are not content to just quietly solidify power over their own societies. They are also pioneering a new form of international collaboration, creating formal and informal networks of ties aimed at enshrining their legitimacy, making money, enhancing their national and personal security, and, most importantly, ensuring their grip on power. Often their international joint ventures, alliances, and shared activities with other leaders who also utilize 3P strategies are conducted under a mantle of utmost secrecy. This new form of ultrasecret diplomacy is aimed at creating bonds of solidarity among rulers who may differ markedly in their ideology but share a distinctive conception of power as permanent and checks on it as unacceptable and avoidable.

Alliances between nations are the bread and butter of international relations. Therefore, there should be nothing special about leaders who rely on populism, polarization, and post-truth to stay in power entering into alliances with other states, as other leaders do. The difference is that the alliances sought by 3P leaders, rather than advancing the national interest, aim to boost and protect their personal interests.

The 3P rulers quickly understand that they can't survive in isolation.

In an interconnected world, isolated power is always precarious. If they're going to be able to keep a steady grip on power, they need to project power beyond their borders, and exploiting solidarity with like-minded leaders achieves that. These foreign allies allow them to create illiberal coalitions that defend them against the liberalizing efforts of important parts of the international community.

Moreover, these transnational arrangements between autocrats serve as a mutual support system. Collaborating with other autocratic nations and their like-minded 3P leaders creates foreign sources of support and, importantly, boosts their legitimacy at home.

But it isn't just autocratic alliances that have gone global, it's also repression itself. The think tank Freedom House calls it "transnational repression," defining it as what happens when "governments reach across borders to silence dissent among diasporas and exiles, including through assassinations, illegal deportations, abductions, digital threats, Interpol abuse, and family intimidation."[1] Freedom House has documented more than six hundred such cases in recent years, affecting dissidents from thirty-one different countries ranging from Sudan and Russia to Equatorial Guinea and Uzbekistan.

Going global opens new and attractive opportunities for 3P leaders and their cronies. They can team up with old-school dictatorships, with democratically elected leaders who have autocratic propensities, or both, each one helping in different ways to put a veneer of diplomatic legitimacy on modes of government outside the liberal norm.

For all their bluster against globalism, 3P autocrats increasingly form their own parallel global network—a kind of upside-down version of the liberal order that can be termed *pseudointernationalism*, the global incarnation of pseudolaw. For these leaders, pseudointernationalism means having one another's back in formal settings: supporting one another's priorities, personnel nominations, and positions in international institutions from Interpol and the International Criminal Court to FIFA, the World Chess Federation, and various United Nations agencies. It means promoting one another's points of view on one another's propaganda organs and advancing mutual interests through the entire spectrum of diplomatic tools, from the vanilla (speeches, position papers, conferences, summits, photo ops) to the decidedly sketchy (Twitter bot armies, active measures, bypassing embargos, financial subterfuges). It means teaming up to launch sophisticated broadcasting systems that beam propaganda directly into the homes of people living in open societies. It means conferring symbolic legitimacy on one another publicly and pooling the resources for holding power privately.

The 3P autocrats seem to find it easy to establish personal bonds with their peers, building strong links even across wide ideological gulfs with those who have adopted the 3Ps and the weakening or even the outright canceling of checks and balances as the keys to amassing and wielding power. This is how the 3P power goes global—by building a tacit, decentralized, and often stealthy network of partnerships between nations governed by illiberal leaders to help each other further common interests. How does this brotherhood operate? Who leads it? How? And what difference does it make?

"DO NOT CONGRATULATE":
The Politics of the Election Night Call

It was a moment that encapsulated the unsettling new normal of today's big-power rivalry. On March 18, 2018, Vladimir Putin won by a landslide in an election virtually no one thought worthy of the name. Even though he had disqualified, jailed, or exiled all of his most credible opponents and shut them entirely out of the broadcast media, Putin had nonetheless felt the need to bolster his win with millions of stuffed ballots, earning him an unseemly 76.7 percent of the vote in Russia's quinquennial charade of democracy.

The world's established democracies grasped that there wasn't much they could do to push back. All they could do was withhold the symbolic legitimacy that comes with international recognition. This had plainly become a matter of concern in Washington, where National Security Council staffers shared the wider consensus that saw Russia as a strategic threat to be contained in the wake of its violent annexation of Crimea in 2014 and its interference in the U.S. presidential elections. Alas, those same National Security Council staffers had become only too aware that President Trump rarely read the briefing materials prepared for him with the greatest of care.

In the end, their solution was simple: they wrote "DO NOT CONGRATULATE" in large print atop the president's briefing notes. It didn't work. Indeed, it backfired. Within days of receiving the briefing, President Trump had called Putin to extend the congratulations his staff had made it a priority to withhold. It was a crucial and coveted signal of American acceptance that, among other similar gestures, gave Putin the confidence it took to reform Russia's constitution in 2020 to allow him to remain in power through 2036.

The leaking of the "DO NOT CONGRATULATE" memo provides a fascinating clue to the dynamics of the congratulations economy. On a world stage where autocrats are increasingly eager to pass themselves off as what they are not, the entire question of the post-election congratulatory phone call has shifted from polite routine into a diplomatic minefield to degrees unthinkable just a few years ago.

Election night congratulations often reveal more about the leaders offering them than about those receiving them. As a rule, the 3P autocrats congratulate both the conventionally elected and their fellow autocrats—a subtle means of erasing the distinction between the two. It is asymmetric, though: leaders of bona fide democracies refrain from personally congratulating those elected in questionable circumstances. When diplomatic necessity imposes an acknowledgment, they will often delegate it to the foreign minister, preserving a little distance. Even for them, it can be risky: in his role as UK foreign secretary, Boris Johnson was roundly criticized for congratulating Victor Orbán on his 2018 election win. In some cases, such as in Angela Merkel's famous 2016 election-eve message to Donald Trump, they'll smuggle a subtle warning into a congratulatory message:

> Germany and America are bound by common values—democracy, freedom, as well as respect for the rule of law and the dignity of each and every person, regardless of their origin, skin color, creed, gender, sexual orientation, or political views. It is based on these values that I wish to offer close cooperation, both with me personally and between our countries' governments.[2]

It doesn't take a master diplomat to read the message in between the lines here.

For the 3P autocrats, piling up congratulatory calls is a valuable means of projecting strength—and the higher-profile the congratulator, the better. When in 2017 Recep Tayyip Erdoğan won a referendum to overhaul the Turkish constitution in order to increase his power, he fielded congratulatory calls from Azerbaijani president Ilham Aliyev, Qatari emir Sheikh Tamim bin Hamad Al Thani, Palestinian president Mahmoud Abbas . . . and Donald Trump. It is easy to see which message will have done most to bolster him.

This talk of congratulations may seem frivolous and arcane; it is not. The 3P leaders are, almost by definition, insecure about the legitimacy of their leadership and centrally concerned with inflating it. In such conditions, questions of protocol and ritual can become an obsession.

The power that rests on these leaders critically needs to veil its autocratic core: that is why they devote considerable resources to sustaining a narrative that legitimates them, however obviously belied by the facts. Any sense that they are out of step with the international mainstream is one of the most serious threats to this narrative. They need to convince their own people that the rest of the world respects them, accepts their governing practices, and treats them as equals. Where sustaining an illusion of normal democratic order is a priority, care must be taken that international blowback doesn't undo the hard-won achievements of domestic propaganda.

The pitfalls are real. When Venezuela's Nicolás Maduro won an election in 2018 widely seen as rigged, the question of who would lend it a patina of legitimacy by showing up in person to witness his inauguration became a kind of fixation. In the event, only a handful of foreign personalities went to witness the charade, most of them fellow Latin American leaders of the far left. From the rest of the world, just two leaders came: Anatoly Bibilov, president of South Ossetia, and Raul Khajimba, president of Abkhazia. Both are breakaway slices of Georgia that act, effectively, as Russian puppet states. Their independence is recognized by almost no one in the rest of the world, save for Russia and a handful of its clients: Syria, Nicaragua,

Venezuela, and Nauru. Far from bolstering Maduro's standing, his dramatic inability to attract leaders of greater standing only under-scored how his fraudulent election failed to bestow the democratic legitimacy he coveted.

Maduro's predicament was not his alone. In many cases, the 3P leaders can produce only a thin façade of democratic rule. It is an artificial construct that does not withstand much scrutiny because it is not designed for people interested in very much scrutiny. What they need from the international arena is not very deep: just enough, in terms of international validation, to be able to reinforce the domestic democratic charade.

This is why Putin congratulates Duterte, who congratulates Orbán, who congratulates Daniel Ortega, who congratulates Nicolás Maduro, who congratulates Putin in a closed circle of autocratic soli-darity. This circle—call it Autocrats Without Borders—is increasingly becoming a relevant factor in international affairs.

The international ties built through congratulatory diplomacy be-comes tangible through personal contact. Experts at stagecraft and the projection of power, the 3P autocrats have learned to respect the power of image. Bringing them together either with other 3P autocrats or with old-school dictators, the manipulated summit becomes a key asset in a bid to dispel any doubt about the legitimacy of their power.

Sometimes attempts to do this go spectacularly wrong, drawing merciless ridicule. On President Trump's first overseas trip in May 2017, he was photographed alongside Saudi king Salman bin Ab-dulaziz Al Saud and Egyptian president Abdel el-Sisi handling a mys-terious glowing orb that seemed lifted directly out of a comic book villain's lair. The occasion was the official opening of Riyadh's Global Center for Combating Extremist Ideology, but it hardly mattered: the over-the-top optics ran away with the photo op, turning it into an instant social media sensation and drawing comparisons to every-thing from *Star Trek* and Harry Potter to the conclave of witches in *Macbeth*.

Later, on the sidelines of the 2019 G7 summit in Biarritz, France, Donald Trump would greet Egypt's el-Sisi with an effusive "Where's my favorite dictator?"[3]—an instance of the kind of "saying the quiet part out loud" that the American president was becoming known for. In the past this would have been seen as just a diplomatic gaffe. In the autocrats' world, however, this is how true, macho presidents "tell it like it is."

Such shoddy showmanship would never be tolerated in Putin's Moscow. As in so much else, the Russian president leads the way when it comes to projecting power through the pomp and circumstance of summits, bilateral encounters, and carefully staged international "conferences." In a series of highly choreographed tripartite meetings with the leaders of Iran and Turkey, the Kremlin showed how mastery of the optics can not only bolster legitimacy but lead to real diplomatic advances on the ground.

But it would be a mistake to think the 3P autocrats turn to the international arena solely for strategic reasons, whether international or domestic. For many, ego is a powerful driver. All politicians of any vintage share a marked tendency toward narcissism. In this respect, however, autocrats are often more explicit in letting the world know that they possess special and unique talents, marking them out from the rest of humanity. One of the occupational hazards of being a 3P autocrat is being deluded by the belief that they are destined for the world stage, that their genius and historical weight are too vast to be contained within a single country. Narcissism, it turns out, can be a power tool.

Take ALBA, Hugo Chávez's much-trumpeted Bolivarian Alternative for the Americas.[4] Offered up as an alternative to the ill-fated Free Trade Area of the Americas (Spanish acronym: ALCA), the Bolivarian Alternative was peddled as an off-ramp for neoliberalism, a palpable incarnation of the old leftist trope that "another world is possible." Never shy about voicing his ambitions, Chávez promoted ALBA in grandiose terms as the first step in realizing Simón Bolívar's nineteenth-century dream of a union of Latin American nations strong enough to offer a counterweight to the United States. As the Pink Wave of center-left and leftist governments swept into power through the first decade of the twenty-first century, ALBA meetings became the "it" affairs on the region's diplomatic calendar: the place where the dream was to be built.

Hypertrophic proposals followed. Chávez announced he would build a rail line between Caracas and Buenos Aires, a gargantuan project whose financial, environmental, engineering, and commercial viability nobody had made a serious attempt at assessing, but which made for irresistible headlines all the same. Later it was a trans-Andean natural gas pipeline designed to skirt around Brazil, apparently because its government had expressed skepticism about the project. That the projects made really no sense at all except as flashy signaling devices about ALBA's ambitions seemed to bother no one very much. The announcements acted more as messaging, signposts of strategic direction, and, especially, very public assertions of unbridled power, not actual plans for real-world projects.

None of these projects were ever completed. What money was allocated to them was never accounted for, vanishing in the puff of corruption that enveloped every major initiative of the Chávez era. The promises served as cover for a grand act of state larceny, yes, but they did more than that. They projected a grand narrative scaled up to match the autocrat's ego.

An Invasion of Bot Armies: Catalonia and Beyond

To see this Russian ambition in action, consider the "sharp power" approach it used to undermine the Spanish state. The label, coined by Christopher Walker and Jessica Ludwig, encompasses the kinds of disruptive active-measures campaigns Putin's Russia has made its trademark.[5] And while sharp power has been deployed all around the globe, few uses have been as successful as the online war that Russia coordinated around Catalonian separatists' ill-fated quest for independence from Spain in late 2017.

Catalonian nationalism was precisely the kind of social fault line the Kremlin loves to expose and exploit: a long-standing fissure ready to be tapped for geopolitical advantage. To be sure, the Russians did not create it, but then their modus operandi has always been to opportunistically seek out social fault lines that arise spontaneously and jump on them with a vengeance.

The Kremlin had understood that Spain was heading toward a

major crisis, with populist nationalists in Catalonia building up a head of steam in favor of secession that could destabilize one of Western Europe's big economies. Moscow had amassed vast experience conducting these kinds of influence operations online, picking out countries' big internal fault lines and mining them for all their destabilization potential. They were good at this.

But in Catalonia, the Russians had a thorny problem. Their bots were in the wrong language. For years, the Kremlin had been building up its army of online bots, custom-making them to wreak havoc on English-speaking public opinion. Those bots had been programmed to follow one another's social media accounts, helping each simulate having a large audience, which helped them build up a substantial following of real humans as well. But English bots were no use in trying to get at the debate over Catalonia that was becoming the critical fault line in Spain. You obviously can't destabilize the Spanish public sphere with thousands of bots tweeting and posting in Russian or in English. What they needed was a different bot army *en español*.

Some of the bots they made up on the fly, but for the rest, the Kremlin leaned on an ally. For the better part of a decade, Venezuela's Ministry of Communications had been amassing its own bot army. It had been designed to manipulate Venezuela's public opinion, not Spain's, but it was connected with plenty of humans. And humans who spoke Spanish, at that.

Soon the campaign began. Augmented by the Venezuelan bots, the Russian bot army set off a storm of tweets, messages, and links to fake stories all minutely calculated to deepen the Catalan separatist crisis. The tools of surreptitious manipulation had burst their national boundaries, coming together to advance their common interest in sowing chaos and undermining democratic institutions everywhere.

Russian and Venezuelan bots joined together to sow FUD: fear, uncertainty, and doubt. Stories of cops beating up old ladies lining up to vote were exaggerated, sensationalized, and relentlessly repeated. Baseless stories about Madrid planning martial law for Barcelona were whipped up by Russian propaganda outlets and then repeated until they became widely believed. Preying on real fault lines in Spanish society, a few dozen people in Moscow and Caracas at the helm of a massive botnet army were able to aggressively destabilize a consolidated Western democracy.

The 2017 Russian-Venezuelan pincer movement on Catalonia's public sphere shows just one of the ways in which the 3Ps can assert themselves by turning democracy's core strengths against it. Twitter had been built as an open platform for debate, a place with no barriers to entry where anyone could engage with anyone else on any topic. This strength could prove its undoing.

The cyberarmies developed for Venezuela extended the use of these tools well beyond Catalonia. First they made a splash in Mexico, where the 2018 presidential election campaign was suffused with charges and countercharges of foreign digital meddling. With the outgoing president, Enrique Peña Nieto, already notorious for employing armies of trolls and bots (memorably dubbed "Peñabots") to slander opponents, the 2018 campaign was soon flooded with unverifiable claims of outsiders seeking to influence Mexico's 71.3 million internet users. Peña's supporters charged that as much as 83 percent of the social media content about the election that favored the eventual winner, Andrés Manuel López Obrador (AMLO to his many followers), originated in Russia and Ukraine.[6] AMLO's campaign countered that the ruling party's bots were still active on behalf of the ruling party's candidate, José Antonio Meade. The fog of accusations and counteraccusations produced precisely the kind of impenetrable sense of uncertainty that peddlers of disinformation thrive on.

But perhaps the most destabilizing use of the Russian-Venezuelan bot armies came in late 2019, when a spasm of social unrest gripped large swaths of Latin America. As so often happens, the bots did not start the trouble. Instead, they identified rising unrest early and rode the wave with relish. According to research by Constella Intelligence, a Spanish data analysis firm:

> During the weeks following the emergence of the sociopolitical crises, Constella's analysts identified a small number of accounts that generated a large volume of publications in relation to street protests. In Colombia, 1% of users analyzed generated 33% of the analyzed

results, and in Chile, 0.5% of users generated 28% of results. These high activity profiles flood the digital public debate with their comments and content and are considered statistically anomalous given the level of frequency of their activity over the period analyzed. This is a key indicator of information disorder. . . . Constella's analysis has identified a total of 175 anomalous identities that were actively participating in both crises. When researching the public geolocation indicated by these users or profiles, 58% of those publicly sharing their geolocation were geolocated in Venezuela.[7]

Many of these suspect accounts specialized in amplifying content from Russian and Venezuelan state propaganda organs: RT, Sputnik, Telesur, and similar media.

Beyond the Russian-Venezuelan bot army universe, digital meddling is rife. An increasingly polarized and populist Israel under Bibi Netanyahu leveraged its own military veterans to form the backbone of a cyberintelligence industry that created highly sophisticated software often sold to autocrats to spy on their own dissidents. A sprawling investigation by *Ha'aretz*, Israel's main center-left paper, found evidence of Israeli firms selling military-derived software for repressive ends around the world, from Mexico and Angola to Azerbaijan, Ethiopia, Indonesia, Uganda, Uzbekistan, and elsewhere. In many cases, software was used to spy on regime opponents. While the commercial transactions were legal and the Israeli companies involved were private, the technology has military origins, and promoting exports is a government priority.

Cuban counterintelligence expertise, Chinese riot control equipment, Israeli cyberintelligence, Russian electronic communications intercepts, Iranian sanctions-busting, and dark-banking expertise: each old-style autocracy has specialized in producing a few of the goods and services autocrats need to cement their power. And they're happy to share. The global trade in means of repression is shrouded in secrecy and its scale difficult to guess at. What requires no guesswork is this: today's autocrats can secure all the tools they need to hang on to power indefinitely with just a few calls to friendly capitals around the world. The new autocrats like their globalization.

As the 3Ps go global, silence has been rediscovered as a guiding principle for the international order. Working on a pre–World War II vision of the international order, they hold the principle of national self-determination sacrosanct. Or rather, they leverage the phraseology of noninterference indiscriminately as an all-purpose alibi to undermine any international challenge to the legitimacy of an autocratic government.

This professed love for noninterference needs to be read laterally. That it is superficial and not what it pretends to be almost goes without saying. The 3P autocrats happily meddle in their neighbors' affairs when it suits their interests. While Recep Tayyip Erdoğan is quick to blame Western meddling in Turkish affairs for any setback his administration faces, Turkish troops have actively occupied a 3,460-square-kilometer chunk of the Aleppo governorate in northern Syria since 2016. Venezuela's Hugo Chávez made the ritual denunciation of U.S. meddling in Venezuelan affairs a centerpiece of his rhetoric, yet evidence keeps emerging that his government funded far-left movements everywhere from Argentina and Ecuador to Spain and Lebanon, with the occasional discovery of suitcases full of cash being artlessly smuggled through foreign customs houses to provide comic relief. Enough has been written already about Russian meddling in foreign elections around the world, less on China's systematic efforts to bolster autocrats through lucrative loans and development projects. And Iran's global network of influence, largely in the hands of its Lebanese proxy Hezbollah, has been used to do everything from blowing up the Israeli Embassy in Buenos Aires and a Jewish community center in the same city to trafficking weapons in Paraguay to laundering money in Vancouver and wholesaling Colombian cocaine destined for Europe.

The 3P autocrats' principled stand against "foreign meddling" is a ruse: sleight of hand used to conceal an agenda too sordid to be acknowledged. What the 3P autocrats object to is not interference in the abstract but rather one quite specific form of it: the use of international norms and standards to constrain a ruler's ability to wield power arbitrarily. The autocrats want, above all else, to wield their power without hindrance. To the extent international norms become a hindrance, they will band together to oppose them.

It is this hostility to norms that hem them in that's at the root of the loose confederation of 3P autocrats, what I think of as Autocrats Without Borders. Under the banner of noninterference, the 3P autocrats champion a hollowed-out form of internationalism: solidarity without constraints.

The liberal international order is, in the million-times-repeated mantra, "rules-based"—and there's nothing the members of the 3P autocracies more reliably oppose than rules designed to constrain them. From the Brexiteers' enormous disdain of European banana regulations to Rodrigo Duterte's scorn for international human rights treaties that prevent cops from killing people for any or no reason, rejection of international limits on sovereign power is an obsession to the autocrats.

Invisible Armies, Artificial Islands, and Little Green Men

One way to avoid being constrained is to avoid being seen—or, if seen, being identified—and on this score, the stealthocratic capacities developed by today's autocrats shine in their ambition. For much of human history, it had been taken for granted that large-scale military operations could not be kept secret. Armies are big, noisy things; move them around and people will notice. Today, though, stealth has moved to cover even this most-impossible-to-hide of domains.

Take China and its aggressive move to build military bases in parts of the South China Sea it claims as its own, a claim that is not internationally recognized. It is a classic lesson in how power can somehow be plainly obvious and shrouded in mystery at the same time.

Trillions of dollars' worth of trade passes through South China Sea waterways each year. The area is an inevitable corridor for ships carrying goods to and from some of the world's most buoyant economies: China, Singapore, Malaysia, Indonesia, Vietnam, Taiwan, the Philippines, and the tiny oil-rich sultanate of Brunei. Some of the channels in these busy waterways need to be dredged to be kept open to shipping. China long ago realized that by depositing the silt that results from dredging along a few strategically placed shallow-water points in the seabed, it could create artificial islands that it could then use to project its power and strengthen its territorial claims in the South China Sea.

The policy was deeply controversial: islands were being built in parts of the sea subject to a baffling multiplication of overlapping claims. China, Brunei, Vietnam, the Philippines, and Taiwan all separately claim sovereignty over the areas where China "created" these new silt islands. The United States, whose naval supremacy in the Pacific has long been the linchpin of security arrangements in the region, greeted China's island-building with alarm, warning it could set the entire region on a course to war.

China's response was very twenty-first century. It couldn't exactly deny it was building the islands—the gargantuan engineering project was plainly visible to passing ships, aircraft, and satellites. So it settled on a policy of obfuscation: denying, against all plausibility, that the project had military purposes. It described the first artificial island as a shelter for local fishing boats.[8] As it grew, the cover story morphed. By 2018, a spokesperson for the Chinese Academy of Engineering was describing what had grown to a network of fourteen artificial islands, six of them large enough to host military installations, as intended for "marine meteorological monitoring, warning, forecasting, prediction, and scientific research."[9]

That the claim was preposterous was, in some ways, the core of its appeal. Long after China had successfully built three large, sophisticated naval and aerial bases on human-made atolls in the region, complete with port installations, air and surveillance facilities, wind turbines, and large barracks and administrative buildings, its officials continued to maintain that it was merely building weather stations and shelters for small fishing boats.

By early 2019, as Beijing began to move sophisticated surface-to-air and surface-to-sea missile installations onto the bases—easily visible in satellite photos of the islands—its massive stealth sea grab was mostly a fait accompli: China now controls the South China Sea in fact, if not in law. Even then, the regime stuck by its claim of being just highly committed to meteorological research.

Notice again the juxtaposition of spectacle and stealth here. Needless to say, China did not expect its denials to be believed. Satellite and aerial photos of the sites left no real room for doubt about its intentions. Yet a policy of deadpan issuances of plainly absurd denials shows the synergy between stealth and post-truth. It is all of a piece with Facebook's repeated declarations that user privacy is a paramount concern, Sepp Blatter's pious declarations of concern about clean governance in world football,[10] and Kris Kobach's adamant declarations of deep worry about voter fraud.[11] The point of these kinds of declarations is not to be believed, exactly—at least not beyond a tiny fringe of committed partisans with a material interest in the lie. They are, instead, instances of post-truth, designed to generate just enough confusion and doubt to create room to maneuver in seeking to reach or keep power.

Nor is China's effective takeover of the South China Sea the most egregious case of military stealth. That crown goes to Russia and its stunningly effective stealth encroachment on the territory of its southern neighbor, Ukraine.

In March 2014, following the overthrow of what amounted to a Russian puppet regime in Ukraine, Russia lashed out with an aggressive move to annex Ukraine's Crimean Peninsula. The commandos that soon spread out around Simferopol, the Crimean capital, and other parts of the region didn't wave a Russian flag. Their combat fatigues had no identifying insignia. In fact, although the uniforms looked exactly like the standard-issue green fatigues used by the Russian army, they had been stripped of any markings whatsoever, to the point that locals began referring to them as "little green men."

Back in Moscow, an aggressive campaign of public obfuscation was already underway. On March 3, 2014, Russian foreign minister Sergey Lavrov described the units as Crimean "self-defense forces" created by local ethnic Russians to ward off supposed threats to them by the local Ukrainians.[12] The explanation lacked any semblance of verisimilitude: nobody locally knew any of these people. Their advance was plainly coordinated and executed with professional efficiency. That Crimea was being invaded by the Russian army couldn't seriously be doubted . . . but neither could it be admitted in public, at least not quite yet.

As Russian troops took over the small airport at Simferopol, Russia's ambassador to the European Union continued to obfuscate. "There are no Russian troops whatsoever in Crimea," he said.[13] Again, the point was not so much to be believed as to muddy the waters long enough for the military operation to succeed.

These "self-defense" forces moved with unusual speed to arrange security for a "referendum" on March 16 on whether Crimeans wanted to remain part of Ukraine or would prefer join the Russian Federation. The referendum was designed to provide a paper-thin patina of pseudolegal legitimacy to what everyone could see was a Russian military land grab. No one in the international community recognized it as legitimate: how could they, when people were expected to vote on their own future in the middle of an invasion, with no proper campaign, and under the watchful eye of heavily armed soldiers everyone knew were from the Russian army?

It didn't matter. Nearly 97 percent of Crimeans, we were told, had voted to become part of Russia. The following day, Vladimir Putin "accepted" Crimea's request to join the Russian Federation. In less than three weeks, Russia had become the first country to annex the territory of a neighbor by force of arms since Saddam Hussein's 1991 invasion of Kuwait.

With Crimea as proof of concept, Putin would escalate an aggressive campaign of territorial conquest against Ukraine while steadfastly denying he was doing any such thing. In 2015, Putin launched a secret war to gain control over the easternmost regions of Ukraine: the Donets Basin region known as the Donbass. Unlike Crimea, which historically had been part of Russia and where ethnic Russians made up an overwhelming majority, the Donbass was mixed: ethnic Russians made up a large minority of the region, around 38 percent, but were the majority in urban areas, including the major cities of Donetsk and Luhansk, which had received large numbers of Russian workers during the Soviet period. It was these areas that Moscow would mostly target in a war it would publicly claim it wasn't fighting.

The initial idea seems to have been to run the Crimean playbook once more, pretending it was local ethnic Russians who were in the driver's seat of a struggle for self-preservation. Of course, in mainland Ukraine, making a grab for its second-largest city, they ran into much more determined resistance. The result was a two-year war that left over ten thousand dead and displaced some 1.4 million Ukrainians from their homes. By the end, although Russia refrained from annexation, Ukraine had lost control of its two major eastern cities.

To this day, the Kremlin continues to maintain the fiction that its troops are not involved in the fighting. The claim has been maintained against an overwhelming mountain of evidence, including clear evidence that only Russian military units could have been in a position to fire the sophisticated Buk surface-to-air missile that shot down a Malaysian airliner on July 17, 2014.[14] Officially, Russia continues to deny to this day having ever deployed any anti-missile batteries to Ukraine or participated in the Donbass war at all. That mind-bending, post-truth approach to knowing and not knowing at the same time is especially visible in the Donbass war: a presidential decree signed by Vladimir Putin in May 2015 classifies "peacetime deaths" suffered by the Russian military as a state secret, which makes it a crime to discuss (or even acknowledge) the casualties of a war that, officially, Russia is not involved in at all.[15]

Yet what was Vladimir Putin to do? Deep into the twenty-first century, it is diplomatically untenable for a country to project its military power into a neighbor's territory openly. To project military power in today's context, it is necessary to cloak it in a cloud of secrecy that need not be minimally believable to accomplish its goals.

Or take Iran. Though locked in an immensely tense diplomatic confrontation with the United States, Iran is not a considerable military power in any traditional sense. Yes, the Islamic Republic has long worked to secure a nuclear weapon, but there is a huge gap, a "missing middle" between its nuclear ambition and its conventional military posture. Since the catastrophic folly of the Iran-Iraq War in the 1980s, the mullahs have understood that their comparative advantage could not lie in conventional military forces. So instead they've developed the Quds Force, an offshoot of the elite Islamic Revolutionary Guard that's been described as perhaps the world's most sophisticated proxy force: an invisible army stretching out throughout most of the Islamic world and beyond, with an estimated 250,000 fighters in total.

By the start of the 2020s, Iranian proxies controlled much of Lebanon and Yemen as well as important parts of Syria, the Palestinian territories, and Iraq. Its most ambitious and forward-leaning proxy, Hezbollah, runs cells throughout Latin America. Other proxies operate freely in lightly governed parts of Southeast Asia, such as remote areas of Indonesia, and the Philippines. Through its proxies, Iran has attacked targets in Buenos Aires and plotted to blow up the Saudi ambassador at Café Milano, a Washington, DC, restaurant popular among the city's power elites. Iran has a third-rate conventional army but a first-rate ability to project military force worldwide, invisibly.

But the projection of state power need not be military. Cuba has pioneered the use of doctors, nurses, and sports trainers as spearheads of complex foreign influence operations. Under the banner of a program called Cuban Medical Internationalism, Cuba sends tens of thousands of skilled workers—around half of them doctors—to work in communities all around the world.

Many of the doctors are in fact pseudodoctors, quickly and shoddily trained and given diplomas as medical doctors so they can be made pawns of Cuban diplomacy. Part moneymaking scheme (the communist regime retains the vast bulk of the payments countries make for this aid), part influence operation, Cuban doctors concentrate in areas of strategic interest to the regime in Havana. At one point, upward of forty thousand of them were at work in Venezuela alone, an ally whose oil shipments supplied nearly all of Cuba's energy and supported the government as well. While intelligence professionals assume some number of these medical professionals are, in fact, spies remitting valuable information back to Havana, the precise percentage is unknowable. What is known, however, is that Cuban Medical Internationalism has allowed Havana an unprecedented degree of plausible deniability as it extends Cuba's substantial intelligence capabilities around the world. After all, who would be so cynical as to suspect a doctor?

Dawn of the GONGOs: The Scourge of Fake NGOs

A casual viewer not privy to the background would be hard-pressed to identify World Without Nazism as anything but what it purports to be: a civil society organization devoted to fighting the resurgence of Nazi ideology in Europe. And who could be opposed to that?

Considerable care has been taken to sustain this perception. As James Kirchick put it in a landmark investigative piece on the group, "on the surface, World Without Nazism (WWN) has all the trappings of an international non-governmental organization (NGO) committed to fighting the scourges of bigotry and anti-Semitism: Glitzy conferences in European capitals. Dry, thousand-page reports full of data. Concerned speeches by its leaders calling for vigilance."[16] But WWN is not a civil society organization. Instead, it is a GONGO: a government-organized nongovernmental organization. A fake NGO.

In the case of WWN, the agenda bears all the hallmarks you would expect given its KGB-era active-measures pedigree. WWN's modus operandi seems to be to emulate the actions of governments opposed to Moscow and attack them as stemming from a hidden neo-Nazi agenda. The line dovetails directly with the Kremlin's propaganda line regarding the conflicts on its borders, where any move by Ukraine or one of the Baltic states to establish some diplomatic distance from Moscow is ascribed to a sinister, fascist hidden agenda. Perhaps grasping that this line would be a tough sell in the West if it was being peddled solely by Russian state organs, the Kremlin went to the considerable trouble of faking a human rights NGO to make its line more appealing outside Russia's own borders.

Like any good active-measures campaign, the WWN succeeded because it contained a grain of truth. Ukraine really does have a neo-Nazi movement that mobilized in the conflict with Russian-backed forces beginning in 2014. Groups like Right Sector and the Azov Battalion (an extremist Ukrainian militia) espoused an extremist ideology that could be fairly described as neo-Nazi. Russian propaganda and WWN rode those groups for all they were worth, enormously overstating their size and influence and portraying them as the hidden hand guiding the entire Ukrainian reform movement. This was backed with outright fabrications: in October 2014, for instance, news was simply invented of anti-Semitic attacks on elderly Jewish residents of Odessa at the hand of Right Sector, and WWN duly noted that it was incensed. But the report was, as the chief rabbi of Ukraine stressed, an outright lie.[17, 18]

Or take Chongryon, the General Association of Korean Residents in Japan. Nominally an NGO, it operates dozens of Korean schools and even a Korean university in Japan. Chongryon has its own banks and, by some estimates, around a third of the pachinko gambling parlors ubiquitous in Japan. Chongryon publishes its own magazines and a daily newspaper, sponsors cultural activities and sports teams for Koreans in Japan in addition to a science and technology association, and operates a travel agency; it even runs three Korean restaurants. Together, Chongryon's businesses may take in hundreds of millions of dollars each year.

And what happens to all that money? It gets remitted back to Chongryon's real owner: the Democratic People's Republic of Korea. Chongryon is a lightly disguised GONGO—in effect a quasi-official arm of the North Korean government in Japan. Five senior Chongryon officials have seats in the DPRK's Supreme People's Assembly. Chongryon's headquarters in Tokyo serves as a sort of unofficial North Korean embassy, providing basic consular services such as issuing North Korean passports and visas. Debate over the legitimacy of Chongryon is a mainstay of Japanese political polemic, especially on the right.

Or take the grandly titled International Organization for Relief, Welfare, and Development. An Islamic aid agency, the IORWD runs programs for disadvantaged people throughout the Muslim world: funding hospitals for victims of the Syrian civil war, schools for the poor in Sudan, and mosques in multiple countries. Through its branches in Indonesia and the Philippines, it also did something somewhat less laudable: it helped fund the 9/11 attacks.

IORWD is a second-degree Saudi GONGO, depending almost entirely for its funding on donations from another Saudi GONGO, the Muslim World League, which receives essentially all its funding from the Saudi state and its royal family. Known until recently as the International Islamic Relief Organization (IIRO), it operates as the humanitarian and development arm of the Muslim World League, which has been deeply implicated in spreading Saudi Arabia's Wahhabi strand of Islamism worldwide since its foundation in 1962. That Osama bin Laden, himself a product of the Saudi elite, would figure out a way to use parts of this organization to fund his terror plots is entirely unsurprising. Indeed, in 2006, the U.S. Treasury Department designated the Indonesian and Philippines branch offices of IIRO as terrorist organizations.

GONGOs are sometimes mobilized in the service of a particular type of falsehood strategy: to simply drown out the voices of legitimate NGOs on an issue. During the United Nations' Universal Periodic Review of Human Rights in Venezuela in 2016, the UN invited civil society organizations to submit reports on the situation in the country. An astronomical 519 reports were filed on Venezuela, the vast majority introduced by NGOs no one had ever heard of before and which, coincidentally, had only glowing praise for the Venezuelan regime's human rights record. UN secretary-general Ban Ki-moon and the UN High Commissioner for Human Rights eventually denounced this as "fraud on a massive scale," but ultimately, the task of telling apart the real Venezuelan NGOs from the fake ones defeated the UN's bureaucrats, who ended up producing a noncommittal report that generated no pressure on Venezuela to actually improve its human rights practices.[19]

GONGOs can be put to a wide variety of uses. Daniel Baer, the Obama-era U.S. ambassador to the Organization for Security and Cooperation in Europe, has described the way governments use GONGOs to gum up the work of the OSCE. At meetings designed to allow civil society activists to interact directly with OSCE diplomats, swarms of GONGOs act like the in-person equivalents of internet trolls, constantly derailing conversations with rants that have little bearing on the questions at hand. Baer describes how GONGO officials would book meeting rooms at the conference with no plans to use them, simply to deprive legitimate NGOs of the space. He even describes GONGOs swarming around the refreshment table at the beginning of each coffee break and making off with every last scrap of food. It is a nuisance, of course, but it is more than that. "At side events hosted by bona fide civil society organizations," Baer explains, "states sometimes dispatch their GONGOs to intimidate human rights defenders by sending a 'big brother' message that brave advocates' words and actions are being monitored and reported back to their capitals."[20]

GONGOs come in all shapes and sizes, from the small, obscure organizations sent to gum up OSCE meetings to global household names like Hezbollah, which in some ways is little more than an Iranian GONGO.

Of course, it is not only autocracies that use GONGOs. The U.S. National Endowment for Democracy (NED), on whose board I served, is arguably the textbook definition of a GONGO. NED styles itself a "a private, non-profit foundation dedicated to the growth and strengthening of democratic institutions around the world," and I can attest to the fact that it guards its political independence zealously. Yet while it may not be government *controlled*, it's undeniably government *funded*, receiving nearly all its funding from the U.S. government. It is precisely the success of organizations like NED in carrying out its mission that made the model attractive for emulation by autocratic opponents of the liberal order, who camouflage their 3P agenda by noting their superficial similarity with organizations like NED.[21]

GONGOs work well for 3P autocrats because in today's media environment the distinction between different kinds of news outlets and different kinds of sources has become blurred. Appealing to the moral authority of an NGO is a powerful mechanism for manipulating opinion. In previous chapters, we've seen how the 3P autocrats buy up existing media outlets to put them beyond the reach of their critics. That's a winning formula domestically, but when the purpose is to project power beyond your borders, GONGOs can play a similar kind of role.

GONGOs succeed through the same kind of isomorphic mimicry

that makes pseudolaw so hard to spot. These pseudo-NGOs piggy-back off of the legitimacy of real civil society organizations to bolster precisely the opposite sorts of values.

The panorama becomes especially muddled when GONGOs don a journalist's cap. Here, enunciating the differences between a legitimate state-supported broadcaster and a propaganda outfit mimicking one is an especially fraught exercise. After all, if Britain has the BBC, Germany Deutsche Welle, and Japan the NHK, why shouldn't Russia have Russia Today, Venezuela and its Latin American allies Telesur, and Iran Press TV? The honest answer ("because the former are real news-gathering organizations and the latter propaganda outlets") is both true and trivially easy to counter with the accusation, "I'm not fake news, you're fake news."

3P autocracies with international ambitions have learned that it pays to mimic the look and feel of international news. It is how you pass off the propaganda you dream up as straight news to willing consumers in their own living rooms, all around the world. A KGB hand from the Cold War era of active measures would scarcely have believed it possible.

Mind the Tipping Point: From 3P Autocracy to the New Normal

It is remarkable how quickly autocratic backsliding has advanced so far in this century. The techno-utopianism of the early 2000s, when the spread of the internet and the rise of social media seemed an insurmountable problem for the world's autocracies, looks like ancient history today. From Russia to China, today's leading autocracies have mastered the internet as a tool of control—a purpose for which it turns out to be far better suited than liberation.

In the first few years of the century, the few democracies that seemed to be backsliding into some flavor of neopatrimonialism looked like oddities. Berlusconi's Italy and Thaksin's Thailand were seen as curiosities, not as threats to the global order. Their leaders look isolated, not menacing.

Those were the good old days.

In the intervening years, autocrats have closed in on critical mass:

a tipping point where so many voices in so many places treat autocracy as normal that it is the other side that begins to feel isolated.

Out of the twenty-five most-populated countries on earth, four are autocracies that did not come to power on the basis of 3P strategies (China, Egypt, Vietnam, and Thailand), and a further ten have seen leaders rise to power through the deployment of populism, polarization, and post-truth: India, the United States, Brazil, Russia, Mexico, the Philippines, Turkey, Iran, the United Kingdom, and Italy. These are big, powerful countries. The 3P framework has been deployed with varying degrees of success in three member countries of the Group of 7 leading industrialized nations. In 2019 and 2020, four out of the five permanent members of the UN Security Council were led either by autocrats or by populists. Only France has held out so far, and its prospects are not secure. Or look at it this way: out of the 5.7 billion people who lived in the world's twenty-five most-populated countries, 4.3 billion were living in countries experiencing either autocracy or autocratic drift.

Such drift is not the marginal phenomenon it looked like a decade ago. And while in many of these countries it has mobilized hugely passionate countervailing forces in society, it is far from certain today whether democrats in those societies will have the wherewithal to restore democratic normalcy. The experience of Italy since 1994, as we have seen, gives ample room for pessimism. It is entirely possible that a few additional countries will fall into some variation of the maladies we've outlined so far, whether it is an anti-politics spiral, a 3P autocracy, or a full-blown mafia state.

This is not a call for fatalism. Far from it. The centrifugal forces that counteract this drive toward autocratic drift are still in operation. The forces that made power harder to gain, easier to lose, and harder to use in normal circumstances have not disappeared.

10

POWER AND PANDEMIC

The research for what became this book began years before the first case of a strange new form of pneumonia was reported in Wuhan, China, at the end of 2019. Through 2020 and 2021, as the COVID-19 pandemic took center stage worldwide, it was fascinating to watch how each of the themes developed in the previous chapters came into their own in a world under siege. Whether discerning the effects of polarization or post-truth, of pseudolaw or foreign military adventurism, of economic inequality or healthcare populism, the coronavirus pandemic neatly illustrates the operations of the 3P framework amid extreme and unprecedented circumstances.

As previous crises had already shown, the long-term effects of major disruptions are often more a function of governmental reaction (and overreaction) to a destabilizing event than of the event itself. The vast, global response the United States mustered to the terrorist attacks on September 11, 2001, transformed the world far more than the attacks themselves. The changes in the economy and society of many countries prompted by the reactions to the 2008 financial crash were deeper and more long-lasting than those of the initial financial accident per se.

The coronavirus will be remembered in the same way. The pandemic itself was, of course, a major global event with lasting consequences. Yet the political, economic, military, corporate, social, and international responses to the virus were more transformational than the immediate impact of the pandemic was.

As a first approximation, it is easy to see the pandemic as a powerful new centripetal force that concentrates power in the hands of those who already have it. The unsettling reality of an unknown deadly virus raging out of control on every continent placed governments at the center of the response and revealed what those in power could and could not do. In most places, the coronavirus emergency vastly expanded the range of government actions people were willing to tolerate and might even demand. From face mask mandates and widespread lockdowns to enormously expansive economic interventions or hitherto unacceptable surveillance, citizens everywhere showed remarkable tolerance for invasive expansions of state power: music to the ears of dictators and 3Ps autocrats.

Worldwide, autocrats jumped at the opportunity, riding the coronavirus wave to further cement their grip on power. As early as April 2020, as Frances Brown, Saskia Brechenmacher, and Thomas Carothers explained in a report for the Carnegie Endowment for International Peace (CEIP, where I am also a fellow), it was already obvious that the pandemic would disrupt democracy and governance worldwide in a startling multiplicity of ways.[1] That early list was long and mostly negative. Just in the first half of 2020, the pandemic would centralize power, close off democratic spaces, ease the path to the abridgment of fundamental rights, expand state surveillance, enable states to banish protests, disrupt elections, undermine civilian control of militaries, and hamper civilian mobilizations. Together, they argued, the novel coronavirus had the potential to "reset the terms of the global debate on the merits of authoritarianism versus democracy."

Some, like China, an old-school dictatorship with a sophisticated and massive police state, took the opportunity to quell festering centers of discontent while moving provocatively to settle border disputes with neighbors on aggressive terms. Others, like the leaders of Hungary and Russia, saw the ongoing crisis as the perfect chance to entrench their power for good while destabilizing their democratic adversaries. Still others, like the leaders of Brazil, Mexico, the United States, and the United Kingdom, relished the pandemic as a chance to burnish their populist bona fides by theatrically displaying their contempt for expert advice. Many more, from Thailand and Turkey to Cambodia and China, relished a new pretext to crack down on dissident speech. In every case, populism, polarization, and post-truth shaped the reactions of the powerful and guided how they sought to leverage the virus as a source of more (and more stable and lasting) power.

Yet it was also quickly apparent that it wouldn't be as simple as the pandemic making life easier for 3P autocrats. According to a campaign postmortem carried out in late 2020 by Trump campaign pollster Tony Fabrizio, bungling the pandemic response in all likelihood cost Donald Trump a second term in office.[2] In societies where authoritarianism still faces real competitive constraints, underperformance in office amid a major crisis has its costs.

So the virus did claim at least one major political scalp, and a centrally important one. But each country experienced the pandemic in accordance with its own reality. Generalizations are fraught—yet from the start, some early patterns are already apparent.

Riding the Coronavirus Wave

Autocratic regimes everywhere had little difficulty grasping that the coronavirus pandemic provided an opportunity to strengthen their grip on society. With governments imposing unprecedented restrictions on their citizens' movements on health grounds, measures that would have seemed heavy-handed in any other circumstance came to look normal, even banal.

Perhaps no other autocratic leader moved as boldly to capitalize on the centripetal potential of the virus as Xi Jinping. The Chinese dictator moved aggressively against adversaries across a series of fronts that had long been irritants to Beijing. Most visibly, in 2020 he dealt a decisive blow to Hong Kong's pro-democracy movement, approving a security law that effectively did away with Hong Kong's quasi-autonomous status under the "one nation, two systems" principles agreed to with the United Kingdom when the former colony was returned to Chinese sovereignty in 1997. The move quickly curtailed the raucous street movement that had rocked Hong Kong with protests in 2019 and also the entire tradition of civic activism in the former British colony.

Hong Kong wasn't the only long-festering problem Xi decided to solve once and for all under cover of the coronavirus. China's remote, complex, and ambiguously demarcated Himalayan border with India was another. In a series of aggressive moves beginning in early 2020, Xi sent Chinese soldiers to occupy territories that had long been administered by India. Xi decided to send a message that China would continue to wield its power in defense of its borders.

The pandemic helped Xi with this plan in ways that are far from obvious. Chinese intelligence appears to have picked up on a serious readiness crisis in the Indian military, which faced a series of COVID-19 outbreaks in the barracks. In the event, it must not have been hard for the Chinese to crack India's military signals: the Indian army relied on Chinese telecom infrastructure for its internal communications.

China's belligerence in the wake of the virus put all its competitors and neighbors on edge. From Vietnam and the Philippines, with whom China has complex territorial disputes in the South China Sea, to Japan and South Korea, Xi's assertiveness threatened to become the aspect of the pandemic with the most disruptive long-term consequences.

But none of China's neighbors greeted the coronavirus with the trepidation of Taiwan, a territory the People's Republic considers its own, despite eight decades of de facto independence. The sight of Beijing reneging on the long-standing commitments of "one country, two systems" in Hong Kong buried the hopes of some Taiwanese that reunification with the mainland could be achieved under an arrangement that preserved the island's openness, economic success, and vibrant democratic traditions.

The virus also allowed China to deepen and expand its campaign of repression against the ethnic Uighurs of Xinjiang province in its far west. The government in Beijing vastly expanded its distant, and largely invisible, gulag archipelago of sinister "reeducation camps" with virtually no international scrutiny.

In each of these cases, the pandemic served as the perfect smoke-screen for China: allowing it to move aggressively on different fronts and face much less pushback than it would have expected in normal times. These moves by the Chinese government would have proba-bly happened anyway even without the excuse provided by the pan-demic. But the health emergency surely catalyzed them.

That, of course, is not the only way to capitalize on the virus. When it comes to creative uses of the pandemic to crack down on dissent, the only limit is imagination. Take Azerbaijan's dictator, Il-ham Aliyev. His interpretation of lockdown rules included banning dissident organizations for breaking social distancing rules after they were found to have brought four people together in a downtown office for a meeting.

Hungary's president, Viktor Orbán, was another of the world's leaders who swiftly and effectively exploited the pandemic to con-centrate his power. He used the public health measures that warned about the heightened risk of infection in large gatherings as a justi-fication to shut down parliament and put off elections indefinitely. As a result, Orbán gained full control of the state apparatus and was able to rule by decree.

In Bolivia, interim president Jeanine Áñez similarly took the chance in 2020 to postpone presidential elections not once but twice under cover of the virus. Her precarious standing in the polls was, she explained to the nation, merely a coincidence. (Áñez would lose office to the left that same year after withdrawing from a race where she was polling fourth—more, in fairness, because of her dismal per-formance in office than because of the pandemic as such.)

In fact, in 2020 the International Foundation for Electoral Systems (IFES) recorded postponements of elections in sixty-four countries and eight territories, with a total of 109 election events postponed.[3] Chile, Ethiopia, Iran, Kenya, North Macedonia, Serbia, and Sri Lanka are some of the nations that postponed nationwide votes for president, parliament, state and local governments, or referendums. Not all of these postponements amount to power grabs, of course: some are motivated by genuine health concerns. That's precisely why the pretext is credible enough to be useful to those exploiting the pandemic for political gain.

Of course, postponing an election for bogus health reasons is only one path to manipulation: refusing to postpone one despite legitimate health concerns is another. Poland refused to postpone an election that Andrzej Duda, the populist president, was believed to be likely to win. And win it he did, with 51 percent of the vote in the second round.

In fact, Poland's populists were far from shy about exploiting the pandemic for their own purposes. As Joanna Fomina of the Polish Academy of Sciences noted, they took the opportunity to pass legislation on hot-button social issues that had faced strong popular opposition before the pandemic. Bills to criminalize sex education and further restrict access to abortion had provoked raucous street demonstrations before the virus struck. Once it did, the government banned street protests (alleging the need to maintain social distancing) and approved the bills in the dead of night.

Almost everywhere, the pandemic has strengthened the executive branch in relation to the other branches of government and expanded the range of measures seen as appropriate for it to take. Australians were, for a time, banned from leaving their own country: what had been unimaginable became unobjectionable. This shift has far-reaching effects across many dimensions, not the least of which is that it created new and attractive opportunities for corruption. With officials under immense pressure to approve procurement contracts for pandemic supplies quickly, opportunities for corruption and graft proliferated, and in states already run as de facto criminal enterprises, they were almost certainly used as opportunities for illicit enrichment.

When it comes to responses to the virus that undermine civil liberties, worldwide moves against free speech were among the most destructive. One could argue that the coronavirus became a global crisis in the first place as a result of censorship: the Chinese government's moves to silence Dr. Li Wenliang and his colleagues in Wuhan, who first tried to raise the alarm over this strange disease in December 2019, squandered the critical early period when the first outbreak might have been contained locally. Dr. Li's subsequent death from COVID-19 in February 2020 made him not only the pandemic's first martyr but freedom of speech's latest one as well.

The pattern of governments using their power to snuff out inconvenient information about the virus was not limited to China. As Jacob McHangama and Sarah McLaughlin wrote for *Foreign Policy*, the early months of the coronavirus saw a global pandemic of censorship, with autocratic governments around the world cracking down on dissent under the guise of banning disinformation about the virus.[4] In Cambodia, dozens were arrested on fake-news charges for comments they made about the pandemic, including members of banned opposition groups who were then held for lengthy pretrial detentions. In Thailand, an expansive definition of virus disinformation led to arrests of people merely criticizing the government's response as insufficient. In Turkey, dozens of people were targeted for "unfounded and provocative" social media posts about COVID-19, and at least nineteen of them were arrested on charges of "targeting officials and spreading panic and fear" by criticizing the government's response.

In 2020, instances of harassment of journalists covering the health crisis, its economic consequences, and governments' responses were common. Azerbaijan, Egypt, Honduras, India, Iran, the Philippines, Russia, and Singapore were just some of the many governments that tried to silence the media. In every case, governments claimed to be moving in the interest of public health to snuff out untrue stories about the virus. In a suspiciously high proportion of cases, those "untrue stories" happened to unveil the ineptitude of the government's handling of the crisis.

In some cases, the pandemic has pushed repressive governments into new areas of information control. In Turkey, for instance, mainstream media was already tightly controlled by the Erdoğan regime long before the virus struck. But the pandemic became the occasion for the government to launch stern rules to "limit disinformation" that, in practice, banned whole categories of speech. The regime used the pandemic as the justification to approve, in mid-2020, a new law that effectively banned Facebook, Twitter, and YouTube unless the heads of these platforms agreed to comply with Ankara's government censorship.[5] Failure to implement court orders to take down content that the government censors found offensive would result in hefty fines and crippling losses of bandwidth.

Brown, Brechenmacher, and Carothers also found an expanded use of high-tech state surveillance capabilities, ostensibly to fight the virus.[6] South Korea, Singapore, and Israel, for example, pioneered the use of cellphone surveillance for contact tracing. It became almost an afterthought to note that if a government is allowed to use such technology to know if you have been in contact with a virus carrier, it can also use it to track whom you have been in proximity to for any other reason.

"While enhanced surveillance is not per se antidemocratic," they write, "the risks for political abuse of these new measures are significant, particularly if they are authorized and implemented without transparency or oversight."

In India, health authorities require people under quarantine to periodically upload selfies with geolocation features enabled to ensure the photo is taken at the person's home. In Hong Kong, incoming travelers were forced to wear an electronic location-tracking device similar to that imposed on people under house arrest. The potential for any of these measures to be abused is overwhelming.

What's more, throughout the world the pandemic strengthened the hand of the armed forces. The military played an expanded role in setting and enforcing public health decisions in Iran, Israel, Pakistan, Peru, and South Africa, in some cases leading to claims that overzealous soldiers abused their power. Then again, just to show that for every trend there is often at least one counterexample, Amr Hamzawy and Nathan J. Brown, researchers at the Carnegie Endowment, found that in Egypt, the response to the pandemic strengthened the hand of the technocratic-civilian faction within El Sisi's authoritarian government at the expense of the influence of the military-centered national security apparatus.[7] Since the 1930s, the use of emergency powers has been identified as the key to entrenching autocratic power. Special opportunities arise when a real emergency coincides with autocratic aspirations. The pandemic was a clear example of this. More than fifty countries declared states of emergency in response to the crisis—many for perfectly legitimate public health reasons. Yet in other places, emergency declarations all but openly trumpeted their authoritarian intent.

In evaluating the potential for a declared emergency to be abused to autocratic ends, scholars look carefully at two aspects in particular: whether the emergency declaration is limited in time, and whether it is limited in scope. An emergency declaration without a carefully circumscribed field of action or end date courts abuse. And the pandemic has seen a disturbing number of such declarations proclaimed.

In the Philippines, the parliament gave President Rodrigo Duterte a grant of emergency power without any limiting principles. In Cambodia, Prime Minister Hun Sen similarly saw his authority to use martial power extended to infinity.[8] As a team of researchers at the University of Gothenburg led by Anna Luehrmann found, Europe was no exception to this trend.[9] For example, the emergency powers parliament granted to Viktor Orbán lacked any specified end date and included prison sentences for distributing fake news about the pandemic. Poland's emergency declaration, while not as broad, also lacked an end date and restricted some media freedoms. In Bulgaria, emergency powers have been used to harass the Roma minority, while in Romania, they have been used to restrict freedom of speech and have set off instances of police abuse in enforcing curfew measures.

A Pandemic of Post-Truth

To the Kremlin, which has long been on the lookout for social fracture points in adversaries in order to exploit them, the pandemic provided ample opportunities to spread disinformation to anxious and confused populations. As an EU report from March 2020 found, Russian intelligence agencies mounted "a significant disinformation campaign" to try to worsen the crisis the pandemic would generate for its adversaries in Europe.[10] Its goals? To destroy confidence in the democracies' emergency response.

Hewing closely to long-standing principles of FUD—fear, uncertainty, and doubt—Russian-backed activists spread stories aimed at undermining people's faith in their own governments. The EU identified eighty different pieces of COVID-19-related disinformation beginning as early as January 22, 2020, more than six weeks before the pandemic had led to the first wave of widespread, and economically painful, lockdowns. Many of the social media bots leveraged for this operation had a long record of aiding Kremlin initiatives to spread disinformation on subjects such as the Syrian civil war, the French yellow-vest protests, Catalonian independence, and others. The campaign was widespread, including content not just in English but in Spanish, Italian, German, and French as well.

As is so often the case, the disinformation campaign pursued a variety of messages simultaneously. In some cases, Russian bots spread the message that the coronavirus was "a human creation, weaponized by the West." But in countries where people are especially distrustful of the government, like Italy, they stressed stories that painted the government as incompetent and unable to rise to the challenge. Messages in Spanish, meanwhile, advanced apocalyptic stories or blamed capitalists for trying to benefit from the virus and "emphasize[d] how well Russia and Putin are dealing with the outbreak," according to the report.[11]

Nor were the accounts marginal players in their public spheres. RT Spanish, the Spanish language arm of Russia Today, Russia's public international broadcaster, counted some 6.8 million "shares" on its stories just in the first few weeks of the pandemic. Russian propaganda might strike sophisticates as crude, but it was brutally effective at shaping perceptions for broad swaths of its target societies.

Certainly, the United States was not immune from the charge, and the evidence of a similar push there was quickly detected. Aiming at an eager and combustible public opinion climate, it met with considerable success. In February 2020, the U.S. State Department accused Russia of conducting a pandemic disinformation campaign that leveraged hundreds of Facebook, Twitter, and Instagram accounts to push narratives including the idea that the CIA had created the novel coronavirus as a bioweapon.[12] The tech giants were once more obligated to shut down accounts suspected of spreading disinformation. But they seemed to be constantly behind and forced to play catch-up.

Apparently impressed by Russian success in the field of pandemic disinformation, China soon joined the fray, launching its own coronavirus post-truth operations aimed at the West. Its interest in breaking the perceived link between China—the site of the original outbreak—and the pandemic's human and economic costs seems to have been paramount for the Chinese, who focused on spreading the notion that China had "been framed"—blamed for a virus actually originating elsewhere.

China was able to project its power in this way thanks to its hugely sophisticated foreign influence infrastructure, with Chinese state television now beaming directly into households everywhere from Kenya to Portugal. But China's power isn't just advanced through its broadcasters; it also uses the kinds of online disinformation campaigns more usually associated with Russia, which the Chinese have been quick to emulate.[13] In June 2020, the European Union blamed China for being behind a "huge wave" of virus disinformation aimed at maligning European governments' responses to the crisis.[14]

China's efforts in this regard are often coordinated with those of other autocracies. As the Alliance for Securing Democracy, an independent NGO, found through sophisticated network research, there is clear evidence that official Chinese messengers piggyback on Iranian and Russian propaganda networks.[15] Since November 2019, three of the top five most-retweeted news outlets, not including Chinese state-backed outlets, were funded by the Iranian or Russian governments (PressTV, RT, and SputnikNews were the third-, fourth-, and fifth-most-retweeted outlets, respectively). In addition, several individuals associated with Russian-government-funded outlets or pro-Kremlin websites were among the one hundred accounts most retweeted by Chinese accounts.[16]

Such results are increasingly shared across internet watchdog organizations. Philip Howard, head of the Oxford Internet Institute, painted a similarly stark rise in disinformation coming in the wake of the coronavirus. "We've seen quite a significant uptick in misinformation generated by foreign state actors, particularly from Russia and China," Howard told CBC News in an interview. "In fact, 92 per cent of the misinformation from state-backed agencies around the world originates from Russia and China."[17]

Such tracking efforts have typically found that state-sponsored post-truth is growing not just more widespread in the pandemic era but also more sophisticated. Organizations such as Russia's Internet Research Agency have grown far more adept at covering their tracks, preventing the kinds of rookie mistakes that made their influence easy to document in, for example, the 2016 Brexit and U.S. presidential votes. Some of it is as simple as improving the copyediting of bot tweets to avoid telltale grammatical and syntax mistakes that give them away as not the work of native English-speakers. But some of it goes much further. As a CNN investigation found, Russia has even begun to outsource some of its disinformation work to NGOs and contractors in Nigeria and Ghana, effectively paying Africans to stoke racial tensions in U.S. social media as anti-racism protests gripped America in the summer of 2020. Some of the African trolls, CNN found, did not actually know that the ultimate paymasters behind their efforts were in Moscow.[18]

How Big a Backlash?

The pandemic, then, was the great centripetal, power-concentrating force of our time, right?

Not really. There's a great danger of oversimplification when faced with such an unprecedented crisis. Early assumptions can quickly prove unfounded, and intuition is no guide to uncharted waters.

To take just one example, one of the earliest conclusions analysts reached about the coronavirus in the early months of 2020 was that it would spell the end of the period of social unrest and street protests that had been spreading around the world in years prior, from Catalonia to Hong Kong to Chile and many other countries. The shelf life of this prediction proved short: by June 2020, the world's hardest-hit country, the United States, was alight with social protests against racist policing, and street protests had resumed from Algeria to Zimbabwe. No one was immune: by August 2020, massive street protests rocked Belarus, destabilizing one of the world's fiercest old-school dictators, Alexander Lukashenko. Just six months later, mass protests with little precedent struck throughout Russia—and not just in the bigger cities—after the Putin regime tried to poison and then imprisoned its most ardent critic, Alexey Navalny. Navalny's explosive publication of information about an enormous Black Sea palace he described as the biggest bribe in Russia's history rocked the Kremlin. The fate of the protest movement is unknown at the time I write this, but the sight of Russians protesting in the streets in the dead of winter set to rest any notion that the virus has weakened people's will to protest.

Could some of the early assumptions of the virus as a power-concentrating force prove just as wrong in the medium term? There is some reason to believe so. Some of the early scholarship on the impact of the virus suggests that its political effects vary enormously across national settings, depending not only on preexisting social fissures and the characteristics of the government but also on the response of the powerful.

It is a view forcefully put forward by my colleague Thomas Carothers, the head of the Carnegie Endowment for International Peace's ambitious research project on this very subject. In a series of case studies on the early effects of the crisis, Carothers found that although the virus did heighten damaging political polarization in Brazil, Indonesia, Poland, Sri Lanka, Turkey, and the United States, the same could not be said of countries such as Chile, India, Kenya, and Thailand.[19]

But to see the pandemic's potential to become a *centrifugal* force wresting power away from autocrats, it is wise to turn first to the three largest countries in the Americas, where some of the world's most powerful 3P autocrats—Jair Bolsonaro, Andrés Manuel López Obrador, and Donald Trump—saw their countries' death tolls soar amid a response riddled with scientific denial, appeals to magical thinking, and straight-up lies. In the short term, polarization ensured that, despite the debacles, all three leaders retained the support of a substantial portion of the population, including a large majority for Mexico's López Obrador, even as untold thousands contracted the virus and died, and millions more lost their livelihoods. But how sustainable will this model prove in the end?

These Western Hemisphere populists' disastrous responses, marked by contempt for scientific advice, show the other side of the pandemic's complex relationship with post-truth. Whereas in Russia and China leaders cynically deployed disinformation as a weapon against their opponents, Jair Bolsonaro in Brazil and Donald Trump in the United States appeared personally convinced of some of the most far-fetched conspiracy theories they peddled. Post-truth can be a potent strategy tool for cynical autocrats, but it can also create disastrous blind spots for credulous ones.

Frustration over virus conditions mobilized Russians' anger toward Putin, spilling over into mass street protests that rocked Moscow and St. Petersburg in the summer of 2020. With Russia home to a very serious COVID-19 outbreak, the government's credibility came under severe strain. Even so, in the early days of the crisis, before tempers had boiled over, Vladimir Putin put in place an audacious drive to extend his term limits through to 2036.

But if many 3P leaders' bunglings has cast a cloud of doubt over their futures, the comparatively effective response of some of the world's best-functioning democracies initially gave rise to hopes that not all is lost for the liberal camp. Denmark, Iceland, Germany, New Zealand, South Korea, and Taiwan stood out for the efficiency of the public response to the crisis: they were able to contain early outbreaks through the decisive, scientifically informed judgment of their scrupulously democratic and, in all but one case, *female* leaders.

Vaccines Are Power

But the COVID-19 pandemic also put a renewed spotlight on the technological capabilities of various countries when it came to producing and distributing a vaccine. Here, long-forgotten mental habits of rank protectionism and scientific chauvinism came back to the fore, as the United States, the European Union, Britain, Russia, and China raced to outshine one another with the speed and reliability of their response. In the early months of 2021, vaccine prioritization became a kind of worldwide obsession. China and Russia, taking full advantage of the latitude their autocracies give them, moved to prioritize exports of vaccines to client countries, in some cases even ahead of their own vulnerable populations. Western allies, facing furious demand for rapid immunization, could hardly be seen to divert their own limited supplies at such a time.

Reality on the ground sometimes matched preexisting stereotypes and sometimes diverged from it. It surprised no one that Israel, with its small population, hypersophisticated life sciences research capabilities, and permanent military footing, approached herd immunity first. But the European Union, despite its enormous scientific and research base and its reputation for technocratic efficiency, stumbled badly out of the gate, failing to secure anywhere near enough supplies for its vast population and falling well behind the leading countries in inoculating the world.

In time, it is likely that the vaccine race of 2020 will be remembered more for providing proof of concept for the viability of mRNA therapies than for anything else. The startlingly high-tech new procedures used to deliver the Moderna and Pfizer-BioNTech vaccines point the way to an entirely new generation of pharmaceuticals that open new avenues for the treatment of a vast range of human ailments. If the pandemic is remembered for having sped the development of such treatments, the early skirmishes over distribution are likely to be forgotten, and the prestige prize for the countries that developed the technique—mostly the United States and Germany, along with their close allies—will overshadow the administrative snafus. By the year 2100, the pandemic could be remembered for little beyond having accelerated the development of precision medicine and reestablishing the prestige of the democracies whose scientists delivered that revolution.

This last point illustrates our central premise for this chapter: like all major crises of recent times, the pandemic's impact will be remembered much more for the second- and third-order effects than for the initial crisis itself. Undoubtedly, the coronavirus reshaped the world.

But once again, governmental responses, and societies' reactions to those responses, are likely to be as consequential as the virus itself—if not more.

There is one possible future, then—to be clear, just *one* of several possible futures—where the coronavirus is remembered as the moment when the world turned the corner on the new 3P autocrats. If, within a few years, it becomes clear that countries that honored scientific expertise and the free flow of information systematically outperformed those that remained committed to post-truth, the legitimacy of know-nothing autocrats will have suffered a severe blow.

11

FIVE BATTLES WE NEED TO WIN

According to "Freedom in the World," an annual report released by Freedom House, a respected American think tank, seventy-three nations had a lower "freedom score" in 2020 than the year before.[1] Only twenty-eight nations saw their scores rise. Ominously, the report noted that 75 percent of the world's population lives in countries that experienced a diminution of voters' rights. "For the first time in this century," as the British historian Timothy Garton Ash has observed, "among countries with more than one million people, there are now fewer democracies than there are non-democratic regimes."[2]

The threat to global democracy could not be more real. The assaults on freedom are global, sustained, and formidable.

Governments of all ideological stripes, including many that style themselves as paragons of democracy, have seized opportunities to weaken the checks and balances that constrain their power. As we have discussed in these pages, in some countries these attacks are blunt and visible; in others they are subtle and stealthy.

Democrats must prevail in the existential contest against enemies who prefer a world in which power is concentrated and unchecked. Yet how best can we fight a war that rages on multiple fronts, against

3P adversaries adept at exploiting democracy's weaknesses and tapping into popular frustrations and discontents that democracies have failed repeatedly to address? In this latter-day incarnation of President John F. Kennedy's "long twilight struggle," democracy's defenders must choose their battles wisely to prevail.[3]

Of the many that lie ahead, I believe that these five stand out as the most important:

1. The battle against the Big Lie
2. The battle against criminalized governments
3. The battle against autocracies that seek to undermine democracies
4. The battle against political cartels that stifle competition
5. The battle against illiberal narratives

In what follows, I sketch what we must do to win in each of these five battlefields. I offer no magic bullets but concentrate instead on identifying the key objectives to be met and the most promising avenues for meeting them.

The Battle Against the Big Lie

Any strategy to defend democracies and ensure that the political system works for the good of society hinges on restoring the ability of citizens to differentiate truth from lies. As Timothy Snyder, one of the most astute chroniclers of contemporary tyrannies, has warned, "Post-truth is pre-fascism . . . to abandon facts is to abandon freedom."[4]

Yet around the world, political leaders increasingly see the appeal of lying in pursuit of power. And by lying I mean not fibbing or spinning, as politicians have always done but telling the kind of lies that poison democratic coexistence and undermine the very possibility of democracy. Count on Donald Trump to show the way: in May 2021, more than five months after blaming his reelection loss on mythical claims of fraudulent voting, he brazenly declared that "the

Fraudulent Presidential Election of 2020 . . . will be, from this day forth, known as THE BIG LIE!"[5]

Big Political Lies belong in a completely different category from political fibbing. The Kremlin's framing of Chechen separatists for the gruesome 1999 bombings of four apartment blocks in Moscow and other Russian cities is a terrifying illustration of how the Big Lie was used to consolidate power, in this case by Vladimir Putin after an ailing Boris Yeltsin designated him as prime minister. Whether it's Putin blaming Chechens, Turkey's Erdoğan alleging a shadowy conspiracy of Gulenist wreckers, or Donald Trump claiming a nefarious "deep state" was arrayed against his administration, the Big Lie enables 3P politicians to justify their power grabs. Every populist pitch has a Big Lie at its core, casting the aspiring autocrat as the only hope of the noble, downtrodden, and betrayed people against a shadowy elite that hates them.

Until recently, the reputational damage of being caught telling a Big Lie served to check the most egregious behavior by aspirants for high office in established democracies. But the rise to power of Trump, Erdoğan, Modi, Duterte, Orbán, and Bolsonaro, among others, suggests a dangerous shift in the cost-benefit balance of telling a Big Lie. No democracy can survive if the propagation of Big Lies is consistently rewarded with power. Draining Big Lies of their power will require a huge amount of political will, legal creativity, and technological and journalistic innovation. But if we lose this particular battle, success in the others will be moot.

Much attention has focused on the role of the internet as a force multiplier for Big Lies. There's some exaggeration involved in this. After all, three centuries before the internet was invented, Jonathan Swift was already quipping that "falsehood flies, and the Truth comes limping after it."[6] But the internet has tilted the playing field so heavily in favor of the liars that people no longer trust the institutions that exist to sort truth from lies. The strong propensity of online algorithms to favor the flashy but false over the humdrum but true has left truth-telling in a kind of crisis, an epistemic muddle that threatens the entire democratic project.

As Anne Applebaum and Peter Pomerantsev have argued, this trend can be reversed. "The internet," as they put it, "doesn't have to be awful."[7] Creative approaches to improving the quality of online civic engagement have been tried with some success in places from Taiwan and Brazil to Seattle and Vermont. Some innovations have tried to strip away the anonymity that stokes toxic online speech; others have sought to create platforms that encourage and reward consensus-building and depolarize the online public square.

The lessons from these initiatives need to be adopted by the online behemoths that now form oligopolies of online search and advertising—through their own choice if possible and by regulation if necessary. The financial, legal, and reputational incentives of the tech giants need to be aligned with society's broader interests.

Twitter's decision to ban Donald Trump following his four-year tsunami of daily lies from the Oval Office will be remembered as the first, if partial and problematic, step in this fight. But the ensuing debate over the effectiveness and justice of deplatforming Trump from Twitter and Facebook (the latter used an independent board to review such decisions, evoking as much scorn as praise) is a reminder of how much more needs to be done. The broad protection from liability granted to the big tech companies in the United States will rightly continue to be a target for legislative attention. Profit-motivated firms with business models built on maximizing user engagement, which falsehood drives in ways that truth cannot, can't be relied on to detoxify their platforms of their own volition.

Traditional media, too, faces a reckoning. In 2020, for the first time, fewer than half of all Americans said they trust traditional media, according to data from Edelman's annual trust barometer. Fifty-six percent of Americans agree that "journalists and reporters are purposely trying to mislead people by saying things they know are false or gross exaggerations." Fifty-eight percent think that "most news organizations are more concerned with supporting an ideology or political position than with informing the public." When Edelman polled Americans after the 2020 U.S. presidential election, the figures had deteriorated even further, with 57 percent of Democrats trusting the media and only 18 percent of Republicans.[8] Journalism used to act as a bulwark against the Big Lie—but it can't play that role if the stories that journalists report are not believed.

Overcoming this crisis will mean revising, and in some cases renouncing, old journalistic impulses. The entrenched habit of "bothsidesism"—the tendency to try to find moral equivalence where there is none—must be rejected if one of those sides is attacking the democratic system.[9]

As Lionel Barber, the former editor of the *Financial Times*, has argued, this does not mean journalism must be openly partisan. So long as arguments are made in good faith and on the basis of evidence, both sides *do* need to be heard. However, when good faith is not on offer or when evidence is maliciously manipulated or ignored, a respectful hearing is not only unwise but potentially destructive.[10] Journalists and commentators cannot be allowed to establish their bona fides as impartial observers by remaining equidistant between the people peddling Big Lies and those resisting them. Aspiring autocrats have long exploited such corrosive moral relativism as part of their 3P strategy.

The principle that a Big Lie disqualifies those who tell it from high office must be reasserted. Leaders who set out to nullify democratic decisions—such as the Republican members of Congress who endorsed Donald Trump's campaign to overturn the results of the 2020 U.S. election—must have no future in politics if democracy is to survive. As Alexander Hamilton wrote in 1787: "The hope of impunity is a strong incitement to sedition; the dread of punishment, a proportionally strong discouragement to it."[11] Yet instead of embracing this principle, after the election the Republicans in thrall to Trump purged those in their party who endorsed it.

A hardening of sanctions against malicious lying would not be as unprecedented as it is often made out to be, nor as unusual. All Western nations have safeguards, for example, to prevent advertisers from making unfounded medical claims. The recognition that false or exaggerated claims on behalf of medicines marketed to sick people can harm them is not controversial, nor should it be. Regulators scrutinize such communications, looking for the claims that cannot be made on behalf of a drug and the warnings and disclaimers that must be included, as anyone who has turned on a television set in the United States knows. To treat this as a violation of speech rights would be outlandish. The falsehoods that national politicians have delivered to their constituents regarding the 2020 election and the pandemic (not to mention climate change) have brought a sharp reminder that political lies can be just as deadly as medical lies.

The instinct that balks at regulating political speech has deep and honorable roots. Legally mandating that such speech be truthful would put us on a slippery slope. After all, if we accept the principle that some political speech is allowed and some is not, what happens when those called on to make the distinction are our adversaries? Such arguments will rightly command scrutiny from judges called on to adjudicate challenges of any new legal framework to protect against Big Lies. But in a world where the viability of democracy as a system is in doubt, such arguments can no longer be admitted as the final word on the matter. Prudence requires that we do better.

Citizens should also be better armed with a robust understanding of the mechanics of democratic governance. Civic education was once a mainstay of secondary education around the world. In too many cases, such lessons have simply been canceled, giving way in the curriculum to flavor-of-the-month approaches that don't give students the historical context and knowledge to assess the debates immanent in democracy. Indeed, a 2018 survey found that only one in three Americans could pass a multiple-choice test drawing on items from the U.S. citizenship examination.[12] The consequences of this ignorance are plain for all to see.

Getting "back to basics" and teaching teenagers how a bill becomes a law is not enough. Today's technological environment places unprecedented demands on information consumers to make choices about what to trust. A generation ago, decisions about which ideas would gain wide currency were relegated to a small cadre of elite editors in a handful of cultural capitals. No longer. Today, every news consumer is his or her own editor. In unschooled hands, this is a recipe for rampant disinformation.

Denying charlatans a receptive audience will require a new focus on digital hygiene. Democracies must develop and support a curriculum for their students that imparts the mental skills to filter the torrents of disinformation that digital life puts before internet users. Technology needs to be enlisted as an ally in this larger effort. AI-enabled tools can measure the credibility of participants in online debates and their adherence to usual standards of verification and truth-telling. Today's online giants already have the technology needed to rank their users according to their vulnerability to disinformation and could put in place mechanisms to protect the vulnerable from the most misleading and corrosive material.

Informed and responsive citizens are the first line of defense against the Big Lie. Where citizens lack the tools to perform their citizenship duties, today's 3P autocrats are more likely to entrench themselves. The costs of inaction on this front are just too high to countenance.

It is imperative that we accelerate the development and adoption of new laws, institutions, technologies, and incentives that give citizens a fighting chance to repeal the barrage of lies deployed against them by existing or aspiring autocrats. This is an eminently achievable goal.

The Battle Against Criminalized Governments

The second battle we must win is against criminalized governments. Don't misunderstand this as another call to fight corruption. Criminalized government is to corruption as the Big Political Lie is to traditional political fibbing. Democracies can coexist with a certain amount of corruption—indeed, they always have. But democracy cannot survive where officials at the highest levels of governments are also the top leaders of sprawling criminal organizations that control critical public institutions (police, the military, intelligence agencies, the diplomatic service, the tax authority, customs, regulatory agencies, etc.) and lucrative private ones (protected state-owned enterprises, industries that exploit natural resources, private monopolies, etc.). These criminal organizations enrich their leaders and their cronies and enable them to attack and repress adversaries at home and abroad. Democracy cannot work in mafia states that rely on organized crime's strategies, tactics, and methods and have the backing of a sovereign state.

From Russia, Syria, and Kosovo to Venezuela, North Korea, and Honduras, mafia states radiate lawlessness, exporting gangland tactics even as they offer safe harbor for the world's criminals. Their financial institutions shield ill-gotten gains from around the world, their diplomacy undermines the democratic aspirations of people everywhere, and their security services terrorize dissidents. A mafia state anywhere is a threat to democracy everywhere.

In today's international system, Vladimir Putin's Russia plays an outsized role in sustaining this loose global confederation of mafia states. Russian diplomats, spies, hackers, and trolls poison the waters for democrats everywhere. Russia's size and geostrategic weight create space for the criminalization of other states. Which is why, in the near term, the battle against criminalized statecraft must take the form of a tough line against the projection of Russian power and an insistence on preventing the Russian criminal elite from enjoying its loot. Beyond Russia, countries that put gangland techniques at the center of their statecraft must be met with determined resistance. In the era of 3P autocracy, the threat to democracy is a challenge not to liberal ideology but to the principle of governance based on law and truth. The routine uses of murder, intimidation, racketeering, and disinformation by a state must never go unchallenged.

The campaign to bring today's mafia states to heel will be a war of attrition. Although spectacular wins may be elusive, it can gradually reduce the threat that mafia states pose.

The first step is simple: follow the money. Ramp up the discovery and sanction of places where mafia state leaders stash away their assets, and you've greatly undermined their model's attractiveness. Yet despite a huge upsurge in enforcement activity in recent decades against illicit financial transactions, leaks, hacks, and investigations continue.[13] It is no secret that leaders and cronies from mafia states are still using some of the world's biggest banks to move and hide vast sums of money in offshore havens.

In that effort, each mafia state is supported by an unseen web of highly paid professionals toiling to make crime pay. Lawyers, accountants, wealth managers, private bankers, public relations and communications experts, corrupt law enforcement, and those serving as fronts must coordinate carefully to disguise and protect mechanisms for laundering ill-gotten loot. Without them, the leader of a mafia state is confined to his own country, a fate few of them are willing to accept. Democracies need to boost the resources they allocate to targeting this ecosystem: the 2020 budget for the U.S. Treasury's Financial Crimes Enforcement Network, for instance, was only $120 million, a puny sum set against several trillion dollars in illicit flows.[14] Democracies must make it harder to create anonymous shell companies by creating more beneficial ownership registries and making the data public. They must curb the dubious practice of selling citizenship, which has given mafia state members hideaways and footholds not only in Caribbean tax havens but also, via Malta and Cyprus, in the European Union.

The leaders of criminalized states are obsessed with reputation laundering, giving "generously" to charities and nonprofits that exist largely for this purpose. Find those fake charities, name them, and shame them. Criminal state hierarchs enjoy the perks of foreign travel and foreign property ownership; withdraw it from them. Take care to raise, one by one, the costs and risks associated with their line of business. When the opportunity arises, jail them. Criminal activity calls for law enforcement responses, whether the perpetrator is a mob boss or a cabinet minister.

The Battle Against Autocracies That Seek to Undermine Democracies

As any student of history knows, states have meddled in one another's affairs for as long as they have existed. Back in the fifth century BCE, Thucydides, a general and one of the first historians, had already identified how Greek city-states used propaganda, rumors, and misinformation to undermine their rivals' morale, foster divisions among their elites, and install allies to lead the enemy's troops and, at times, even its government.[15]

Modern times have been no different, whether what's at issue are the machinations behind revolutions and wars on the European continent or the bluster, subterfuge, and manipulations of the global Cold War. The political scientist Dov H. Levin has found, for instance, that on a worldwide level, the United States and the USSR/Russia "intervened in one of every nine competitive national level executive elections between 1946 and 2000."[16] In the twentieth century's contest between autocracies and democracies, the latter gained ground after the fall of the Soviet Union. By 2007, most of the seventy-five countries rated as autocracies in 1987 by the Center for Systemic Peace's Polity IV dataset had become democracies or had mixed systems.[17]

As we have seen, the momentum in that struggle is shifting. The swelling power and sway of an authoritarian China have upended expectations of democracy's inexorable triumph. So has a revanchist Russia. Together, they have extended their shared interest in overturning the existing international order through new groups, initiatives, and institutions, whether BRICS (Brazil, Russia, India, China, and South Africa), China's Belt and Road Initiative, or the Shanghai Cooperation Organization. Indeed, globalization and interdependence have superheated the competition between democracies and autocracies in once obscure multilateral bodies like the World Health Organization (WHO), the Universal Postal Union, the Internet Corporation for Assigned Names and Numbers, and the International Civil Aviation Organization.

Yet for all these changes, perhaps the most unprecedented and insidious disruption we have recently witnessed has been the malicious use of state power to undermine the political legitimacy of democratic rivals abroad through new online communications technologies. Meddling in other countries' politics has become far easier and cheaper in the twenty-first century, so much so that this tool is no longer available only to superpowers. North Korea, Turkey, Brazil, and Iran are just some examples of midsized, poor countries from which cyberattacks have been launched against politicians, governments, and private companies in larger, wealthier countries like the United States, France, or Spain.

We have come to grips with the scale of this problem only gradually. To Britons, the realization came as evidence emerged that Russia interfered in their 2016 Brexit referendum. For Americans, it came when evidence began to pile up of Moscow's meddling in the presidential elections of 2016 and 2020. Spaniards learned the same lesson ahead of Catalonia's wildcat independence referendum in October 2017. And many Chileans came to suspect the same after a subway fare hike triggered widespread protests in October 2019. Time and again, foreign disinformation campaigns emanating from autocracies destabilized what had been seen as a consolidated democracy. Influence operations like these are deeply asymmetrical: they're heavily stacked in favor of the instigator. With costs so low and potential rewards so high, such attacks are certain to proliferate.

Take the case of the foreign disinformation onslaught in the last two U.S. elections. As I have written before, this cyberconfrontation was asymmetrical not because America was at a technological disadvantage (the United States is a global leader in the technologies needed to wage cyberwars), but because Russia, China, and other autocracies were able to exploit the vulnerabilities of a democracy. What made America susceptible to the attack from an authoritarian Russia encapsulates the weaknesses that make all democracies susceptible to foreign political cyberattacks. For one thing, Russia targeted the democratic process. In the words of the intelligence community's January 2017 report, the hacks and leaks worked to "undermine public faith in the U.S. democratic process."[18]

They aimed to take advantage of the free flow of information in a democratic society, the effect of that information on public opinion, and the electoral mechanisms through which public opinion determines a country's leadership. Moreover, not only are democratic politicians more vulnerable to leaks, but democracies are also more likely to produce leakers to begin with. The legal protections afforded to individuals in democratic states make it hard to deter this type of behavior.

Why haven't Western democracies made the necessary reforms to adapt to the threat? Why have they let countries like Russia get the upper hand, not in capabilities but in practice? One reason is surely the checks and balances that limit the concentration of power and slow down governmental decision-making. While all bureaucracies, including those of authoritarian regimes, move slowly, Putin and Xi are far less encumbered by laws and institutional constraints than their democratic counterparts.[19]

These genetic democratic weaknesses can also hamper the ability of democracies to forge a united multilateral front against 3P autocrats. Look, for instance, at how voting structures in the European Union have prevented it from holding Viktor Orbán to account or from stopping Hungary from blocking criticism of China and Russia. The Trump administration's frustrations with the challenges and democratic niceties of multilateral diplomacy caused it to withdraw from bodies such as the UN Human Rights Council, citing the membership of malefactors such as China, Venezuela, and the Democratic Republic of Congo. Yet as former congressional representative Eliot Engel noted, that withdrawal just allowed "the council's bad actors to follow their worst impulses unchecked."[20] The way to strengthen democracy is not to withdraw from universalist bodies, which are the battleground for influence, but to build up alliances and complementary groups and use them more effectively. For instance, democracies account for 80 percent of funding for the WHO: properly concentrated, such power could have blunted the effort of China, which contributes only 2 percent, to distort the organization's initial investigations into the origins of the coronavirus pandemic.[21] Yet the effort to build better coalitions cannot come at the expense of principles: democracies lose more than they gain when they uncritically welcome, for strategic reasons, 3P leaders such as Modi, Erdoğan, Orbán, and Duterte to their ranks.

Thomas Carothers has called for democracies to "make collective, mutually supportive commitments to improve their own democracies and to stand up for democracy whenever it is threatened in other countries."[22] Such a commitment should be at the center of an agenda for democratic renewal focused tightly "on three priorities: fighting corruption, defending against authoritarianism, and advancing human rights."[23] Solidifying the commitment of a small group of core established democracies to support one another vigorously along these three axes would be a major achievement in guarding against foreign subversion.

That commitment needs to be public, solemn, and backed by specific action, because like a cancer, autocracy metastasizes. Left unchecked, it seeks out new organs to infect, both across and within borders. Democracy protection, then, is no mere matter of liberal do-goodism: it is a vital national security priority.

The Battle Against Political Cartels

Democracy is a way of organizing political competition. In a democracy, those unhappy with the current state of affairs can change things, but only if they can persuade enough fellow citizens to vote for them. Ensuring fair and lawful political competition is the central purpose of democratic checks and balances. Impartial courts, term limits, and checks on executive power in general exist to bar those who hold office from subverting the system to remain in power indefinitely.

Nearly every negative trend in today's democracies stems from the rise of *anti-competitive pressures* in the political system. In all the different ways we have seen in this book, 3P autocrats enlist the power of the state—its judges, cops, soldiers, media, civil servants, and regulators—in the service not of the nation but of their side. Their goal is to rig the game, plain and simple, and to consolidate their power.

In the business world, anti-competitive practices have been closely regulated for well over a century. Laws protect consumers from competition-stifling practices such as price-fixing, cartels, and predatory pricing. We must now extend this same reasoning to the political realm. 3P autocrats are all in when it comes to anti-competitive politics. They corner the market on political donations, erecting huge financial barriers to entry for competitors. They gerrymander safe districts for themselves. They drive their opponents off the airwaves, stack the courts with judges who will rule against those who threaten their power, and create artificial barriers to voting in order to disadvantage their opponents. In short, 3P autocrats act as consummate political monopolists.

To defeat them, we need a kind of political anti-trust doctrine, one designed to protect the competitive dynamic at the heart of democracy. Whether dealing with campaign finance, redistricting, voter registration, or media regulation, policymakers must squarely confront one question: Do the current rules foster fair and constructive competition? Where the answer is no, a strong prima facie case exists for intervention and reform.

The United States deserves special mention in this context. To reestablish its role as a stabilizing force in the international system, the United States needs to reimagine its central political institutions, beginning with the presidency, to curb the threat of autocratic backsliding. It needs to reform how Congress is elected and how it operates to allow it to make timely and difficult decisions. It needs to revolutionize an election system that produces intractable partisan gridlock and rancor by default. Most urgently, America needs to rethink the role of money in politics to curb the plutocratic takeover of its most important institutions.

From Bolivia to India, from Italy to the Philippines, many other countries will need reforms on a similar level of ambition and scope to tackle the threats democracy now faces. The obstacles to such a program are well-known. Entrenched interests too often mean that deep reforms are politically inviable, while those that are viable are often too shallow.

This reality, however, is no grounds for despair. The outer limits of what is viable can alter rapidly in a crisis, and 3P autocrats are pinwheels of crises. Nothing exercises the political imagination like the sudden realization of peril, and amid the onslaught of 3P autocracy, those who still believe in the relevance of democracy are motivated as seldom before.

The Battle Against Illiberal Narratives

Donald Trump decried "the swamp" and promised to drain it. Hugo Chávez called his opposers "the squalids" and threatened them with jail or worse. Spain's Pablo Iglesias and Italy's Beppe Grillo slam "the caste": their country's monied political and economic elites. In the United Kingdom, Boris Johnson derided "Brussels" as the home of unelected bureaucrats who used the European Union to impose silly rules and abusive regulations on Britain. Hungary's Viktor Orbán attacked "the globalists" who wanted to fill the country—and Europe—with illegal immigrants, while Turkey's Recep Tayyip Erdoğan is obsessed with "Gulenists," whom he describes as members of a cult-like terrorist organization led by dissident cleric Fethullah Gulen. "Cabal" trips off the tongues of all 3P autocrats, who use it as a cudgel to attack their rivals. Their named enemies may be as diverse as their societies, political backgrounds, and ideologies. Yet the stories that 3P autocrats tell their followers follow a familiar pattern. Mutatis mutandis, they are the same narrative. All 3P leaders define themselves in opposition to an enemy beholden to nefarious interests at home and abroad. In this narrative, the traitor to the nation, and especially to the working class and the poor, is a cancer that needs excision. Sometimes the enemy is a rival political leader, in other cases an institution, and often another country or social, racial, or ethnic group.

Like all good narratives, this one has clear villains and heroes as well as artfully crafted combinations of facts and fictions. As Cas Mudde, a Dutch political scientist who focuses on extremism and populism in Europe and the United States, has shown, the damsel in distress in this fairy tale is always the same, the "noble people" abused by predator elites. The savior hero is also always the same: the necessary autocrat called on by destiny to protect the poor and defeat the elite.[24]

Conspiracy theories abound in the narratives that populist leaders use to radicalize their followers. And the early twenty-first century has provided plenty of raw material to work with. Poverty, immiserating economic crashes, inequality, pandemics, armed conflicts, ruinous climate change, job-destroying technologies, and a long list of grievances and dashed expectations are realities that autocratic leaders did not create. What they did create are narratives that mobilize fear and anger and propose fanciful solutions designed to energize their followers. They offer a promised land where predatory elites are tamed and problems go away—provided, of course, that the 3P leader is given unlimited power.

It is hard for democrats to compete against this 3P narrative. As the political scientist David Runciman has lamented about Donald Trump, "His tweets, his this, his that, it's like a knife through the butter of information space. I thought people would have worked out barriers, and they haven't. Trump's way of doing politics just continues to cut through."[25]

Post-truth populists don't need to stick with hard facts. They're free to promise painless, instantaneous solutions that rekindle hope, boost expectations, and promise revenge. At the moment, this toxic tale feels good to their followers. And therein lies its power.

What do democrats offer in reply? Abstract ideas and process. The rule of law. Checks and balances. Freedom. The power of the market and the possibilities opened by economic opportunity. All attractive ideas for those who don't have to worry about basic needs. To a chronically unemployed father who needs to provide for his hungry children, these ideas are remote, irrelevant, and surely not a solution to his family's problems. Liberals offer a complicated explanation for why conducting politics in a certain way will lead to the best results for all. Not only is this counternarrative full of abstract ideas, but it often lacks an identifiable hero and villain. Our "good guys" are just those willing to commit to a set of abstract ideals and procedural rules, and our "bad guys" are those who refuse to do so. The entire package can feel lifeless, bloodless, hatched in a lab. I passionately believe it is correct . . . but I also have to accept that it doesn't get people's adrenaline pumping the way a 3P narrative does.

This imbalance is baked in to the terms of the debate. It's an unfair disadvantage that those of us who stand up for democracy will always have to face—notwithstanding the exceptional rhetorical gifts of inspiring democratic leaders like Martin Luther King Jr., Robert F. Kennedy, Nelson Mandela, B. R. Ambedkar, and Vaclav Havel. But while we can never entirely overcome it, we can blunt the impact of the 3P autocrats' advantage by stressing that freedom and democracy lead to human flourishing in a way autocracy never can. We can give people something substantive to be for, not just against. We can make an argument for a good life with deep roots in the traditions of the West that may not be intoxicating but remains honest.

The populist frame is too powerful to be defeated permanently. Like a virus, it reappears in outbreaks again and again throughout history. But the rhetoric is hollow. And pointing out that hollowness gives us an opening we must exploit to sell people once more on the promise of democratic life.

Sobriety is in order. The fact that democracy has survived over the last three centuries in no way guarantees that it will prevail against its enemies once more. But if we can defeat the Big Lies, sideline criminalized governments, parry the attempts at foreign subversion directed at democratic elements, face down the political cartels that stifle competition, and beat back the illiberal narratives that sustain autocratic onslaughts, we'll have won the war to preserve democracy.

AFTERWORD

Bringing the Politically Homeless in from the Cold

Around the world, especially in democracies facing autocratic challenges, broad swaths of the electorate have been left politically homeless by polarization. As hyperpartisans take over political institutions and social media, regular people find themselves choosing between parties they barely recognize and that don't fully represent their values and interests. Typically, the result is that they turn away from politics altogether or fall in line with whichever side their family, friends, and neighbors back in order to keep a sense of identity, of group belonging. Their alienation prepares the ground for one of the worst maladies of our time: anti-politics.

Institutional innovations can help bring these politically homeless citizens in from the cold. A few examples illustrate the possibilities of reforming the status quo.

Consider ranked-choice voting, the reform on offer that is perhaps most likely to drain the life out of aspiring 3P autocrats. Under the system, rather than casting a single vote, each voter ranks candidates on the ballot by order of preference. If a voter's top-ranked candidate receives the smallest number of votes in an election, he or she is eliminated from contention and their voters' preferences are transferred to their second-choice candidate. The system is designed to sideline candidates who capture a small number of voters while turning off the majority. Such extreme candidates can sometimes be elected in a divided field, even when most voters reject them. The selection of Donald J. Trump as the Republican nominee in 2016 is a classic example of that dynamic at play.

Under ranked-choice voting, Trump would still have received more first-choice votes than any of his contenders. But as his adversaries' second-choice votes were counted, it would have become obvious that his appeal was too narrow.

A political system that uses ranked-choice voting to elect its representatives will, as a rule, elect politicians who try to embody the preferences of the broad center of the political spectrum. Under ranked-choice voting, politicians still compete—fiercely!—for power. But now they do it under rules that channel competition toward the broader good. By giving candidates a positive incentive to try to gain as many second-choice votes as possible, it turns negative campaigning into a losing strategy. Ranked-choice voting rewards politicians for treating each other as adversaries to be brought on board, not as enemies to be destroyed, and yields officeholders who more closely match the preferences of the average voter. And it's no chimera: the system is already in use in general elections in Australia, New Zealand, and Ireland and in mayoral elections in the United Kingdom as well. Even in the United States, it's already in use in local races in twenty-one jurisdictions from California to Maryland, including in New York City, and statewide in Maine and Alaska. Ranked-choice voting remains unfamiliar to many. That ought to change.[1]

Imagine what would happen to the U.S. political system if ranked-choice voting was adopted more widely. The fear of primary challenges that keeps politicians wedded to their party's most extreme wing would subside, allowing politicians to represent the broad middle of their electorate more honestly. With less to gain and more to lose from harsh attacks against one's opponents, the tone of campaigning would change. The temperature of the public sphere as a whole would come down. And the voice of reason might just begin to break out above the din.

Another illustrative example of high-impact reforms is the widespread adoption of citizens' juries and citizens' assemblies—representative groups of citizens randomly selected and then brought together to discuss a specific problem and devise recommendations on how to address it. In its most ambitious iterations, citizens' assemblies convene people for extended stays in a secluded location to be briefed by experts and afforded the opportunity to question them at length before crafting a recommendation. Probably no country has done this better than Ireland, which uses these panels to present official recommendations on which the parliament must then vote. The Irish have not relegated citizens' assemblies to dealing with obscure second-tier or technical issues. On the contrary, in Ireland, the legality of abortion was left in the hands of ninety-nine citizens who previously did not know one another: homemakers, students, former teachers, truck drivers, and professionals deliberated over five weekends in a North Dublin hotel at the end of 2016 and presented recommendations that, eventually, were accepted as the thirty-sixth amendment to the Irish constitution via a nationwide referendum.

It's easy to dismiss reforms such as ranked-choice voting or citizens' assemblies as unrealistic. Such experiments can sound utopian, and certainly any attempt to redirect power from entrenched machine politicians to citizen philosopher-kings will face strong pushback. Radical experimentation of this sort is not to be entertained lightly—and wouldn't need to be entertained at all if the current system did not face mortal threats. But it does face such threats.

Reforms such as ranked-choice voting and citizens' assemblies could, over time, help redraw the norms of political discourse, disempowering extremists and fostering competition that yields consensus rather than chaos. Over time, the extremism that has marked the U.S. Republican Party could subside, giving rise to a modern party of the center right—forward-looking, engaged with the economic and social concerns of its members, and devoted to effective limited government, along the lines of Germany's Christian Democratic Union, for example.

Now, reforms such as ranked-choice voting and citizens' juries are no panacea. They are just two examples of the kinds of institutional innovations that deserve consideration. And innovations are just *tactics* to be deployed in pursuit of a broader goal. They can help bring the politically homeless in from the cold and promote a political system where competition for power is lively and intense but also fair, lawful, and constructive.

In much of the democratic world, an experimental, disruptive mindset is embraced in the private sector but largely absent from the political realm. While futuristic new technologies like precision medicine and quantum computing receive lavish funding from the world's venture capitalists, our political decision-making seems stuck in a time warp. Many practices trace their lineage, directly or indirectly, to America's now 245-year-old revolution. And that revolution, in turn, was made by people obsessed with saving America from the same fate as the Roman Republic. Should we really continue to accept as an article of faith that the problems of the twenty-first century can always be addressed with two-century-old mechanisms inspired by two-millennia-old concerns?

Across the developed world, bold, inventive, paradigm-shifting scientists and disruptive, knowledge-based corporations offer a bracing contrast to the gray, tradition-bound, dour public sector and the politicians who control it. Left unaddressed, this imbalance in creativity and energy will cripple democrats' ability to overcome the 3P challenges we face.

The times call for bold experimentation in government—not just innovative policies, but also innovative ways of making policy. Digital technologies and fifty years' worth of research in cognitive science and social psychology have upended our understanding of how best to make collective decisions. If we want to bring the politically homeless in from the cold, we must be willing to take some risks on new methods of collective decision-making. As Runciman has noted, pointing to the growing technological complexity of policy problems:

> Solving problems is better than not solving them. But the solutions
> are often beyond democratic control—the input of the voting public

is getting downgraded all the time. We wait for others to provide
the answers. It's undignified. That produces resentment and the inevitable backlash against expertise.[2]

Our job, then, is to try many ways of making public decisions,
across different geographies and levels of government, to begin to get
a sense for what works and what doesn't and to allow the best ideas
to diffuse across the democratic world. For all we know, the truly
transformational ideas have not even been conceived yet. Winning
the war against 3P autocrats will require the revolutionary courage
and creativity that gave birth to modern representative democracy
in the first place. If we fail, we'll bequeath our children and grand-
children a world that gradually drifts away from the principles of
freedom and self-government that ought to be their birthright. And
so, win this war we must.

ACKNOWLEDGMENTS

"We do not know what is happening to us, and that is precisely the thing that is happening to us, the fact of not knowing what is happening to us. . . . Such is always the vital sensation which besets man in periods of historical crisis." Thus wrote the famed Spanish philosopher José Ortega y Gasset in the early 1930s, a time of social and political upheaval in Europe.

Ortega y Gasset's observation is applicable to today's world. Our time is also one of great turmoil and uncertainty. It's easy to sense that profound changes are afoot and that they will impact us, our families, friends, employers and employees, cities, nations, and, yes, the world as a whole. Discerning how these changes will affect us in practice is the challenge of this book; it is my attempt to sort out "what is happening to us." Over the several years it took me to research and write it, I was fortunate to count on colleagues and friends whose knowledge and intellectual rigor are only exceeded by their generosity.

Foremost among them is Francisco "Quico" Toro, a cherished colleague and dear friend. He was the first reader to whom I would send my rough drafts or float an idea, a dilemma, or a doubt. His pointed questions, smart suggestions, and careful corrections helped me refine my thinking and clarify the way I conveyed my thoughts. James Gibney, a good friend and one of the best editors I have worked with, also greatly helped me sharpen my arguments and my writing.

Mike Abramowitz, Bill Bradley, Jessica Mathews, Jonathan Tepperman, and Bob Zoellick read and carefully commented on several earlier drafts. This book is much better thanks to them.

I am also deeply indebted to Madeleine Albright, Anne Applebaum, Frank Fukuyama, Adam Grant, Alan Murray and David Rubinstein for their useful observations and their generous comments.

Roger Abravanel, Cayetana Alvarez de Toledo, Ricardo Avila, Sebastian Buckup, Gustavo Coronel, Javier Corrales, Liza Darnton, Luca d'Agnese, Uri Friedman, Enrique Goni, Francisco Gonzalez, Gianni di Giovanni, Brian Joseph, David Kamenetzky, Julie Katzman, Ricardo Lagos, Ed Luce, Thierry Malleret, Maurizio Molinari, Luis Alberto Moreno, Yascha Mounk, Anne Neuberger, Ben Press, Jose Rimsky, Gianni Riotta, Gerver Torres, Christopher Walker, Andrew Weiss, and Brian Winter read some chapters or the entirety of the manuscript and offered useful comments and encouragement.

I have had a long and fruitful association with the Carnegie Endowment for International Peace, the Washington-based think tank where I work. It has been my intellectual home for decades, and the way I think about the world and the forbidding challenges we confront or the amazing possibilities we face is, in large measure, molded by my years at Carnegie. Bill Burns was Carnegie's president between 2014 and 2021, when he left to become the director of the Central Intelligence Agency. That is also the period in which I researched and wrote much of this book and thus benefitted from Bill's support. Tom Carothers is Carnegie's senior vice president for research and one of the world's most respected students of democracy and its perils. These are central themes of this book, and I was lucky to have Tom's comments and suggestions. My thanks to Bill, Tom, and the many Carnegie colleagues who, over the years, shared their knowledge and ideas with me. Martha Higgings, the director of Carnegie's library, and her team were immensely helpful in tracking down texts or pointing me toward relevant materials.

Tim Bartlett, an executive editor at St. Martin's Press, was the editor of my previous book, *The End of Power*, as well as this one. His deep understanding of the subject matter, combined with his long experience steering authors and making their ideas shine, make him an ideal editor. I feel fortunate to have had his support during all these years. Gail Ross, my literary agent, offered invaluable advice and support, as did Miguel Aguilar at Penguin Random House in Spain and Gianluca Foglia at Feltrinelli in Italy.

My indomitable assistant, Angelica "Angie" Estevez, performed innumerable tasks with precision, effectiveness, and grace. She also helped with research and the production of the analytical index. Lara Ballou, Christina Lara, and Valentina Cano, my assistants at different times during this project, were immensely helpful. My thanks to all of them.

I feel very lucky to have a family whose members were not only willing to read the multiple drafts of this book but were also great at detecting its flaws and helping me correct them. My infinite thanks to my wife, Susana, our children, and their spouses.

This book is dedicated to Nusia Feldman, who despite having witnessed firsthand the very worst of malignant power, kept a warm smile, a gentle soul, and an unshakable trust in the innate goodness of people.

NOTES

Introduction

1. Cas Mudde and Cristóbal Rovira Kaltwasser, *Populism: A Very Short Introduction* (New York: Oxford University Press, 2017).
2. Timothy Snyder, *On Tyranny: Twenty Lessons from the Twentieth Century* (New York: Penguin Random House, 2017).
3. Yascha Mounk, *The People vs. Democracy: Why Our Freedom Is in Danger and How to Save It* (Cambridge, MA: Harvard University Press, 2018).
4. Daron Acemoglu and James Robinson, *Why Nations Fail: The Origins of Power, Prosperity and Poverty* (New York: Penguin Random House, 2013).
5. Anne Appelbaum, *Twilight of Democracy: The Seductive Lure of Authoritarianism* (New York: Doubleday, 2020).
6. Enrique Krauze, *El pueblo soy yo* (Madrid: Random House, 2018).
7. Larry Diamond, *Ill Winds: Saving Democracy from Russian Rage, Chinese Ambition, and American Complacency* (New York: Penguin Books, 2019).
8. Francis Fukuyama, "Against Identity Politics," University of Pennsylvania, accessed March 18, 2021, https://amc.sas.upenn.edu/francis-fukuyama-against-identity-politics.
9. Steve Tesich, "A Government of Lies," *The Nation*, January 20, 1992.
10. "Word of the Year 2016," Oxford Dictionaries, https://languages.oup.com/word-of-the-year/2016.
11. Sean Illing, "A Philosopher Explains America's 'Post-Truth' Problem," Vox, August 14, 2018.
12. Barbara A. Biesecker, "Guest Editor's Introduction: Toward an Archaeogenealogy of Post-truth," *Philosophy and Rhetoric* 51, no. 4 (2018): 329–41.
13. David Stasavage, *The Decline and Rise of Democracy: A Global History from Antiquity to Today* (Princeton, NJ: Princeton University Press, 2020).

14. Francis Fukuyama, "The End of History?," *The National Interest* 16 (Summer 1989): 3–18.

15. François, duc de La Rochefoucauld, *Reflections or Sentences and Moral Maxims*, trans. J. W. Willis Bund and J. Hain Friswell (London: Simpson Low, Son, and Marston, 1871), 218.

16. Erica Frantz, *Authoritarianism: What Everyone Needs to Know* (Oxford: Oxford University Press, 2018).

17. Jackson Diehl, "Putin and Sissi Are Putting on Elections. Why Bother?," *Washington Post*, March 4, 2018.

1. The Global War on Checks and Balances

1. Joanna Berendt, "Polish Government Pushes Legislation to Tighten Control over Judges," *New York Times*, December 21, 2019.

2. "CBI Raids at Prannoy Roy's Residence—Read What NDTV and Roys Are Accused Of," OpIndia, June 5, 2017, https://www.opindia.com/2017/06/cbi-raids-prannoy-roy-ndtv-396-crore-icici-bank-fraud.

3. "Bolivian Court Clears Way for Morales to Run for Fourth Term," Reuters, November 28, 2017.

4. Charlie Savage, "Trump Vows Stonewall of 'All' House Subpoenas, Setting Up Fight over Powers," *New York Times*, April 24, 2019.

5. Steve Coll, *Private Empire: ExxonMobil and American Power* (New York: Penguin Books, 2013).

6. David Michaels, *The Triumph of Doubt: Dark Money and the Science of Deception* (Oxford: Oxford University Press, 2020).

7. Javier Corrales, "Trump Is Using the Legal System Like an Autocrat," *New York Times*, March 5, 2020.

8. Ronald L. Numbers, *The Creationists: From Scientific Creationism to Intelligent Design* (Cambridge, MA: Harvard University Press, 2006).

9. Paul Volcker, "Paul Volcker's Final Warning for America," *Financial Times*, December 11, 2019.

10. "Putin for Life: State Duma Resets Presidential Term-Limit Clock to Zero," Warsaw Institute, March 25, 2021, https://warsawinstitute.org/putin-life-state-duma-resets-presidential-term-limit-clock-zero.

11. Mila Versteeg, Timothy Horley, Anne Meng, Mauricio Guim, and Marilyn Guirguis, "The Law and Politics of Presidential Term Limit Evasion," *Columbia Law Review* 120, no. 1 (January 2020): 173–248.

12. James Worsham, "The 'Gerry' in Gerrymandering," National Archives, June 21, 2018, https://prologue.blogs.archives.gov/2018/06/21/the-gerry-in-gerrymandering.

13. Paul Krugman, "American Democracy May Be Dying," *New York Times*, April 9, 2020.

14. Sean Illing, "David Frum on Why Republicans Chose Trumpocracy over Democracy," Vox, October 26, 2018.

15. David Frum, *Trumpocracy: The Corruption of the American Republic* (New York: Harper Collins, 2018).

16. Robert Siegel, "Cleric Accused of Plotting Turkish Coup Attempt: 'I Have Stood Against All Coups,'" NPR, July 11, 2017.

17. Girish Gupta, "Special Report: How a Defrocked Judge Became the Chief Legal Enforcer for Maduro's Venezuela," Reuters, November 15, 2017.

18. Will Doran, "Roy Cooper Loses a Lawsuit in His Power Struggle Against the NC Legislature," *News and Observer*, December 21, 2018.
19. Patrick Kingsley, "As West Fears the Rise of Autocrats, Hungary Shows What's Possible," *New York Times*, February 10, 2018.
20. "Would-Be Autocrats Are Using Covid-19 as an Excuse to Grab More Power," *The Economist*, April 25, 2020.
21. Viktor Orbán, speech at the 25th Bálványos Free Summer University and Youth Camp, July 26, 2014, Băile Tuşnad (Tusnádfürdő), trans. Csaba Tóth, *The Budapest Beacon*, July 29, 2014, https://budapestbeacon.com/full-text-of-viktor-orbans-speech-at-baile-tusnad-tusnadfurdo-of-26-july-2014.

2. The Politics of Fandom

1. Gabriel Garcia Marquez, *The Autumn of the Patriarch* (New York: Harper Collins, 2006).
2. Ryszard Kapuściński, *The Emperor: Downfall of an Autocrat* (New York: Penguin Random House, 1989).
3. Donald H. Reiman and Neil Fraistat, *Shelley's Poetry and Prose* (New York: W. W. Norton, 2002).
4. Aaron Couch and Emmet McDermott, "Donald Trump Campaign Offered Actors $50 to Cheer for Him at Presidential Announcement," *Hollywood Reporter*, June 17, 2015.
5. "Full Text: Donald Trump Announces a Presidential Bid," *Washington Post*, June 16, 2015.
6. Alex Altman and Charlotte Alter, "Trump Launches Presidential Campaign with Empty Flair," *Time*, June 16, 2015.
7. Roderick P. Hart, *Trump and Us: What He Says and Why People Listen* (London: Cambridge University Press, 2020).
8. Silvio Berlusconi, "1994—Discesa in campo di Berlusconi," campaign launch speech from 1994, posted by liberalenergia, YouTube, August 11, 2009, 00:05, https://www.youtube.com/watch?v=B8-uIYqnk5A.
9. Berlusconi, "1994—Discesa in campo di Berlusconi," 00:23.
10. Ruben Durante, Paolo Pinotti, and Andrea Tesei, "The Political Legacy of Entertainment TV," *American Economic Review* 109, no. 7 (July 2019): 2497–530.
11. "Survey of Adult Skills (PIAAC)," Programme for the International Assessment of Adult Competencies, OECD, last modified November 15, 2019, https://www.oecd.org/skills/piaac.
12. Ruben Durante, Paolo Pinotti, and Andrea Tesei, "Voting Alone? The Political and Cultural Consequences of Commercial TV," Paolo Baffi Centre Research Paper No. 2013–139, June 6, 2013, available at SSRN, https://ssrn.com/abstract=2290523 or http://dx.doi.org/10.2139/ssrn.2290523.
13. Alexander Stille, *The Sack of Rome: Media + Money + Celebrity = Power = Silvio Berlusconi* (New York: Penguin Random House, 2007).
14. John Lloyd, "The New 'Italian Miracle,' 1993," *Financial Times*, May 9, 2008.
15. Max Weber, *The Theory of Social and Economic Organization* (New York: Oxford University Press, 1947).
16. Max Weber, *Economy and Society* (Berkeley: University of California Press, 1978).
17. David A. Fahrenthold, "Trump Recorded Having Extremely Lewd Conversation About Women in 2005," *Washington Post*, October 8, 2016.

18. Simon Kuper, "Trumpsters, Corbynistas and the Rise of the Political Fan," *Financial Times*, July 20, 2017.

19. Maggie Haberman, Glenn Thrush, and Peter Baker, "Trump's Way: Inside Trump's Hour-by-Hour Battle for Self-Preservation," *New York Times*, December 9, 2017.

20. Patrick R. Miller and Pamela Johnston Conover, "Red and Blue States of Mind: Partisan Hostility and Voting in the United States," *Political Research Quarterly*, March 30, 2015.

21. Shanto Iyengar and Sean J. Westwood, "Fear and Loathing Across Party Lines: New Evidence on Group Polarization," *American Journal of Political Science* 59, no. 3 (July 2015): 690–707.

22. Francis Fukuyama, "Against Identity Politics," University of Pennsylvania, accessed March 18, 2021, https://amc.sas.upenn.edu/francis-fukuyama-against -identity-politics.

23. Thomas E. Mann and Norman J. Ornstein, *It's Even Worse Than It Looks: How the American Constitutional System Collided with the New Politics of Extremism* (New York: Basic Books, 2016).

24. Fukuyama, "Against Identity Politics."

25. Andrew Sullivan, "America Wasn't Built for Humans," *New York Magazine*, September 18, 2017.

26. Beppe Grillo, "Reset!" show in Rome, March 30, 2007, posted by Grilli quotidiani, YouTube, August 2, 2017, https://www.youtube.com/watch?v=8sR6pSLDFdU.

27. Alberto Nardelli and Craig Silverman, "Italy's Most Popular Political Party Is Leading Europe in Fake News and Kremlin Propaganda," BuzzFeed News, November 29, 2016.

28. Nick Gass, "Trump on Small Hands: 'I Guarantee You There's No Problem,'" Politico, March 3, 2016.

29. Hugo Chávez, *Aló Presidente* no. 30, Caracas, February 13, 2000, http://todochavez .gob.ve/todochavez/3822-alo-presidente-n-30.

30. "Lula, Kirchner y Chávez acuerdan construir 'el gran gasoducto del sur,' que atravesará Suramérica," *El Mundo*, January 20, 2006.

31. Naomi Klein, "The Media Against Democracy," *The Guardian*, February 18, 2003.

32. Michael Wolff, *Fire and Fury: Inside the Trump White House* (New York: Henry Holt, 2018).

33. Juan Forero, "Venezuela's Chavez Marks 10 Years with Talkathon," NPR, May 29, 2009.

34. Toby Meyjes, "Leaders of These Countries Say the Press Is the 'Enemy of the People,'" *Metro*, February 20, 2017.

35. Max Weber, "The Nature of Charismatic Authority and Its Routinization," in *The Theory of Social and Economic Organization*, trans. A. M. Henderson and Talcott Parsons (New York: Oxford University Press, 1947).

36. Marshall McLuhan, *Understanding Media: The Extensions of Man* (Boston: Massachusetts Institute of Technology Press, 1964).

3. Power Tools

1. Anders Aslund, *Russia's Crony Capitalism: The Path from Market Economy to Kleptocracy* (New Haven, CT: Yale University Press, 2019).

2. Sydney P. Freedberg, Scilla Alecci, Will Fitzgibbon, Douglas Dalby, and Delphine Reuter, "How Africa's Richest Woman Exploited Family Ties, Shell Companies,

and Inside Deals to Build an Empire," *International Consortium of Investigative Journalists*, January 19, 2020, https://www.icij.org/investigations/luanda-leaks /how-africas-richest-woman-exploited-family-ties-shell-companies-and-inside -deals-to-build-an-empire/.

3. E. J. Dionne Jr., Norm Ornstein, and Thomas E. Mann, "How the GOP Prompted the Decay of Political Norms," *The Atlantic*, September 19, 2017.

4. Steven Levitsky and Daniel Ziblatt, "The Crisis of American Democracy," *American Educator* 44, no. 3 (Fall 2020): 6.

5. George Packer, "The President Is Winning His War on American Institutions," *The Atlantic*, April 2020.

6. Timothy Snyder, *On Tyranny: Twenty Lessons from the Twentieth Century* (New York: Penguin Random House, 2017).

7. Timothy Snyder, "House Committees Accelerate Impeachment Inquiry," interview by Rachel Maddow, *The Rachel Maddow Show*, MSNBC, September 27, 2019, transcript, https://www.msnbc.com/transcripts/rachel-maddow-show /2019–09–27-msna1285286.

8. Anne Appelbaum, "History Will Judge the Complicit," *The Atlantic*, July/August 2020.

9. Francesca Gina and Max Bazerman, "When Misconduct Goes Unnoticed: The Acceptability of Gradual Erosion in Others' Unethical Behavior," *Journal of Experimental Social Psychology* 45, no. 4 (July 2009): 708–19.

10. Clare Baldwin and Andrew C. Marshall, "How a Secretive Police Squad Racked Up Kills in Duterte's Drug War," Reuters, December 19, 2017.

11. Chieu Luu, Tiffany Ap, and Kathy Quiano, "Philippines President 'Ordered Death Squad Hits While Mayor,' Alleged Hitman Claims," CNN, September 16, 2016.

12. Eduardo Galeano, *Open Veins of Latin America: Five Centuries of the Pillage of a Continent*, trans. Cedric Belfrage (New York: Monthly Review Press, 1997).

13. Pablo Neruda, *Un canto para Bolívar*, ed. especial (Madrid: Visor Libros, 2014).

14. Silvio Berlusconi, "1994—Discesa in campo di Berlusconi," campaign launch speech from 1994, posted by liberalenergia, YouTube, August 11, 2009, 00:18, https://www.youtube.com/watch?v=B8-uIYqnk5A.

15. David A. Graham, "Really, Would You Let Your Daughter Marry a Democrat?," *The Atlantic*, September 27, 2012.

16. Belinda Luscombe, "Would You Date Someone with Different Political Beliefs? Here's What a Survey of 5,000 Single People Revealed," *Time*, October 7, 2020.

17. Lisa Bonos, "Strong Views on Trump Can Be a Big Dating Dealbreaker, and Other Takeaways from a Survey on Love and Politics," *Washington Post*, February 7, 2020.

18. Frank Newport, "In U.S., 87% Approve of Black-White Marriage, vs. 4% in 1958," Gallup, July 25, 2013, https://news.gallup.com/poll/163697/approve-marriage -blacks-whites.aspx.

19. Francis Fukuyama, *Identity: The Demand for Dignity and the Politics of Resentment* (New York: Farrar, Straus and Giroux, 2018).

20. Michael Gove, "Gove: Britons 'Have Had Enough of Experts," interview with Faisal Islam of Sky News on June 3, 2016, posted by rpmackey, YouTube, June 21, 2016, 01:02, https://www.youtube.com/watch?v=GGgiGtJk7MA&t=61s.

21. BBC News, "EU Referendum," BBC, June 2016, https://www.bbc.co.uk/news /politics/eu_referendum/results.

22. Joe Twyman (@JoeTwyman), "Over two thirds of Leave supporters (+ quarter of Remainers) say it is wrong to rely too much on 'experts'. #EURef," Twitter, June 15, 2016, https://twitter.com/JoeTwyman/status/743079695986622464?s=20.

23. Daniel W. Drezner, *The Ideas Industry: How Pessimists, Partisans, and Plutocrats Are Transforming the Marketplace of Ideas* (New York: Oxford University Press, 2017).

24. Representatives Fred Upton [R-MI-6], Spencer Bachus [R-AL-6], Ed Whitfield [R-KY-1], Sue Wilkins Myrick [R-NC-9], Tim Murphy [R-PA-18], Lee Terry [R-NE-2], Judy Biggert [R-IL-13], and Robert E. Latta [R-OH-5], H.R. 5979—United States Nuclear Fuel Management Corporation Establishment Act of 2010, July 29, 2010, https://www.congress.gov/bill/111th-congress/house-bill/5979/cosponsors?s=3&r=1&overview=closed&searchResultViewType=expanded.

25. Brad Johnson, "Rep. Fred Upton on Global Warming: 'I Do Not Say That It Is Man-Made,'" ThinkProgress, February 8, 2011.

26. Zachary Coile, "Pelosi, Gingrich Team Up for Global Warming TV Ad," SFGate, April 18, 2008.

27. Michael O'Brien, "Gingrich Regrets 2008 Climate Ad with Pelosi," *The Hill*, July 26, 2011.

28. Michael Young, *The Rise of the Meritocracy* (Oxfordshire: Routledge, 1994).

29. Hugo Chávez, *Aló Presidente*, no. 131, Caracas, December 15, 2002, http://todochavez.gob.ve/todochavez/4138-alo-presidente-n-131.

30. Hannah Arendt, *The Origins of Totalitarianism* (New York: Harcourt Brace Jovanovich, 1973), 339.

31. A. G. Sulzberger, "The Growing Threat to Journalism Around the World," *New York Times*, September 23, 2019.

32. Philip Bennett and Moisés Naím, "21st-Century Censorship," *Columbia Journalism Review*, January 5, 2015.

33. "Poland's Campaign Against the Press Could Devastate What's Left of Its Democracy," editorial, *Washington Post*, October 23, 2020.

34. Thomas R. Lansner, ed., "Capturing Them Softly: Soft Censorship and State Capture in Hungarian Media," WAN-IFRA, 2013, http://m.wan-ifra.org/sites/default/files/field_article_file/WAN-IFRA%20Soft%20Censorship%20Hungary%20Report_0.pdf.

35. Krisztián Simon and Tibor Rácz, "Hostile Takeover: How Orbán Is Subjugating the Media in Hungary," *Focus on Hungary*, Heinrich Böll Stiftung, August 22, 2017, https://www.boell.de/en/2017/08/22/hostile-takeover-how-orban-subjugating-media-hungary.

36. Carl Schmitt, *Political Theology: Four Chapters on the Concept of Sovereignty* (Chicago: University of Chicago Press, 2006).

4. The Hunt for Culprits

1. Roberto Stefan Foa and Yascha Mounk, "The Danger of Deconsolidation: The Democratic Disconnect," *Journal of Democracy* 27, no. 3 (July 2016): 5–17.

2. Alexis de Tocqueville, *Democracy in America: And Two Essays on America*, trans. Gerald E. Bevan (London: Penguin, 2003).

3. Samuel P. Huntington, *Political Order in Changing Societies* (New Haven, CT: Yale University Press, 1968).

4. Stanley Feldman, "Authoritarianism, Threat, and Intolerance," in Eugene Borgida,

Christopher Federico, and Joanne Miller, *At the Forefront of Political Psychology: Essays in Honor of John L. Sullivan* (Oxfordshire: Routledge, 2020), chap. 3.

5. Christopher Johnston, B. J. Newman, and Y. Velez, "Ethnic Change, Personality, and Polarization over Immigration in the American Public," *Public Opinion Quarterly* 79, no. 3 (January 1, 2015): 662–86.

6. Michele Gelfand, Joshua Conrad Jackson, and Jesse R. Harrington, "Trump Culture: Threat, Fear and the Tightening of the American Mind," *Scientific American*, April 27, 2016.

7. Diana Rieger, Lena Frischlich, and Gary Bente, *Propaganda 2.0: Psychological Effects of Right-Wing and Islamic Extremist Internet Videos* (Cologne: Wolters Kluwer Deutschland, 2013), 37.

8. Marc J. Hetherington and Jonathan D. Weiler, *Authoritarianism and Polarization in American Politics* (Cambridge: Cambridge University Press, 2012).

9. Philip E. Converse "The Nature of Belief Systems in Mass Publics (1964)," *Critical Review* 18 (2006): 1–74.

10. Yascha Mounk, *The People vs. Democracy: Why Our Freedom Is in Danger and How to Save It* (Cambridge, MA: Harvard University Press, 2018).

11. "Meet ALICE," United for ALICE, accessed March 19, 2021, https://www.unitedforalice.org.

12. Stephanie Hoopes et al., *United Way ALICE Report—The Consequences of Insufficient Household Income* (New Jersey: United Way, 2017), https://www.unitedforalice.org/Attachments/AllReports/17UWALICE%20Report_NCR_12.19.17_Lowres.pdf.

13. Board of Governors of the Federal Reserve System, *Report on the Economic Well-Being of U.S. Households in 2017* (Washington, DC: Federal Reserve, 2018).

14. Anne Case and Angus Deaton, *Deaths of Despair and the Future of Capitalism* (Princeton, NJ: Princeton University Press, 2020).

5. Corporate Power

1. Thomas Philippon, *The Great Reversal: How America Gave Up on Free Markets* (Cambridge, MA: Harvard University Press, 2019).

2. Tom Orlik, Justin Jimenez, and Cedric Sam, "World-Dominating Superstar Firms Get Bigger, Techier, and More Chinese," Bloomberg Economics, May 21, 2021, https://www.bloomberg.com/graphics/2021-biggest-global-companies-growth-trends/?srnd=politics-vp&sref=nXmOg68r.

3. John Maynard Keynes, *The General Theory of Employment, Interest, and Money* (Camden: Palgrave Macmillan, 2021).

4. Alberto Cavallo, "More Amazon Effects: Online Competition and Pricing Behaviors," *Jackson Hole Economic Symposium Conference Proceedings* (Kansas City: Federal Reserve Bank, 2019).

5. Alan B. Krueger, "Luncheon Address: Reflections on Dwindling Worker Bargaining Power and Monetary Policy," speech, Federal Reserve Bank, Kansas City, MO, August 24, 2018.

6. Whole Foods Market, "Amazon and Whole Foods Market Announce Acquisition to Close This Monday, Will Work Together to Make High-Quality, Natural and Organic Food Affordable for Everyone," news release, August 24, 2017.

7. Robert H. Bork, *The Antitrust Paradox: A Policy at War with Itself* (New York: Free Press, 1993).

8. Lina M. Khan, "Amazon's Antitrust Paradox," *Yale Law Journal* 126, no. 3 (January 2017): 564–907.
9. Charlie Warzel, "Mark Zuckerberg Is the Most Powerful Unelected Man in America," *New York Times*, September 3, 2020.
10. Javier Espinoza and Sam Fleming, "EU Seeks New Powers to Penalise Tech Giants," *Financial Times*, September 20, 2020.
11. Jerrold Nadler and David N. Cicilline, "Investigation of Competition in Digital Markets," U.S. House of Representatives, October 6, 2020, https://fm.cnbc.com/applications/cnbc.com/resources/editorialfiles/2020/10/06/investigation_of_competition_in_digital_markets_majority_staff_report_and_recommendations.pdf.
12. Khan, "Amazon's Antitrust Paradox."
13. Nadler and Cicilline, "Investigation of Competition in Digital Markets."
14. Thomas Philippon, "Commentary: Understanding Weak Capital Investment: The Role of Market Concentration and Intangibles," paper presented at Jackson Hole Economic Policy Symposium 2018, Federal Reserve Bank, Kansas City, MO, https://www.kansascityfed.org/documents/6978/philippon_JH2018.pdf.
15. Ufuk Akcigit and Sina T. Ates, "Slowing Business Dynamism and Productivity Growth in the United States," paper presented at Jackson Hole 2020, October 8, 2020, https://www.kansascityfed.org/documents/4952/aa_jh_201008.pdf.
16. "America's Concentration Crisis," Open Markets Institute Report, accessed March 19, 2021, https://concentrationcrisis.openmarketsinstitute.org.
17. "Fortune's List of America's Largest Corporations in 1990," *Fortune*, accessed March 19, 2021, https://archive.fortune.com/magazines/fortune/fortune500_archive/full/1990.
18. Andrea Murphy, Hank Tucker, Marley Coyne, and Halah Touryalai, "Global 2000: The World's Largest Public Companies," *Forbes*, May 13, 2020.
19. Dino Grandoni, "Big Oil Just Isn't as Big as It Once Was," *Washington Post*, September 4, 2020.
20. Per-Ola Karlsson, Deanne Aguirre, and Kristin Rivera, "Are CEOs Less Ethical Than in the Past?," *PwC* 87 (Summer 2017): 5.
21. Dan Marcec, "CEO Tenure Drops to Just Five Years," Equilar Inc., January 19, 2018, https://www.equilar.com/blogs/351-ceo-tenure-drops-to-five-years.html.
22. Director of National Intelligence, "Background to 'Assessing Russian Activities and Intentions in Recent US Elections': The Analytic Process and Cyber Incident Attribution," Office of the Director of National Intelligence, January 6, 2017, https://www.dni.gov/files/documents/ICA_2017_01.pdf.

6. Anti-Politics

1. Javier Corrales, "Beware the Outsider," *Foreign Policy*, March 16, 2016.
2. Roberto Stefan Foa, A. Klassen, M. Slade, A. Rand, and R. Collins, "The Global Satisfaction with Democracy Report 2020," Centre for the Future of Democracy, Cambridge, UK, 2020, https://www.cam.ac.uk/system/files/report2020_003.pdf.
3. Mancur Olson, *The Rise and Decline of Nations: Economic Growth, Stagflation, and Social Rigidities* (New Haven, CT: Yale University Press, 1982).
4. David Mora, "Update: We Found a 'Staggering' 281 Lobbyists Who've Worked in the Trump Administration," ProPublica, October 15, 2019.
5. "GDP Growth (Annual %)–Italy," World Bank, accessed March 19, 2021, https://data.worldbank.org/indicator/NY.GDP.MKTP.KD.ZG?locations=IT.

6. "Tax Dodgers Cost Italy €122 Billion in 2015," The Local Italy, December 16, 2015, https://www.thelocal.it/20151216/bosses-put-italys-tax-dodging-bill-at -122bn-euros.

7. Rakesh Kochhar, "Middle Class Fortunes in Western Europe," Pew Research Center, April 24, 2017, https://www.pewresearch.org/global/2017/04/24/middle -class-fortunes-in-western-europe.

8. "Italian Elections 2018—Full Results," *The Guardian*, March 5, 2018.

9. José Meléndez, "Ellos son los expresidentes centroamericanos en prisión," *El Universal*, February 14, 2018.

10. Moisés Naím, "Politician-Eating Beasts," *El País*, May 1, 2019.

7. Power After Truth

1. "George Washington and the Cherry Tree," National Park Service, accessed March 19, 2021, https://www.nps.gov/articles/george-washington-and-the-cherry -tree.htm.

2. Jay Rosen (@jayrosen_nyu), "Phrases like 'rewriting history' and 'muddying the waters' do not convey what is underway. It's an attempt to prevent Americans from understanding what happened to them through the strategic use of confusion," Twitter, April 13, 2020, https://twitter.com/jayrosen_nyu/status /1249885575655632896.

3. Alan Rusbridger, "Breaking News—A Summary of the Book's Arguments for Medium," ARusbridger.com, December 9, 2018, https://www.arusbridger.com/blog /2018/12/9/breaking-news-a-summary-of-the-books-arguments-for-medium.

4. "Post-truth," *Collins Dictionary*, accessed March 19, 2021, https://www .collinsdictionary.com/us/dictionary/english/post-truth.

5. Hannah Arendt, *The Origins of Totalitarianism* (New York: Harcourt Brace Jovanovich, 1973), 474.

6. Michael Isikoff and David Corn, *Russian Roulette: The Inside Story of Putin's War on America and the Election of Donald Trump* (New York: Twelve Books, 2018).

7. Andrew S. Weiss, "Vladimir Putin's Political Meddling Revives Old KGB Tactics," *Wall Street Journal*, February 17, 2017.

8. John B. Dunlop, *The Moscow Bombings of September 1999: Examinations of Russian Terrorist Attacks at the Onset of Vladimir Putin's Rule*, 2nd ed. (Stuttgart: Ibidem, 2014).

9. Michael McFaul, "The Smear That Killed the 'Reset,'" *Washington Post*, May 11, 2018.

10. Committee on Intelligence of the 116th Congress, 1st sess., "Report on Russian Active Measures Campaigns and Interference in the 2016 U.S. Election; Volume 2: Russia's Use of Social Media with Additional Views," U.S. Senate, accessed March 19, 2021, https://www.intelligence.senate.gov/sites/default/files /documents/Report_Volume2.pdf.

11. Melissa M. Lee, "Subversive Statecraft: The Changing Face of Great-Power Conflict," *Foreign Affairs*, December 4, 2019.

12. Christopher Paul and Miriam Matthews, *The Russian "Firehose of Falsehood" Propaganda Model: Why It Might Work and Options to Counter It* (Santa Monica, CA: RAND Corporation, 2016).

13. "Bot Army," *Collins Dictionary*, accessed March 19, 2021, https://www .collinsdictionary.com/us/dictionary/english/bot-army.

14. Sinan Aral, *The Hype Machine: How Social Media Disrupts Our Elections, Our Economy, and Our Health—and How We Must Adapt* (New York: Penguin Random House, 2020).

15. Soroush Vosoughi, Deb Roy, and Sinan Aral, "The Spread of True and False News Online," *Science* 359, no. 6380 (2018): 1146–51.

16. AFP, "Facebook Closes Fake News Pages in Poland: Rights Group," Yahoo! News, May 17, 2019.

17. Roberto Saviano, "Facebook Closes Italy Pro-Government Fake News Pages: Rights Group," Yahoo! News, May 13, 2019.

18. Natasha Lomas, "Facebook Has Quietly Removed Three Bogus Far-Right Networks in Spain Ahead of Sunday's Elections," TechCrunch, April 23, 2019.

19. Oxford Internet Institute, "State-Backed Media from China and Russia Targets European and Latin American Audiences with Coronavirus News," press release, Oxford Internet Institute, June 29, 2020.

20. Katarina Rebello, Christian Schwieter, Marcel Schliebs, Kate Joynes-Burgess, Mona Elswah, Jonathan Bright, and Philip N. Howard, "Covid-19 News and Information from State-Backed Outlets Targeting French, German and Spanish-Speaking Social Media Users: Understanding Chinese, Iranian, Russian and Turkish Outlets," Oxford Internet Institute, June 2020.

21. Elyse Samuels, "How Misinformation on WhatsApp Led to a Mob Killing in India," *Washington Post*, February 21, 2020.

22. Trisha Jalan, "Updated: Tripura Govt Extends 2-Day Internet Ban by 48 Hours," Medianama, January 11, 2019, https://www.medianama.com./2019/01/223-trip ura-internet-shutdown-2019.

23. Bharti Jain, "Lok Sabha Elections: At 67.1%, 2019 Turnout's a Record, Election Commission Says," *Times of India*, May 21, 2019.

24. Snigdha Poonam and Samarth Bansal, "Misinformation Is Endangering India's Election," *The Atlantic*, April 1, 2019.

25. Nikhil Dawar, "Fact Check: Viral Post Claiming Sonia Gandhi Richer than Britain's Queen Elizabeth II Is False," *India Today*, January 9, 2019.

26. Supriya Nair, "The Meaning of India's 'Beef Lynchings,'" *The Atlantic*, July 24, 2017.

27. Dexter Filkins, "Blood and Soil in Narendra Modi's India," *New Yorker*, December 9, 2019.

28. "How WhatsApp Is Used and Misused in Africa," *The Economist*, July 20, 2019.

29. Danny Rayman, "Mexico: How Data Influenced Mexico's 2018 Election," *Tactical Tech Collective*, July 2, 2018, https://ourdataourselves.tacticaltech.org/posts/overview-mexico/.

30. Redacción Desinformémonos, "Con el hashtag #SaqueaUnWalmart bots y mensajes anónimos generan caos y pánico," Desinformémonos, January 5, 2017, https://desinformemonos.org/hashtag-saqueaunwalmart-bots-mensajes-anonimos-generan-caos-panico.

31. John McBeth, "Is Indonesia's Widodo in China's Pocket?," *Asia Times,* December 11, 2017.

32. Andreas Harsono and Tempe McMinn, "'I Wanted to Run Away': Abusive Dress Codes for Women and Girls in Indonesia," Human Rights Watch, March 18, 2021, https://www.hrw.org/report/2021/03/18/i-wanted-run-away/abusive-dress -codes-women-and-girls-indonesia.

33. "Police Question Prabowo Campaigners for Saying Jokowi Would Ban Call to Prayer, Legalize Gay Marriage," Coconuts Jakarta, February 25, 2019, https://coconuts.co/jakarta/news/police-question-prabowo-campaigners-saying-jokowi-ban-call-prayer-legalize-gay-marriage.

34. Mali Walker, "Indonesia's Democracy at Risk from Disinformation," *The Strategist*, Australian Strategic Policy Institute, May 15, 2019.

35. Marshall McLuhan, *The Medium Is the Message: An Inventory of Effects* (London: Penguin Books, 1967).

36. European Union, "Commission Regulation (EC) No 2257/94 of 16 September 1994 Laying Down Quality Standards for Bananas (Text with EEA Relevance)," September 20, 1994, 6–10.

37. Dominic Wring, "Going Bananas over Brussels: Fleet Street's European Journey," The Conversation, June 21, 2016, https://theconversation.com/going-bananas-over-brussels-fleet-streets-european-journey-61327.

38. Sarah Lambert, "Putting the Banana Story Straight," *The Independent*, September 21, 1994.

39. "Guide to the Best Euromyths," BBC News, March 23, 2007.

40. "Euromyths," European Parliament Liaison Office in the United Kingdom, https://www.europarl.europa.eu/unitedkingdom/en/news-and-press-releases/euromyths.html.

41. Damian C. Adams, Michael T. Olexa, Tracey L. Owens, and Joshua A. Cassey, "Déjà Moo: Is the Return to Public Sale of Raw Milk Udder Nonsense?," *Drake Journal of Agriculture Law* 13, no. 305 (2008).

42. Jon Henley, "Is the EU Really Dictating the Shape of Your Bananas?," *The Guardian*, May 11, 2016.

43. Anne Applebaum, "Boris Johnson's Victory Proves It's Fiction, Not Fact, That Tories Want to Hear," *Washington Post*, July 23, 2019.

44. Glenn Kessler, Salvador Rizzo, and Meg Kelly, "Trump's False or Misleading Claims Total 30,573 over 4 Years," *Washington Post*, January 24, 2021, https://www.washingtonpost.com/politics/2021/01/24/trumps-false-or-misleading-claims-total-30573-over-four-years.

45. Chris Cillizza, "Donald Trump Lies More Often than You Wash Your Hands Every Day," CNN, June 10, 2019.

46. Michael Foucault, *The Foucault Reader* (New York: Penguin Random House, 1984).

47. Bruno LaTour, *Science in Action: How to Follow Scientists and Engineers Through Society* (Cambridge, MA: Harvard University Press, 1988).

48. David Frum, *Trumpocracy: The Corruption of the American Republic* (New York: Harper Collins, 2018).

49. Jop de Vrieze, "Bruno Latour, a Veteran of the 'Science Wars,' Has a New Mission," *Science Magazine*, October 10, 2017.

50. Alyza Sebenius, "Microsoft Releases Deepfake Detection Tool Ahead of Election," Bloomberg, September 2, 2020.

51. Peter Pomerantsev, *This Is Not Propaganda: Adventures in the War Against Reality* (New York: Public Affairs, 2019).

8. Mafia States, Criminal Governments

1. Philip Zelikow, Eric Edelman, Kristofer Harrison, and Celeste Ward Gventer, "The Rise of Strategic Corruption: How States Weaponize Graft," *Foreign Affairs*, July/August 2020.

2. Francis Fukuyama, http://www.ridge.uy/wp-content/uploads/2016/05/Fukuyama_Francis.pdf.

3. Charles Tilly, "Warmaking and Statemaking as Organized Crime," CRSO Working Paper No. 256, University of Michigan, February 1982, 8, https://deepblue.lib.umich.edu/bitstream/handle/2027.42/51028/256.pdf.

4. Niccolo Machiavelli, *The Prince* (New York: Bantam Books, 1984).

5. Thomas Hobbes, *Leviathan* (Baltimore: Penguin Books, 1968).

6. Mancur Olson, "Dictatorship, Democracy, and Development," *American Political Science Review* 87, no. 3 (1993): 567–76.

7. Francis Fukuyama, "Political Order and Political Decay," lecture, Chatham House, September 22, 2014, https://www.chathamhouse.org/sites/default/files/field/field_document/20140922PoliticalOrderDecay.pdf.

8. Gordon Tullock, *Rent Seeking*, in *The World of Economics*, ed. J. Eatwell, M. Milgate, and P. Newman (London: Palgrave Macmillan, 1991), 604–9.

9. Anne O. Krueger, "The Political Economy of the Rent-Seeking Society," *American Economic Review* 64, no. 3 (1974): 291–303.

10. Daron Acemoglu and James Robinson, *Why Nations Fail: The Origins of Power, Prosperity and Poverty* (New York: Penguin Random House, 2013).

11. Luke Harding, "WikiLeaks Cables Condemn Russia as 'Mafia State,'" *The Guardian*, December 1, 2010.

12. Paul Klebnikov, "Godfather of the Kremlin: Boris Berezovsky and the Looting of Russia," *Kirkus Reviews*, September 1, 2000.

13. Ruth May, "Putin: From Oligarch to Kleptocrat," *New York Review of Books*, February 1, 2018.

14. Zelikow et al., "The Rise of Strategic Corruption."

15. Leonardo Coutinho, "Hugo Chávez, the Spectre," Center for a Secure Free Society, September 20, 2018, https://www.securefreesociety.org/research/hugo-chavez-the-spectre.

16. Marton Dunai, "How Viktor Orbán Will Tap Europe's Taxpayers and Bankroll His Friends and Family," Reuters, March 15, 2018.

17. Balint Magyar and Balint Madlovics, "Hungary's Mafia State Fights for Impunity," Balkan Insight, June 21, 2019, https://balkaninsight.com/2019/06/21/hungarys-mafia-state-fights-for-impunity.

18. Patrick Kingsley, "Orbán and His Allies Cement Control of Hungary's News Media," *New York Times*, November 29, 2018.

19. "Putin Critic Bill Browder Freed After Brief Arrest in Spain," BBC, May 30, 2018.

9. The 3P Autocrats Go Global

1. Nate Schenkkan and Isabel Linzer, "Out of Sight, Not Out of Reach: Understanding the Global Scale and Scope of Transnational Repression," Freedom House, February 2021, https://freedomhouse.org/sites/default/files/2021–02/Complete_FH_TransnationalRepressionReport2021_rev020221.pdf.

2. Angela Merkel, "Bundeskanzlerin Merkel gratuliert dem designierten Präsidenten der Vereinigten Staaten von Amerika, Donald Trump," *Presse-und Informationsamt der Bundesregierung (BPA)*, November 9, 2016, https://www.bundesregierung.de/breg-de/aktuelles/bundeskanzlerin-merkel-gratuliert-dem-designierten-praesidenten-der-vereinigten-staaten-von-amerika-donald-trump-479452.

3. Nancy A. Youssef, Vivian Salama, and Michael C. Bender, "Trump, Awaiting Egyptian Counterpart at Summit, Called Out for 'My Favorite Dictator,'" *Wall Street Journal*, September 13, 2019.

4. "ALBA," Portal ALBA, accessed March 19, 2021, http://www.portalalba.org /index.php.

5. Christopher Walker and Jessica Ludwig, "The Long Arm of the Strongman: How China and Russia Use Sharp Power to Threaten Democracies," *Foreign Affairs*, May 12, 2021.

6. Kirk Semple and Marina Franco, "Bots and Trolls Elbow into Mexico's Crowded Electoral Field," *New York Times*, May 1, 2018.

7. Constella Intelligence, "Protests in South America: An Analysis of New Trends in Digital Disinformation and Influence Campaigns," Constella Intelligence, February 13, 2020, https://constellaintelligence.com/social-unrest-colombia-chile.

8. Katy Lee, "China Is on a Crazy Mission to Build Artificial Islands. What the Hell Is It Up To?," Vox, March 13, 2015.

9. Lily Kuo, "China Says It's Building Islands and Airstrips in the South China Sea for Better Weather Forecasts," *Quartz*, June 22, 2015.

10. Associated Press, "Sepp Blatter: Fixing FIFA takes time," ESPN, July 27, 2011.

11. Chris Mills Rodrigo, "Kobach 'Very Concerned' Voter Fraud May Have Happened in North Carolina," *The Hill*, December 6, 2018.

12. Carl Schreck, "From 'Not Us' to 'Why Hide It?': How Russia Denied Its Crimea Invasion, Then Admitted It," Radio Free Europe Radio Liberty, February 26, 2019.

13. Bill Chappell and Mark Memmott, "Putin Says Those Aren't Russian Forces In Crimea," NPR, March 4, 2014.

14. "MH17 Ukraine Plane Crash: What We Know," BBC, February 26, 2020.

15. Gabriela Baczynska, "Putin Classifies Information on Deaths of Russian Troops in Peacetime," Reuters, May 28, 2015.

16. James Kirchick, "Anti-Nazi Group Secretly Helping Kremlin Rebuild Russian Empire," *Daily Beast*, April 14, 2017.

17. Halya Coynash, "Russian 'Right Sector War Against Odessa Jews' Debunked," Kharkiv Human Rights Protection Group, September 10, 2014, http://khpg.org /en/1412804893.

18. Halya Coynash, "Chief Rabbi and Others Dismiss Putin's 'Anti-Semitic Extremist' Claims," Kharkiv Human Rights Protection Group, May 3, 2014, http://khpg .org/en/1393978300.

19. UN Watch, "Report: Venezuela Used 500 Front Groups to Subvert Today's UN Review of Its Rights Record," Human Rights Council, November 1, 2016, https://unwatch.org/report-venezuela-used-500-front-groups-subvert-todays-un -review-rights-record.

20. Daniel Baer, "Mind the GONGOs: How Government Organized NGOs Troll Europe's Largest Human Rights Conference," *Medium*, September 29, 2016.

21. National Endowment for Democracy homepage, accessed March 19, 2021, https://www.ned.org.

10. Power and Pandemic

1. Frances Z. Brown, Saskia Brechenmacher, and Thomas Carothers, "How Will the Coronavirus Reshape Democracy and Governance Globally?," Carnegie

Endowment for International Peace, April 6, 2020, https://carnegieendowment
.org/2020/04/06/how-will-coronavirus-reshape-democracy-and-governance
-globally-pub-81470.

2. Fabrizio, Lee & Associates, "Post Election Exit Poll Analysis: 10 Key Target States,"
Politico, December 2020, https://www.politico.com/f/?id=00000177–6046-de2d
-a57f-7a6e8c950000.

3. "Global Impact of COVID-19 on Elections," Election Guide: Democracy Assistance and Elections News, accessed March 19, 2021, https://www.electionguide
.org/digest/post/17591.

4. Jacob McHangama and Sarah McLaughlin, "Coronavirus Has Started a Censorship Pandemic," *Foreign Policy*, April 1, 2020.

5. Zeynep Bilginsoy and Mehmet Guzel, "Turkey: Social Media Law's Passage
Raises Censorship Worries," *Washington Post*, July 29, 2020.

6. Brown, Brechenmacher, and Carothers, "How Will the Coronavirus Reshape
Democracy and Governance Globally?"

7. Amr Hamzawy and Nathan J. Brown, "How Much Will the Pandemic Change
Egyptian Governance and for How Long?," Carnegie Endowment for International Peace, July 23, 2020, https://carnegieendowment.org/2020/07/23/how
-much-will-pandemic-change-egyptian-governance-and-for-how-long-pub
-82353.

8. Sun Narin, "Gov't Defends Draft 'State of Emergency' Law; Rights Groups Remain
Concerned," VOA Khmer, April 2, 2020, https://www.voacambodia.com/a/govt
-defends-draft-state-of-emergency-law-rights-groups-remain-concerned/5356841
.html.

9. Anna Luehrmann, Amanda B. Edgell, Sandra Grahn, Jean Lachapelle, and
Seraphine F. Maerz, "Does the Coronavirus Endanger Democracy in Europe?," Carnegie Endowment for International Peace, June 23, 2020, https://
carnegieeurope.eu/2020/06/23/does-coronavirus-endanger-democracy-in
-europe-pub-82110.

10. Robin Emmott, "Russia Deploying Coronavirus Disinformation to Sow Panic in
West, EU Document Says," Reuters, March 18, 2020.

11. Andrea Dudik, "Russia Aims to Stir Distrust in Europe on Virus Disinformation," Bloomberg Businessweek, March 19, 2020.

12. Amanda Seitz, "State Dept.: Russia Pushes Disinformation in Online Network,"
AP News, August 5, 2020.

13. Sarah Cook, "Beijing's Global Megaphone: The Expansion of Chinese Communist
Party Media Influence Since 2017," Freedom House, 2020, https://freedomhouse
.org/report/special-report/2020/beijings-global-megaphone.

14. Jennifer Rankin, "EU Says China Behind 'Huge Wave' of Covid-19 Disinformation," *The Guardian*, June 10, 2020.

15. Jessica Brandt and Fred Schafer, "Five Things to Know About Beijing's Disinformation Approach," Alliance for Securing Democracy, March 30, 2020,
https://securingdemocracy.gmfus.org/five-things-to-know-about-beijings
-disinformation-approach.

16. Jessica Brandt and Torrey Taussig, "The Kremlin's Disinformation Playbook
Goes to Beijing," Brookings Institution, May 19, 2020, https://www.brookings
.edu/blog/order-from-chaos/2020/05/19/the-kremlins-disinformation-playbook
-goes-to-beijing.

17. Elizabeth Thompson, Katie Nicholson, and Jason Ho, "COVID-19 Disinforma-

tion Being Spread by Russia, China, Say Experts," CBC News, May 26, 2020, https://www.cbc.ca/news/politics/covid-coronavirus-russia-china-1.5583961.

18. Clarissa Ward, "Inside a Russian Troll Factory in Ghana," CNN, March 12, 2020.

19. Thomas Carothers and Andrew O'Donohue, "Polarization and the Pandemic," Carnegie Endowment for International Peace, April 28, 2020, https://carnegieendowment.org/2020/04/28/polarization-and-the-pandemic-pub-81638.

11. Five Battles We Need to Win

1. Sarah Repucci and Amy Slipowitz, "Freedom in the World 2021: Democracy Under Siege," Freedom House, 2021, https://freedomhouse.org/report/freedom-world/2021/democracy-under-siege.

2. Timothy Garton Ash, "The Future of Liberalism," *Prospect*, December 9, 2020.

3. President John Fitzgerald Kennedy, "Inaugural Address," transcript of speech delivered in Washington, DC on January 20, 1961, https://www.ourdocuments.gov/doc.php?flash=false&doc=91&page=transcript.

4. Timothy Snyder, *On Tyranny: Twenty Lessons from the Twentieth Century* (New York: Penguin Random House, 2017).

5. Allan Smith and Leigh Ann Caldwell, "Cheney Hits Back at Trump over Election 'Big Lie,'" NBC News, May 3, 2021, https://www.nbcnews.com/politics/donald-trump/cheney-hits-back-trump-over-election-big-lie-n1266143.

6. Jonathan Swift, *The Examiner*, No. XIV, 1710.

7. Anne Applebaum and Peter Pomerantsev, "The Internet Doesn't Have to Be Awful," *The Atlantic*, March 8, 2021.

8. Felix Salmon, "Media Trust Hits New Low," Axios, January 21, 2021.

9. "Bothsidesing: Not All Sides Are Equal," *Merriam-Webster Dictionary*, accessed May 19, 2021, https://www.merriam-webster.com/words-at-play/bothsidesing-bothsidesism-new-words-were-watching.

10. Lionel Barber, "Lionel Barber: Trump and Truth," Persuasion, January 18, 2021, https://www.persuasion.community/p/lionel-barber-trump-and-truth.

11. Alexander Hamilton, James Madison, John Jay, John Dunn, Donald L. Horowitz, and Eileen Hunt Botting, *The Federalist Papers,* ed. Ian Shapiro (New Haven, CT: Yale University Press, 2009).

12. Patrick Riccards, "National Survey Finds Just 1 in 3 Americans Would Pass Citizenship Test," Woodrow Wilson National Fellowship Foundation, October 3, 2018, https://woodrow.org/news/national-survey-finds-just-1-in-3-americans-would-pass-citizenship-test.

13. Alicia Tatone, "Global Banks Defy U.S. Crackdowns by Serving Oligarchs, Criminals and Terrorists," International Consortium of Investigative Journalists, September 20, 2020, https://www.icij.org/investigations/fincen-files/global-banks-defy-u-s-crackdowns-by-serving-oligarchs-criminals-and-terrorists.

14. Matthew Collin, "What the FinCEN Leaks Reveal About the Ongoing War on Dirty Money," Brookings Institution, September 25, 2020, https://www.brookings.edu/blog/up-front/2020/09/25/what-the-fincen-leaks-reveal-about-the-ongoing-war-on-dirty-money.

15. Thucydides, *History of the Peloponnesian War*, trans. Rex Warner (Baltimore: Penguin Books, 1968).

16. Dov H. Levin, "When the Great Power Gets a Vote: The Effects of Great Power Electoral Interventions on Election Results," *International Studies Quarterly* 60, no. 2 (June 2016): 189–202.

17. Drew Desilver, "Despite Global Concerns About Democracy, More than Half of Countries Are Democratic," Pew Research Center, May 14, 2019, https:// www.pewresearch.org/fact-tank/2019/05/14/more-than-half-of-countries-are -democratic.

18. Director of National Intelligence, "Background to 'Assessing Russian Activities and Intentions in Recent US Elections': The Analytic Process and Cyber Incident Attribution," Office of the Director of National Intelligence, January 6, 2017, https://www.dni.gov/files/documents/ICA_2017_01.pdf.

19. Moisés Naím, "How Democracies Lose in Cyberwar," *The Atlantic*, February 13, 2017.

20. Colin Dwyer, "U.S. Announces Its Withdrawal from U.N. Human Rights Council," NPR, June 19, 2018.

21. Bruce Jones and Adam Twardowski, "Bolstering Democracies in a Changing International Order: The Case for Democratic Multilateralism," Brookings Institution, January 25, 2021, https://www.brookings.edu/research/bolstering-democracies-in -a-changing-international-order-the-case-for-democratic-multilateralism.

22. Frances Z. Brown, Thomas Carothers, and Alex Pascal, "America Needs a Democracy Summit More Than Ever: How to Bring the Free World Together Again," *Foreign Affairs*, January 15, 2021.

23. Ejeviome Eloho Otobo and Oseloka H. Obaze, "Biden's Likely Policy Orientation Toward Africa," *The Guardian*, February 1, 2021.

24. Cas Mudde and Cristóbal Rovira Kaltwasser, *Populism: A Very Short Introduction* (New York: Oxford University Press, 2017).

25. Angus Colwell, "'I Genuinely Think 2020 Is Scary': David Runciman on Trump, Young People, and the Future of Democracy," *Pi*, March 2, 2020.

Afterword

1. "Where Ranked Choice Voting Is Used," Fairvote, May 2021, https://www .fairvote.org/where_is_ranked_choice_voting_used?gclid=CjwKCAjw-e2EBh AhEiwAJI5jg5iKpN7hEJaQvR_M7M_P0CksPS1uwMI8LPViJd37yWilL74evP -RQBoChzgQAvD_BwE.

2. Frank Wilkinson, "Democracy Will Die, Maybe in Its Sleep," BNN Bloomberg, May 22, 2018.

INDEX

MOISÉS NAÍM is a scholar at the Carnegie Endowment for International Peace and an internationally syndicated columnist. He served as editor in chief of *Foreign Policy,* as Venezuela's trade minister, and as executive director of the World Bank.